TURNING POINTS OF GENERAL CHURCH HISTORY

BY

EDWARD L. CUTTS, D.D.

CONDENSED AND REVISED BY

WILLIAM C PIERCY, M.A.

LONDON
SOCIETY FOR PROMOTING
CHRISTIAN KNOWLEDGE
NEW YORK AND TORONTO: THE MACMILLAN CO.

991

AUTHOR'S PREFACE

THIS is an attempt to give, within the limits of a small book, some adequate idea of the history of the Church of Christ to the thousands of intelligent Church-people who have little previous acquaintance with the subject. The special features of the plan are these :— Pains have been taken to show what the Church is—viz., the Body of Christ informed by the Holy Spirit ; the salient points of the history have been selected with a special view to our present ecclesiastical condition ; instead of referring the reader to other books, to which he may not have ready access, for that sketch of secular history which is indispensable to an intelligent grasp of Church history, such a sketch is included.

EDITOR'S PREFACE

THE fact that Cutts' " Turning Points " has, since its publication in 1877, sold to the number of upwards of seventeen thousand and is still in demand, led the committee of S.P.C.K. to decide that a book in a form that has proved so useful should not be allowed entirely to go out of print.

The mere passage of time had necessarily made it a little out of date, and in a few cases later researches of scholarship demanded some emendations or qualifications, and especially it was felt that an abridged edition would be the most useful form for republication. The reduction in size has been done mainly by verbal condensation, with some unimportant omissions, but the editor has endeavoured to leave untouched all that was vital to the original author's point of view, and where any new matter or different estimate has been introduced has indicated his own responsibility therefor.

The one considerable addition he has made, to carry out the author's wish that the book should be specially helpful in " our present ecclesiastical condition " has been in the Chapter (XXXIX) where the history of the doctrine of the Holy Communion is set forth. This has been brought up to date and the omission so frequent in such books of any clear indication of what the term " transubstantiation " really means, and especially how it is distinguished from the doctrine of the Real Presence, has been remedied.

The author's final chapter (with its appendix) on " The Present State of the Catholic Church " was necessarily entirely out of date and has been omitted. There has been no attempt to replace it, as it seemed alien to the purpose of a book which dealt with " Turning Points " merely.

Editor's Preface

As the original work, apart from this, ended with the Reformation period, it seemed best also to leave any later " Turning Points " to be judged in the future in the cool light of history when a like perspective of time can properly reveal their real importance.

For the same reason—that the work deals with " Turning Points "—the editor has resisted a strong temptation to deal more fully with some subjects which may, if that is not borne in mind, appear to our own generation, to be somewhat inadequately dealt with in the original, such as the later influence of monasticism, while with regard to others of special interest to ourselves, such as the respective influence of Celtic, Gallican and Roman missionaries to England, the preparatory causes of the English reformation (including the Renaissance), the impulse to missionary effort in modern days, and the story and influence of Nonconformity, he has reminded himself sternly that this book deals with " General " Church history and that the due proportion between Continental and English Church History must limit his inclinations. He is consoled by reflecting that such important subjects as these are better studied in volumes specially devoted to them than in a general review of this kind, which necessarily partakes of the nature of sketches. But, above all, in the course of a minute reading of this book, has the editor been impressed with, and constantly admired, the clearness, fairness and (within its limits) completeness of the author's original work and how fitted it is even to-day to introduce young students, or beginners, to the essential points and vital crises in the history of the Holy Catholic Church.

EAST HORSLEY, 1928.

CONTENTS

CHAPTER I

THE WORLD PREPARED FOR THE CHURCH

CHAPTER II

THE CHURCH IN THE GOSPELS

CHAPTER III

THE APOSTOLIC CHURCH

CHAPTER IV

SKETCH OF THE ROMAN EMPIRE TO THE CONVERSION OF CONSTANTINE

Contents

Contents

Contents

CHAPTER XIX

THE TRIUMPH OF THE CHURCH

CHAPTER XX

THE EXTENSION OF THE CHURCH OUTSIDE THE EMPIRE

CHAPTER XXI

FATHERS OF THE CHURCH : ATHANASIUS, CHRYSOSTOM, AMBROSE

CHAPTER XXII

MONASTICISM

CHAPTER XXVI

THE EASTERN EMPIRE FROM THE DEATH OF JUSTINIAN TO THAT OF HERACLIUS

CHAPTER XXVII

THE MOHAMMEDAN CONQUESTS

Contents

CHAPTER XXXII

THE CONVERSION OF THE SLAVONIC NATIONS

CHAPTER XXXIII

THE HILDEBRANDINE PERIOD

Contents

CHAPTER XXXVIII

CHAPTER XXXIX

MEDIEVAL DEVELOPMENTS

Contents

CHAPTER XL

THE REFORMATION

TURNING POINTS OF
GENERAL CHURCH HISTORY

CHAPTER I

THE WORLD PREPARED FOR THE CHURCH

GLANCE at the state of the world at the time when our Lord Jesus Christ came into it, lived, suffered, died, rose again, ascended, and on the foundation of the apostles and prophets erected the Church, whose history is our present theme.

We are specially concerned with three great races of mankind—the Greek, the Jewish, and the Roman.

First, the Greek. The human intellect reached, perhaps, its highest development in this glorious race. In history and philosophy, arts and literature, its productions are still the models for mankind. The Greek, first of the ancient races, learnt the falsehood and folly of the popular religion, and directed his researches to the universe around him, and to his own being, and sought from these, by use of human reason, an explanation of the phenomena of Being and of Life—an answer to the questions, What am I, and whence ? what is the true method of life ? what becomes of me after death ? These researches led to the establishment of the various systems of Greek philosophy. The chief were, the Epicurean, the Stoic, and the Platonic.

Epicureanism, as taught by Lucretius, was materialistic. Its theory of human life was that happiness is the highest good, and that a wise man should pursue happiness in a well-regulated enjoyment of all the pleasures which the world affords. It was a religion suited to the acute, worldly-

cp Bethune Bakers" Rise of Xtian Church p 116 ff

minded, pleasure-loving man ; involving no moral responsi-
bilities, calling for no self-denials ; leaving him without fear
or scruple to enjoy life, with no limit except that to indulge
in excess would blunt the keen edge of enjoyment.

The Stoic philosophy was Pantheistic.   The universe
was an organic whole informed by a universal spirit.   All
individual existence has emanated from this universal spirit,
and is absorbed into it again.   Evil and good are only
different necessary forms of the universal life.   The wise
man lives within himself, holding himself superior to the
accidents of life, and retaining his serenity under all
circumstances.   He has the same divine life as the gods ;
manifested in his individuality for a little while, and then
reabsorbed into the whole, and given forth again in new
individuals.   The whole is everything, the individual
nothing.

But the profoundest and noblest philosophy was the
Platonic.   It taught the existence of one Supreme Spirit,
the Maker and Ruler of the universe, Who united in His
Being all perfections.   Man was not a mere transient
phenomenon, but a real permanent individual ; there was a
spark of the divinity in him, purifying him and drawing him
up to a higher mode of existence.   It taught a belief in
virtue and vice—virtue pleasing to God and preparing man
for a happy future life ; vice, displeasing to God and earning
for man a miserable future.

The Eclectic philosophers took one doctrine from one
system, and another from another, and recast them into
a system of their own.

These philosophies took the place of religion to the
educated Greek ; they were an explanation of the universe,
and a guide to human life.   But the philosophers held that
the ancient superstitions were useful for women, children,
and the unlearned vulgar, who were incapable of rising to
such a knowledge of philosophy as would influence their
lives ; and they themselves attended the temples, and paid
respect to the ancient religious observances, in order to
encourage the vulgar belief in them.

Greek colonies and conquests had spread the Greek
culture and philosophy widely over the world.   An adven-
turous, maritime, commercial race, they had established

flourishing communities along the shores of almost the whole Mediterranean Sea. Southern Italy itself was largely peopled by Greeks. The rapid conquests of Alexander the Great were, after his death, divided among his generals into four kingdoms. Ptolemy took Egypt, Arabia, and Palestine ; Cassander had Macedonia and Greece ; Lysimachus had Thrace, Bithynia, and other provinces beyond the Hellespont ; Seleucus took all the rest of Upper Asia, including Syria and Persia, and stretching as far as the Indus. These Greek sovereigns were enlightened and energetic rulers ; they diligently introduced Greek civilisation into the subject countries, built cities, encouraged commerce, patronised learning, philosophy, and the arts. Greek culture became widely diffused. Greek became the language of literature and commerce throughout the civilised world, and the conclusions of Greek philosophy were widely known among educated people.

The Jews, since their return from the Babylonian captivity, had outgrown the narrow limits of their own land, adopted commerce as their pursuit, and spread over the civilised world. Every great city had its colony of Jews, who did not intermarry with, or merge into, the people around, but retained their nationality, religion, and social isolation. At Alexandria its great Macedonian founder assigned them a third part of the city, and gave them the same privileges as the Greeks. At Antioch they were allowed, by Seleucus its founder, the same political privileges, and were governed by their own ethnarch. Everywhere their peculiarities attracted notice, everywhere they were witnesses to the two great truths—the Unity of God, and the Promise of a Saviour. In every city the synagogue was surrounded by a fringe of Gentile " God-fearers," who believed in the Jewish God, and more or less shared the Jewish hope of Messiah. Women especially were attracted by Jewish teaching, and many of them of all ranks (Acts xiii. 50) were its disciples and supporters.

The establishment of the Roman empire was the last great step in the preparation of the world for the Church. It adopted the Greek civilisation and completed the work which Greek conquests, commerce, and philosophy had begun, in breaking down the barriers of race and religion

which divided mankind. Greek commerce found paths
through the seas from one maritime city to another. Roman
conquest made great high-roads, straight over hill and
valley, through forest and marsh, connecting the imperial
city with the furthest frontiers of the empire. Rome had
succeeded to all the Asian and African conquests of Greece,
and added her own European conquests. Roman government and Roman law bound the various nations together
as citizens of one empire. Teachers of Greek philosophy
abounded in the chief cities of the empire. The well-born
youth were sent to Athens, as to a university, to complete
their education. Every Roman considered himself something of a philosopher.

The different races of the world were brought into more
intimate relations and more familiar intercourse than at any
previous period in history. It is astonishing to what an
extent the Roman world was thrown open, and how freely
men moved about in it, regarding it as a common country.
The interminable straight roads led them with perfect ease
and safety from one side of the world to the other ; they
were everywhere under the protection of the same strong
government, the same wise and just laws. In every city
houses, streets, temples, and theatres wore the same aspect ;
the higher classes everywhere wore the same dress, spoke
the same language, had the same manners. Greece and
Rome had made the crooked ways straight, the rough
places smooth, and prepared the way for the coming of the
Lord, that all flesh might see the salvation of God ; and
Judaism, like a herald, had raised a general expectation of
His coming.

CHAPTER II

THE CHURCH IN THE GOSPELS

THE extent to which the Church occupied the mind of our Lord, is shown in the prominent and large space which it takes up in His discourses.

There is no question that by the phrase " kingdom of heaven," or " kingdom of God," our Lord means His Church.* In the great majority of cases it is applied to the state of the Church militant here upon earth ; in a few places it may apply more especially to its state triumphant in heaven, but these are only two phases of the same Church.

The Church had already been foretold in Daniel's great prophecy as the " kingdom of the God of heaven, which shall never be destroyed."† The kingdom of David and Solomon was a type of it, and God had promised to David that the Messiah should be of his seed and should sit upon his throne. Accordingly Christ was born at Bethlehem, David's city, " because He was of the house and lineage of David " ; and the genealogy of St. Matthew traces His descent through the kings. The magi came and worshipped Him as King of the Jews (*i.e.*, of the true Israel). For assuming this title He was arraigned before Pilate, and He claimed before him to be a king, though not in the sense His accusers meant. On this charge He was actually put to death, for " the title of His accusation," put, according to custom, on His cross, in Hebrew, Greek, and

* See Matt. xvi. 18, 19, where our Lord says, " Thou art Peter, and upon this rock I will build My *Church* . . . and I will give unto thee the keys of the *kingdom of heaven* "—the *Church* and the *kingdom of heaven* mean the same thing. Col. i 13, " Who hath translated us into the *kingdom of His dear Son*," means into the *Church* ; and 1 Thess. ii. 12, " Who hath called you unto *His kingdom* and glory," also means into *the Church*.

† Daniel ii. 44, vii. 27.

5

Latin, was, " Jesus of Nazareth, the King of the Jews."
John Baptist's preaching was, " Repent, for the kingdom of
heaven is at hand." *   Our Lord Himself began His ministry
with the same announcement, " Repent, for the kingdom of
heaven is at hand " † ; and He sent forth His apostles to
make the same proclamation.‡   Out of thirty-two parables,
nineteen are parables of the kingdom.   The *sower* speaks of
the first proclamation of the Gospel, and foretells the
different reception it would meet with from different kinds
of hearts.   The *tares* shows that the Church would not
consist of good people only, but that hypocrites would be
found in it.   The *mustard-seed* prophesies the vast extension
of the kingdom from its small beginning, so that the Gentile
nations would seek shelter under it.   The *leaven* illustrates
the way in which, hidden from observation, the power of
the Spirit would work in the world and leaven the mass of
mankind.   The *treasure* and the *pearl* show how some would
come upon the Gospel as by accident, like the Ethiopian
eunuch, and others, like Justin Martyr, as the end of a
careful search after truth.   The *net* tells us how the Church,
having swept through the ages from one end of the world
to the other, will finally land those whom it had caught on
the shore of eternity, and there the separation (already
spoken of in the *tares*) shall take place.   (Matt. xiii.
41, 42, 43.)

But although our Lord generally speaks of His Church
under the title of kingdom, it is to Him we owe the word by
which it has been and is most usually called.   " Upon this
rock " of Peter's confession of His deity " I will build My
Church, and the gates of hell shall not prevail against it "
(Matt. xvi. 18) ; and again, He says that an offending
brother who refuses to listen to private admonition is to be
reported " to the Church ; but if he neglect to hear the
Church " he is to be cast out of its communion (Matt. xviii.
17).   The word translated church (ἐκκλησία) means a body
called out of the general mass of people ; as Abraham and
his seed were called out of the rest of mankind and formed a
separate nation and Church, so individuals are called out of
all nations and formed into a distinct kingdom and Church
of Christ.

* Matt. ii. 2.   † Matt. iv. 17.   ‡ Matt. x. 7.

In His baptism our Lord received the Divine anointing to the kingly office. On the very day after, He began to gather His Church out of those whom John the Baptist had prepared for Him. A little later He laid the foundations of the sacred ministry of His Church. He chose twelve, whom He named apostles, and sent them forth to preach to the lost sheep of the house of Israel " *The kingdom of heaven* is at hand," and gave them power to work miracles in attestation of their authority to make this proclamation of the kingdom. When they returned from their mission, He kept them with Him thenceforward, to be witnesses of all He did and said, that they might be taught and trained for their future work.

The life and teaching of our Lord lead up to the moment when He at length drew from the hearts of His apostles, through the mouth of Peter, the confession of His divinity :—" But whom say *ye* that I am ? And Peter answered, Thou art the Christ, the Son of the living God " ; and from this moment He begins to look forward to and to speak of His death. In response to the apostle's confession of His divinity He prophesies the foundation of His Church, and gives the promise of its indefectibility : " On this rock "—the rock of this confession—" I will build My Church, and the gates of hell shall not prevail against it." The two things are joined together by our Lord—the confession of His divinity and His Church, the one founded on the other. Note again that His last parable, that of the vine, was a type of the deepest mystery of the Church, viz., its incorporation with Christ ; and His last act before His passion was the institution of the great means of maintaining that incorporation.

During the great Forty Days, between His resurrection and His ascension, His Church was the chief subject of His communications with His disciples, " being seen of them forty days, and speaking of the things pertaining to *the kingdom of God* " (Acts i. 3). The evangelists record some of these sayings. On the evening of Easter Day, when He appeared to the apostles assembled in the upper room, " He breathed on them and said, Receive ye the Holy Ghost : whosoever sins ye remit, they are remitted unto them ; and whosoever sins ye retain, they are retained." When

He appeared on the shore of the lake of Galilee He wrought the miracle of the draught of fishes, typical of the work of the commissioned fishers of men, and gave to Peter the command, and through Peter to the rest of the apostles, " Feed My sheep," " Feed My lambs." He appeared to His disciples and said, " All power is given unto Me in heaven and in earth "—as God He possessed all power from all eternity; it was as Son of man that, after His resurrection, He received His kingdom—" Go ye, therefore, and make disciples of all nations, baptizing them in the name of the Father, and of the Son, and of the Holy Ghost ; teaching them to observe all things whatsoever I have commanded you ; and, lo, I am with you alway, even unto the end of the world.   Amen " (Matt. xxviii. 19, 20).

What, then, is the idea of the Church which we gather from the Gospels ? It is a spiritual kingdom, of which Christ is the ever-present King, the Bible its code of laws, the clergy its ministers, and Christian people its citizens ; a kingdom extending into every temporal kingdom, not withdrawing subjects from their temporal allegiance, for the civil magistrates are His ministers attending to this very thing, but setting up a superior claim to a more entire obedience and more devoted allegiance, as extending over a higher province. The apostles are to go into all the world and proclaim this kingdom, and demand belief and obedience to the proclamation under the most awful sanctions. They are to admit men into it by an external act of incorporation, to appoint subordinate officers over every section, to rule the whole with Divine authority. The Church will leaven the whole of society, until it shall have become co-extensive with the world ; and the gates of Hades shall not prevail against it. The apostles are promised supernatural guidance and assistance, equally applying to what they taught in doctrine, and to what they ordained as to organisation.

CHAPTER III

THE APOSTOLIC CHURCH

THE Acts of the Apostles is the history of the establishment and development of the Church of Christ. Incidental notices in the Epistles and the Revelation complete the history of its apostolic organisation.

The Christian Church was supernaturally begun in the upper chamber at Jerusalem on the day of Pentecost. The Lord had prepared it a body, in the 120 gathered together there to await the fulfilment of Christ's promise of the Comforter. As the Holy Spirit breathed into Adam's body the breath of life, so the same Spirit came with a sound as of a rushing mighty wind and filled the house where they were sitting, and tongues of flame lighted upon each of them, and they were all filled with the Holy Ghost ; and the Church—the company of believers, called by Christ, and indwelt by the Holy Spirit, the " one Body and one Spirit " —began its life, against which the gates of hell should not prevail.

The multitude of Jews and proselytes gathered for the feast from all parts of the world, from the Tiber to the Euphrates, from the Euxine to the cataracts of the Nile, flocked together at the rumour of the miracle ; and the apostles, filled with the Holy Ghost, at once began their work of making disciples by the preaching of the Word ; and they, pricked in their hearts, asked, " Men and brethren, what shall we do ? " Peter told them, " Repent, and be baptized every one of you in the name of Jesus Christ, for the remission of sins ; and ye shall receive the gift of the Holy Ghost. For the promise is to you, and to your children, and to all that are afar off, even as many as the Lord our God shall call." " Then they that gladly received his word were baptized," to the number of 3,000.

9

Next we have a statement of the criteria of Church membership. They continued steadfastly—

1. In the apostles' doctrine.
2. In their fellowship.
3. In the breaking of the bread.
4. In the prayers.

The events of the next few days or weeks, or months it may be, are summed up in the words, " And the Lord added to the Church daily those who were being saved (οἱ σωζόμενοι) " (Acts i. 47).

In the third chapter we see how the working of miracles helped the preaching of the word ; for many who saw the miracle of the healing of the lame man at the Beautiful Gate, " believed ; and the number of the men was about 5,000."

The foreign Jews converted on the day of Pentecost, and those who were scattered abroad by Saul's persecution, went everywhere telling what they had learned, and so preparing for the future mission work of the apostles. But the Church, as an organised body, was limited at first to Jerusalem, and all its members were Jews.

The eighth chapter relates its extension to the first circle beyond the Jewish pale. Philip the deacon went down to Samaria and preached Christ ; and the people, seeing his miracles and hearing his teaching, believed, and were baptized, both men and women. When the apostles heard of it they sent down two of their own number, Peter and John, who " laid their hands upon them and they received the Holy Ghost."

The next step was the admission of a Gentile proselyte, in the conversion and baptism, also by the agency of Philip, of the treasurer of Queen Candace. Philip preached to him Jesus, and when the eunuch said, " See, here is water, what doth hinder *me* to be baptized ? " Philip said, " If thou believest with all thine heart, thou mayest." In the eunuch's reply we have a catechumen's baptismal confession of faith : " I believe that Jesus is the Son of God "—the germ of all the creeds ; and Philip baptized him, and the eunuch went on his way rejoicing.

In the tenth chapter we have the history of the extension of the Church to the Gentile world. This was a greater step than that of the admission of Samaritans, or of "God-fearing" proselytes who were already half Jews. This accounts for the elaborate circumstances of the transaction, and the fulness with which they are recorded. A vision of an angel bids Cornelius, the Roman centurion, send for Peter the apostle. A simultaneous vision bids Peter lay aside his Jewish scruples, and go to this Gentile. While Peter is yet speaking, the Holy Ghost falls on the Gentile company, and Peter is able to appeal to this manifest indication of the will of Jesus as his warrant for admitting these uncircumcised Gentiles by baptism into the Church of Christ.

We have seen how, on the day of Pentecost, the Church of Christ, as a visible company of believing people indwelt by the Holy Ghost, began to be ; we have seen the Church spread in widening circles from the upper room to embrace Jews, Samaritans, proselytes, and Gentiles. So far Jerusalem has been the centre of interest, and Peter the most prominent figure of the history, though chap. ix. has told us of the conversation of one Saul who was hereafter to figure more largely in the narrative. In chap. xi. 19 the scene shifts to another series of events—the gradual spread of the Church among the Gentiles.

Some men of Cyprus and Cyrene coming to Antioch, the great and luxurious capital of Syria, preached the Gospel to its heathen inhabitants, and a great number believed and turned to the Lord. When tidings of this came to the ears of the Church at Jerusalem, the apostles assumed the direction of this new work, and sent Barnabas to organise and conduct it. The work so prospered under his hands, that he went to Tarsus to induce Saul to come to help him. It was now seven years since Saul's miraculous conversion. The first three years he seems to have spent in Arabia, and then to have returned to his native city, and to have taken no active, at least no conspicuous, part in the work of the Church. Barnabas knew him personally ; it was he who had (ix. 27) answered for Saul when the brethren at Jerusalem had distrusted the sudden conversion of the recent persecutor. The time was now come for the fulfilment of the purpose which Jesus had revealed to Saul at his conversion : " He is a chosen vessel to bear My name among the Gentiles " (Acts x. 15, and xxvi. 17). He accepted the duty to which Barnabas invited him, and for a whole year they laboured together in the flourishing Gentile Church of Antioch where the name of Christian was first given to the believers.

At the end of that time the Holy Ghost bade the prophets and teachers at Antioch separate Barnabas and Saul for a special mission ; and Antioch became the centre whence the Church began to spread itself over the nations of the world. Barnabas and Saul went first to Cyprus (where Barnabas was known as a landowner, and Saul began to be known as Paul) and preached in its chief cities ; then crossed the sea to the southern part of Asia Minor, and preached in some of its towns—the Pisidian Antioch, Iconium, Lystra, Derbe—ordaining elders everywhere to take charge of the new churches ; then returned in the third year to give an account of their labours to the Church at Antioch.

After about a year's interval, during which they had visited Jerusalem, defended their action against those of the circumcision and received the directions of the Holy Ghost through St. James as president of the Council, Paul undertook a second missionary journey, taking Silas as his companion. First he revisited the Churches of Derbe, Lystra, and Iconium, which he and Barnabas had founded. Then he pushed forward westward through Galatia, and a vision led him to cross the narrow strait which separates the continents, and to carry the Gospel into Europe ; and the sacred historian records his progress through the cities of Macedonia and Greece, Philippi, Thessalonica, Berœa, Athens, Corinth, and Ephesus.

A third journey through the country of Galatia and Phrygia in order, strengthening the disciples, led to a two years' stay at Ephesus, whence Paul travelled again through Macedonia and Greece, and finally up to Jerusalem. Here he was arrested by the Roman captain of the Temple as the cause of a riot in the Temple precincts. He was detained in custody two years at Cæsarea, when at length his appeal to the emperor led to his visit as a prisoner to Rome, where he stayed two years in his own hired house, preaching the Gospel without hindrance. When the sacred history has thus recorded how the Church was established among the three great civilisations—Jewish, Greek, and Roman—its task is accomplished, and it ends.

The Epistles of St. Paul reveal incidentally something of the interior history of several churches of his foundation— those of Corinth, Galatia, Ephesus, Philippi, Colosse, and Thessalonica.

The Revelation (chap. i. 3) gives us a view, at the close of the first century, of one corner of the field of the Church, viz., of the great Ephesian Church, and the daughter Churches which had sprung from her, and were still, and continued to their end, under her jurisdiction—the Churches of Smyrna, Pergamum, Thyatira, Sardis, Philadelphia, and Laodicea.

All the principles of Church organisation and discipline are found to have been established by the apostles acting under Divine inspiration. The Church is seen as a visible body of men gathered out of all nations, admitted by the external ceremony of baptism and the laying on of hands for the reception of the Holy Ghost, assembling together for common worship, obeying the same laws. Consisting of men of different races, scattered in all the cities of the world, the Church of the New Testament is yet one body, an *imperium in imperio*. Its internal unity consists in the one Spirit which dwells in it. Its external bond of unity is the ministry, whose members all derive their authority, through the apostles, from Christ.

The Church is a visible society, into which all, Jew and Gentile alike, are bidden to enter by baptism if they desire salvation through Christ; and having entered, to conform to its laws. So the early Christian writers understood it. Irenæus says : " They who do not come into the Church do not partake of the Spirit, but deprive themselves of life; for where the Church is, there is the Spirit of God." *
And St. Cyprian says : " He cannot have God for his father who has not the Church for his mother." †

The two sacraments hold the same prominent place in the Church of the New Testament that they have ever since held in the Church.

Baptism is the sacrament of entrance. Our Lord had declared to Nicodemus that without baptism no man could

* Irenæus, lib. iii., cap. xi.   † De Unitate Ecclesiæ.

enter into the kingdom of God, *i.e.*, the Church (John iii.).
Our Lord commanded, " Make disciples of all nations,
baptizing them " (Matt. xxviii. 19) ; and in obedience to
this command the converts of the New Testament are
always baptized at once as a matter of course. The three
thousand converted on the day of Pentecost (Acts ii. 41) ;
the Samaritans (Acts viii. 12) ; the Ethiopian proselyte
(Acts viii. 38) ; Paul after his miraculous conversion
(Acts xxii. 16) ; Cornelius and his friends, though they had
already received the Holy Ghost (Acts x. 47, 48) ; Lydia
and her household (Acts xvi. 15) ; the jailer of Philippi and
all his (Acts xvi. 33) ; the twelve disciples of John Baptist
at Ephesus, though they had received John's baptism
(Acts xix. 6) ; Crispus and his house, and many of the
Corinthians (Acts xviii. 8) ; the household of Stephanas
(1 Cor. xvi. 15).

Holy Communion is one of the four criteria of primitive
Churchmanship :—They continued steadfastly in the breaking of the bread. It was so much the centre and chief act
of their worship that the history of St. Paul's doings at Troas
describes the purpose for which the disciples were accustomed to come together every Lord's day as being to break
the bread (Acts xx. 7).

St. Paul (1 Cor. x.) alludes to the veneration in which the
two sacraments were held by the primitive Christians, and
warns them not to trust in these great privileges for salvation unless they continued faithful to their profession and
their grace.

The unity of the Church is plainly set forth : " There is
one Body and one Spirit, one Lord, one Faith, one Baptism,
one God and Father of all " (Eph. iv. 4, 5). The internal
bond of this unity is spiritual unity in the mystical body of
Christ. Christ himself teaches it : " As the branch cannot
bear fruit of itself, except it abide in the vine ; no more can
ye, except ye abide in Me. I am the vine (stem), ye are the
branches " (John xv. 4, 5). St. Paul compares it to the
oneness of a human being : " He is the head of the body,
the Church " (Col. i. 18). " As the (human) body is one, and
hath many members, and all the members of that body, being
many, are one, so also is Christ (the mystical Christ) ; for by
one Spirit are we all baptized into one body " (1 Cor. xii. 13).

The importance of it appears from the admonition,
" Be ye all of one mind " ; from the anxiety of the apostle
to check the rising spirit of partizanship in Corinth, " I
beseech you, brethren, by the name of our Lord Jesus
Christ, that there be no divisions among you " (1 Cor. i. 10,
etc.) ; from the direction to the Romans to avoid the
leaders of schism, " Mark them which cause divisions . . .
and avoid them " (Rom. xvi. 17 ; cf. 1 Tim. vi. 3, 4, 5).

The mode of maintaining this external unity of a society
scattered in groups through every city of the world is to
" continue steadfastly in the apostles' fellowship." When
the Samaritans were baptized the apostles sent two of their
own number to receive the converts into the unity of their
fellowship ; when the Gentiles were converted at Antioch
they sent Barnabas to take charge of the new work.

But how was unity to be maintained when serious differences of opinion arose ? The sacred history tells us. The
first serious question was whether the Mosaic institution
was a permanent one. Some said that though the gates of
God's ancient Church were to be thrown open to the Gentiles, yet the Gentiles must conform to its divinely
sanctioned customs ; others maintained that the Mosaic
institution was a temporary addition to the covenant made
with Abraham, which had served its purpose and was now
to pass away, and Jews and Gentiles were to unite in the
Christian Church, on the basis of the original covenant
with Abraham, with new institutions ordained by Christ.
The question troubled the believers everywhere and was
evidently of the utmost consequence. The way it was
settled, and the unity of the Church preserved was by the
calling of a synod or council : " The apostles and elders
came together to consider of this matter." There it
appeared, from Peter's account of the miraculous sanctions
under which he admitted Cornelius and his friends into the
Church, and by Paul and Barnabas's account of the miracles
which had attended their wholesale admission of Gentiles
everywhere, that Christ had sanctioned their admission into
the Church without their observance of the ceremonial
law. So they drew up a canon in which they boldly affirm,
" It hath seemed good to the Holy Ghost and to us " so to
decree. When the believers read the decree they did not

question its authority ; but, admitting it as an authoritative solution of a difficult and dangerous difference, " rejoiced for the consolation " (Acts xv.).

The threefold ministry is seen fully constituted and established in the Church of the New Testament.   Christ Him self ordained the apostles, and gave them full powers as His representatives, and guided them by the Holy Spirit in the exercise of those powers.

The history of the appointment of deacons is recorded in the sixth chapter of the Acts.*   The selection of these † seems to have been left for obvious reasons to the discontented Hellenist party, but they were ordained to their office by the laying on of the apostles' hands.   Their office was especially to administer the charities of the Church, but we find that some of them at least (Stephen and Philip) also preached and baptized.

The first appointment of presbyters is not recorded.   We find them first mentioned as already existing in the Church of Judea in Acts xi. 30.   When the foreign churches sent their help to the brethren in Judea during the famine, they sent them to the elders by the hands of Barnabas and Saul. Wherever the apostles gathered together a number of disciples, there they ordained an elder to take charge of the flock, over which they themselves, however, retained the chief oversight and supreme government.   Thus Barnabas and Paul " ordained elders in every church " (Acts xiv. 23) to take charge of these separate flocks.   That their appointment was made under the inspiration of the Holy Ghost we learn from St. Paul's address to the elders of Ephesus : " Take heed therefore unto yourselves, and to all the flock, over the which the Holy Ghost hath made you overseers, to feed the Church of God " (Acts xx. 28).   St. Peter assumes the same principles of Church government, and similarly compares the office of an elder to that of a shepherd : " The elders among you I exhort, who am also an elder.   Feed the flock of God which is among you, taking the oversight thereof, not by constraint, but willingly ; not for filthy

* It is possible that this may be only the record of an addition of some Hellenists to the body of deacons already existing ; but it has usually been accepted as the record of the first institution of this order of the ministry.

† All their names are Greek.

lucre, but of a ready mind; neither as being lords over God's heritage, but being ensamples to the flock " (1 Pet. v. 1—3). The duties of the second order of the ministry were, therefore, to rule a particular congregation of believers, subject to the superior rule of the apostles, and to minister the word and sacraments in that congregation.

We find, then, abundant evidence of the existence of three gradations or orders of the ministry in the Apostolic Church. Was this ministry, and this gradation of orders in it, intended to be, and was it in fact, permanent?

When our Lord commissioned some to go and make disciples of all nations, teaching them to observe " whatsoever I have taught you," and promised to be with them to the end of the world, He clearly contemplated the permanent existence of such a body of ministers. St. Paul's direction to Timothy (2 Tim. ii. 2), " The things that thou hast heard of me, the same commit thou also to faithful men, who shall be able to teach others also," likewise contemplates a succession of authorised teachers.

The real question is as to the permanence of the highest order of the ministry. When the apostles died, were the individual congregations left to the rule of the second order, or were any successors appointed to the apostles in whom the office of the supreme government of the churches was continued? In other words, was the permanent government of the Church intended by our Lord to be Episcopal or Presbyterian? Three facts in the history of the New Testament make it at least highly probable that it was intended that the apostles should be, as in fact they were, succeeded by others in their higher office and supreme authority over the other ministers, and over the general body of the Church.

The first is the appointment by the apostles of a Bishop of Jerusalem.

Before they dispersed to their missionary work throughout the world they appointed James to be the Bishop of the Church of Jerusalem. Whether this was James the son of Alphæus the apostle or the son of Joseph by a former wife, all agree that he was a kinsman of our Lord. The ancient fathers constantly affirm that James was Bishop of Jerusalem. The catalogues of the Bishops of Jerusalem, given by the first Christian writers, all place James at the head of the list.   An episcopal throne, or chair, in which it was believed that he used to sit, was still preserved and had in veneration when Eusebius wrote his history early in the fourth century.   The notices of him in the New Testament confirm this statement.   In the early·part of the Acts St. Peter is always spoken of as the leading person in the Church at Jerusalem ; but after the twelfth chapter James always appears to be the chief person in that Church. When Peter was delivered from prison, he bids some of the disciples " go show these things to James and to the brethren "—James was the chief among the brethren. When Paul came up to Jerusalem to give a report of his missionary labours and successes he went to James, and all the elders were present (Acts xxi. 18)—the bishop and his presbyters.   At the Synod of Jerusalem James authoritatively sums up the discussion and pronounces the decree of the synod.   Paul speaks (Gal. ii. 9) of having conferred with " James, Cephas, and John, who seemed to be pillars," where James is put before Peter and John.   The Judaising teachers who went down from Jerusalem to Antioch are said to be " certain who came from James," which implies that he was the head of the Church of Jerusalem.   On the death of James the surviving apostles and disciples assembled together at Jerusalem and ordained Simeon, the son of Cleophas, another kinsman of our Lord, to be his successor. Simeon presided over this Church till the time of Trajan, and was one of the victims of the persecution under that emperor.   After Simeon, succeeded thirteen bishops, all of Jewish name, before Hadrian drove out the inhabitants and razed the city to the ground.   Their names are given by Eusebius, the historian of the early Church.

The second fact is that St. Paul, towards the close of his life, appointed Timothy to exercise in the Church of Ephesus and Titus in the churches of Crete the same authority which he himself had hitherto exercised there. His Epistles to Timothy and to Titus are the written instructions which he gave them to guide them in the execution of their important office, and they were included in the sacred canon as the inspired directions to all the bishops of the Church of Christ   The ancient fathers constantly call

Timothy Bishop of Ephesus, and the subsequent bishops of that see are always spoken of as being his successors ; at the Council of Chalcedon a list of twenty-seven in uninterrupted succession from him was extant.

It is the method of the New Testament history of the Church, as we have seen, to mention examples of Church principles as occasion arises, and to leave to us the inference that the principles thus incidentally mentioned were of general application   We conclude that these are instances of the transition from the rule of apostles keeping an oversight over all the churches of their own foundation, to that of bishops, each succeeding to the apostolic authority in the particular portion of the Church committed to his care.

Would there have been no exhortations to the people or to the presbyters as to the mode of exercising this Church power, when it should suddenly fall into their hands on the apostles' decease ?

The third fact alluded to confirms this view of the question.   The seven epistles in the Book of the Revelation are addressed to the " angels " of the seven principal churches of Proconsular Asia—viz., Ephesus, Smyrna, Pergamum, Thyatira, Sardis, Philadelphia, and Laodicea.   The date of the book is probably about 95 A.D., or two or three years later; and it is clear from the letters themselves that these " angels " are individual men invested with the chief authority in those several churches.   The title "angels" is very nearly the same in meaning as apostles.   St. Augustine and other ancient fathers call these seven angels the bishops of the seven churches.   We know that these churches had bishops at a very early period.   Timothy had been appointed Bishop of Ephesus long before.   Polycarp, a disciple of St. John, is stated by his disciple Irenæus to have been consecrated by the apostles Bishop of Smyrna.   Not long after St. John's time, Sagaris, said to have been a disciple of St. Paul, was Bishop of Laodicea.   Melito was Bishop of Sardis in the time of the Emperor M. Aurelius.   When Ignatius wrote his Epistle to the Philadelphians, which, at most, was not above twelve years after St. John returned from Patmos, they had a bishop, whose gravity, modesty, and other virtues Ignatius commends.   The old Roman martyrology speaks of Carpus, Bishop of Thyatira, who suffered martyrdom under Antoninus. Antipas is said to have been Bishop of Pergamos. So that we have evidence of the presidency of bishops in these seven churches in or soon after the time when the Revelation was written.

In the sub-apostolic age, we find abundant clear statements by the early fathers that these cases of Jerusalem, Ephesus, Crete, and the Apocalyptic Churches, are only examples of that which took place universally—viz., that the apostles everywhere appointed men to continue in the several churches the authoritative government which they themselves had first exercised in them.

Clement, Bishop of Rome towards the end of the first century, who is said to be the Clement mentioned by St. Paul (Phil. iv. 3), says in his First Epistle to the Corinthians, the earliest uncanonical book which has come down to us, " the apostles knew through our Lord Jesus Christ that contentions would arise about the name of episcopacy, and for this reason, being endued with perfect foreknowledge, they appointed certain persons, and handed down an order of succession, so that when they should depart, other approved men should take their office and ministry." [Epis. ad Corinth. I. § 44.]

Clement of Alexandria (A.D. 180—210) says, " The Apostle John, when he settled at Ephesus, went about the neighbouring regions ordaining bishops and setting apart such persons for the clergy as were signified to him by the Holy Ghost " (Strom., *Quis dives salvetur*).

Let us stand at the close of the period to which the sacred history of the Church of Christ brings us—viz., to the close of the first, or early part of the second, century—and look round upon the condition of the Church.

It is the reign of the Emperor Trajan. Turn first to the chief city of Pro-Consular Asia, Ephesus, for there, walking in its stately streets, passing under the shadow of its beautiful Temple of Diana, frequenting its public baths, may still be seen a venerable old man, who forms a living link between the Christians of the day and the Lord Jesus ; for this is the disciple whom Jesus loved—the last survivor of the twelve who went up and down with Jesus. He has lately written, at the pressing request of many, a fourth Gospel, to confirm the three Gospels which have long been in the hands of Christian people, and especially to put on record some of the discourses of the Lord. During his recent exile in Patmos he was favoured with a vision of the Lord, and with revelations of the future history of the Church, and was charged by the Lord Himself with messages to the seven churches.

Our eyes turn naturally to Jerusalem. Alas! the burnt and blackened walls of the Temple, standing amidst the ruins of the half-depopulated city, tell of the Jewish war under Vespasian, ending with the assault of the city and the burning of the Temple under Titus. But there is still a feeble Church in Jerusalem, and Simeon, the brother of the Lord, is its bishop.

Few are left in the world whose bodily eyes saw the Lord. Ignatius, the Bishop of the Church in Antioch, they say, saw Him when a boy. Some say he was the child whom Jesus once took and set in the midst of the apostles to teach them a lesson of humility. But the churches still contain many who had been personally acquainted with one or other of the apostles ; had heard their preaching, witnessed their miracles, been their disciples, had themselves received with the laying on of their hands miraculous gifts of the Spirit. Some who were appointed by the apostles themselves to preside over the churches still survive, and still occupy the bishop's seat. Ignatius is bishop of the venerated mother Church of splendid Antioch ; Polycarp, the disciple of John, is the angel of the Church of Smyrna ; Clement, the companion of Paul, rules the churches of the mistress of the world ; and there are others.

In most of the chief cities of the empire there is a Church. Its history is nearly the same in all. It began at the synagogue, among the Jews and the proselytes, and their sympathisers. After a while it separated from the synagogue and formed a distinct body, which was hated, and, where possible, hindered and persecuted by the Jews and their adherents. Vulgar prejudices were excited against it by horrible stories of monstrous secret rites and licentious practices. But the Christians have steadily increased. They meet together for their simple rites in the large upper room of the house of some devoted disciple ; they lead outwardly peaceful and harmless lives ; they are noted for their mutual attachment ; their societies are organised and affiliated, and are in frequent intercommunication, so that they form a network all over the empire, and even beyond the bounds of the empire. Whatever city a Christian visits, he has only to go to the church in that city, and whether he is Jew, Greek, Roman, or barbarian, rich or poor, bond or free, there he is received as a brother among brethren.

Especially are churches numerous in Asia Minor and Eastern Europe, where they are organised not only in towns but even in country places. There are many in the cities of Egypt ; from Rome and Italy they have spread to Carthage and the rest of Proconsular Africa. There are churches scattered thinly over the Parthian empire and Arabia, and other countries of the East. There are a few churches in Gaul and Spain. Besides and beyond these organised churches the Gospel has been preached and its doctrines embraced by scattered disciples all over the known world. The Christian soldier has spoken of it to his comrades in distant garrisons, the Christian merchant to the dwellers of the countries to which he has travelled ; and the leaven of the Spirit is spreading secretly and mysteriously among the masses of mankind.

CHAPTER IV

THE ROMAN EMPIRE FROM JULIUS CÆSAR TO CONSTANTINE

FROM the time of Nero to that of Constantine, the Church founded by Christ grew from the apparent condition of a mere handful of sectaries, the offspring of a schism in the synagogues, to be the dominant and established religion throughout the Roman empire.

The period is one of special importance ; for while, on one hand, the Church is fully organised, and left to its normal working, on the other hand the Church is still so united, and so near the apostolic age, as to give us some security for the purity of its doctrine and discipline. The disadvantages of the Christian profession have kept out the mere worldly professor, and no alliance with the State had yet modified its constitution. So that we appeal to this period as affording the purest standard of the doctrine and discipline of the Church of Christ.

To obtain a clear notion of the history of the Church of this period some knowledge of the outlines of the history of the Roman empire is necessary.

Seven centuries of conquest had at length made Rome the mistress of a vast congeries of kingdoms, republics, and states, of at least a hundred different races, speaking as many different languages, including along with the most ancient and the most polished civilisations barbarous tribes whose conquest by Rome was their first contact with civilisation—Egypt and Greece, Gaul and Britain. To all these nations the conquerors allowed their municipal governments and their ancestral religions.

But while Rome was rapidly completing the circle of her empire, the political power over it was passing out of the hands of the august body (the senate), which had presided over its earlier fortunes, into the hands of a single master. The wars of conquest had created vast and veteran armies, which knew no country but their camp and no master but their imperator. He who could win the affections of the legions could, if he had ambition and daring, make himself master of Rome and the subject world. JULIUS CÆSAR (B.C. 46) had the ambition to attempt and the genius to accomplish this design. Made perpetual Imperator he retained the sole command of the armies he had so often led to victory. Made perpetual Dictator he controlled with absolute authority all the civil organisation of the State.

His assassination did not restore Rome to its ancient liberty; for after a short struggle, first with the Republican party—Brutus and Cassius and their conspirators—and then with rival aspirants for power, Antony and Lepidus, AUGUSTUS (B.C. 27) succeeded in grasping his uncle's power. Affecting simplicity in his mode of life, and retaining all the forms of the Republican constitution, he was yet absolute master of the Roman world. His policy was to abstain from further territorial acquisitions and to consolidate the provinces together with Rome into a firm and enduring empire. A decree of his, ordering a census to be taken in all the countries under the Roman authority, was the human cause of the journey of the Virgin Mary and Joseph from Galilee to their ancestral city, Bethlehem; where she brought forth her first-born son, and they called his name Jesus.

Five princes of the Julian family thus wielded absolute power under the modest guise of first citizen of Rome. On the death of Augustus his step-son, the gloomy, suspicious, and tyrannical TIBERIUS, succeeded (A.D. 14). In his reign, under the authority of his delegate Pontius Pilate, Procurator of Judea, Jesus was crucified on a charge of treason.

His great-nephew, the furious CALIGULA (A.D. 37) reigned four years. His resolve to have a statue of himself erected in the Temple at Jerusalem, so engaged the thoughts of the Jewish magistracy as to divert them from the persecution of the Christians, and gave to the Church the peace mentioned in Acts ix. 31.

On the assassination of Caligula in A.D. 41, his uncle, the feeble CLAUDIUS, was raised to the purple by the acclamation of the troops. In his reign the conquest of Britain took place, the emperor paying a brief visit to the island to reap the laurels of the first decisive success of his lieutenants, and to return to Rome with the honour of a triumph and the title Britannicus.

NERO, his step-son and son-in-law, succeeded him A.D. 54, and was the Cæsar to whose personal judgment Paul of Tarsus, in the exercise of his right as a Roman citizen, appealed from the subordinate tribunal of the Procurator Festus. In his seventh year (A.D. 61) St. Paul arrived in Rome. He spent two years in an irksome but not severe custody, until his case was brought before the emperor, and he was acquitted and set at liberty. In the following year (A.D. 64) occurred the great fire at Rome, and the horrible persecution of the Christians there, of which we tell in our next chapter. Four years after this (in A.D. 68), Paul was again sent prisoner to Rome, and a very ancient and probable tradition says that he suffered martyrdom there, together with St. Peter, in this last year of Nero's reign.

The atrocities of Nero drove the nobles into conspiracy. GALBA (A.D. 68), a statesman and general, then governing the Spanish province, was induced, in his seventy-second year, to head the revolt. He was called imperator by the Spanish legions, Rome welcomed the tidings, and the senate acknowledged a new master. Nero, deserted by every one, fled in disguise to the neighbouring villa of one of his freedmen, and there found courage to die a Roman's death when his pursuers were already at the door. Within one year Galba, Otho, and Vitellius triumphed and were overthrown in turn ; the last-named by VESPASIAN (A.D. 69), who had been proclaimed emperor by the troops engaged under his command in the Judean war.

With his reign commenced a better era, which lasted during the reigns of the Flavian and Antonine families, embracing eight reigns and about 110 years, until the death of Aurelius. These princes all showed the utmost outward deference to the senate ; the long struggle between the imperator and the nobility, the army and the senate, and sword and the gown, which had drained the life-blood of Rome from Marius to Nero, ceased, and the contending parties seemed to be reconciled. All these emperors with one exception (Domitian), were men of ability, virtue, and public spirit ; it was a period of legal government, of wise, just, and beneficent administration, of tranquil obedience and general prosperity.

Three of the Flavian family reigned—Vespasian and his two sons, Titus and Domitian. The reign of VESPASIAN is connected with ecclesiastical history chiefly by the events which accompanied the suppression of the Jewish rebellion. As general of the armies in Judea, Vespasian had conquered the whole country except Jerusalem. When he marched to Rome to seize the purple, he left Titus to conduct the siege of the Holy City. The horrors our Lord had foretold were fulfilled in that dreadful siege.* At length the city was taken, the Temple, in spite of the anxiety of Titus to save it, was burnt ; the sacred vessels graced the conqueror's triumph on his return to Rome, and their likeness may still be seen sculptured on a panel of the triumphal arch of Titus in the Forum. Before the siege the Christian community, recognising the signs foretold by their Lord, had escaped to the little town of Pella, beyond the Jordan. Of the Jews multitudes had fled to Egypt, where there was already a numerous Jewish population at Alexandria and Cyrene ; others fled to Mesopotamia, and came under the rule of the Parthian monarchy. The slave markets of the world were glutted with captured Jews. At the close of the war, Jerusalem and the great cities were left desolate; the Christians returned and a few Jews, and built huts amidst the ruins of the Holy City. But the Jewish polity was transferred to Tiberias, situated amidst the most prosperous part of the country, and there took root again for a while. The Temple, the priests, and the Sanhedrin were gone for ever. A new school of religious teaching sprang up under the doctors of the law and the rabbis, out of which grew the Mishna, a commentary on the Old Testament Scriptures, and, later, the Gemara, a commentary on the Mishna.

TITUS succeeded his father as sole sovereign in A.D. 79, and after a brief reign was succeeded by his brother DOMITIAN (A.D. 81). Cruel and dissolute, he feared the fate which he was conscious he deserved ; and those who, from

* See Josephus, *War*, Bk. vi.

their virtue, ability, and conspicuous station, were likely rivals were the victims of his apprehensions, while the wealthy were executed that he might seize their confiscated estates. One of the ten general persecutions which historians count is ascribed to his reign, but probably the Christians felt his cruelty merely because they were confounded with the Jews, who were persecuted then, as often in later times, on account of their wealth rather than on religious grounds. He was at length (A.D. 96) assassinated by his friends and officials, whose own lives were in danger from his increasing suspicions of all around him.

The virtuous NERVA (A.D. 96) was invited by the senate to assume the empire, and associated with himself the warlike Trajan, who, after two years, succeeded him.

With Trajan (A.D. 98) begins the reign of the Antonine family—Trajan, Hadrian, Antoninus, Aurelius—the eighty years of whose possession of supreme power was the golden age of the Roman world.

The Antonines, unlike the first Cæsars, did not rule the provinces specially in the interests of Rome, but sought to wield their sovereignty in the interests of all mankind.

TRAJAN (A.D. 98), the first great military emperor since Julius Cæsar, added Dacia to the empire, extended his arms and conquests beyond the Euphrates, and secured the frontiers of the empire by the terror of the Roman discipline and valour. In his reign Pliny the Younger, Governor of Bithynia, wrote to inform the emperor of the growth of Christianity in his province, and to ask instructions for the treatment of its professors, and received an imperial rescript in reply. We shall presently make use of these valuable documents in illustration of the history of the Church. The life of the Apostle St. John extended into the early part of the reign of Trajan. In this reign, too, occurs the martyrdom of Polycarp, of whom more later.

HADRIAN (A.D. 117) abandoned the eastern conquests of his predecessor and devoted himself to the defence of his northern frontiers against the rising power of the northern barbarians. He was especially an administrator. He devoted his attention to the internal affairs of the whole empire, visiting every part of it in person, inquiring into its condition, encouraging everywhere, by his presence and example, the development of its resources and the construction of works of public utility and civic magnificence. He took a philosophic interest in the different religions of the empire, and was especially curious about the religious mysteries ; in Greece he was initiated into the Eleusinian mysteries ; the Jews say that he became a Jewish proselyte ; in Alexandria he was very much impressed with the solemn grandeur of its ancient monuments and rites. In his fourteenth year (A.D. 132) occurred, under Barcochebas, the last revolt of the Jews. It was put down with great severity, and Hadrian banished all the Jews from their country. On the ruined site of Jerusalem he founded a new city called after his own family, Ælia Capitolina. A temple of Jupiter rose on the sacred site of Moriah. The Christians were allowed to remain in the country, and to live in Jerusalem, while he forbade a Jew to set foot in the city on pain of death. The Church of Jerusalem in time regained some degree of prosperity, and was, in the fifth century, raised to the dignity of a patriarchate *causâ honoris* ; but it is remarkable that with all the claims it had upon the veneration of Christendom there was never any tendency to claim for it the place, which Rome afterwards tried to usurp, of the Mother Church and centre of organisation of the Christian world.

ANTONINUS, worthily surnamed PIUS (A.D. 138), an upright, amiable, religious man, passed his well-regulated life in tranquillity between his palace in Rome and his villa in the suburbs. He devoted himself especially, with the help of great jurisconsults, to the establishment of a wise system of imperial law throughout the empire. To him Justin Martyr addressed his great plea for the Christians known as his *Apologia*.

His adopted son and successor, MARCUS AURELIUS, surnamed the Philosopher (A.D. 161), was one of the noblest examples of the wisdom and moral excellence possible of attainment under the influence of mere philosophy.

By these four great princes the provinces were gradually bound together into one majestic and harmonious whole. It is remarkable, and will hereafter be accounted for, that Christianity suffered persecution under the authority of all these virtuous sovereigns, while it was allowed to increase unmolested under some of the vilest and wickedest emperors.

The reign of Aurelius is especially marked by the first general persecution expressly ordered by an emperor.

COMMODUS, his son and successor (A.D. 180), a youth of violent passions and degraded tastes, spent his days with gladiators and his nights in orgies, recklessly dooming to death those who excited his suspicions or his anger. His favourite mistress, Marcia, whom he treated as empress, seems to have been a believer in Christianity or to have had Christian connections, and used her influence to protect its professors. His murder by the officers of his household left the empire without a natural successor.

In future the prize of empire was confessedly the gift of the soldiery, and their nominee did not always pay the senate the courtesy of asking from them the customary acknowledgment of his title.

PERTINAX (A.D. 193), one of the few counsellors of Marcus Aurelius who had not fallen a victim to the jealousy of Commodus, was offered the purple. The strictness of his life and government, however, soon offended the mutinous and insolent Prætorians, and, after eighty-six days, they assassinated him. An old senator, JULIUS DIDIANUS (A.D. 193), outbid the late emperor's father-in-law, who was a rival candidate, and was elected by the venal Prætorians, and acknowledged by the complacent senate. Three of the great provincial governors refused to accept the new emperor, and each took steps to win the empire for himself.

SEPTIMIUS SEVERUS (A.D. 193), a native of Africa, in command of the legions which occupied Pannonia and Dalmatia, reached Rome by forced marches, compelled the Prætorians to surrender and executed their leaders. The senate pronounced sentence of deposition and death against Didianus. Severus successively met and defeated his rivals—Pescennius Niger, the governor of Syria, on his march from Eastern Europe ; and Clodius Albinus, the governor of Britain, in a great battle at Lyons. Severus held the sovereignty during a vigorous and successful reign of eighteen years, and left his two sons, CARACALLA and GETA (A.D. 211), joint heirs of the empire. The murder of Geta left Caracalla sole master. The honours and privileges of Roman citizenship, in former times gradually extended to individuals, to cities, to whole communities, were by this emperor extended to all free inhabitants of the empire. After a six years' reign of cruelty, Caracalla was murdered by his minister MACRINUS, who then procured his own election (A.D. 217), but a successful conspiracy replaced him by the young ELAGABALUS (A.D. 218), the nephew of Severus.

Elagabalus had been priest of the Temple of the Sun at Emesa, and he introduced this worship into Rome, and required the senate to join in the splendid rites with which the emperor-priest honoured his god above all the ancient gods. The religious zeal of Elagabalus did not prevent him from plunging into infinite luxury and infamous lusts. He was murdered by the Prætorians, and succeeded by his young and virtuous cousin ALEXANDER SEVERUS (A.D. 222).

For forty years the Roman world had experienced the vices of tyrants, from Commodus to Elagabalus. Under Alexander it enjoyed thirteen years of calm and good government. Of a devotional turn of mind, he esteemed Christ as one of the great religious teachers of the world, and tolerated His religion ; Christian bishops, as such, were among the habitual attendants at his court.

At length the army revolted and elected to the throne MAXIMIN (A.D. 235), a Thracian peasant, of gigantic stature and strength, who had gradually risen to high command in the army. A mere brutal and jealous soldier, he never during his three years' reign even visited Italy, but from his camp on the Rhine or Danube, surrounded only by soldiers and minions, tyrannised over the Roman world. Christians suffered in his reign, but, perhaps, only as friends of Alexander.

A revolt against the extortion of his African procurator compelled GORDIAN, the Proconsul of Africa, to place himself at its head and assume the purple (A.D. 238). His family was one of the most illustrious of the Roman senate, which embraced his cause against the domination of the soldiery and the tyranny of their nominees. We need not follow the story of rivalry and bloodshed which marked the next eleven years.

In the reign of DECIUS (A.D. 249), took place the first invasion of that people, the Goths, who ultimately broke the Roman power, and in his reign a deliberate and general persecution of the Christians was commanded by the emperor's edict. He perished, after two years' able rule, in an unsuccessful engagement with the Goths, and after the dethronement of GALLUS (A.D. 251), and the murder four months later of ÆMILIANUS, was succeeded by VALERIAN (A.D. 253), who associated with himself his son GALLIENUS. The whole period of the Valerian reign (fifteen years) was one uninterrupted series of confusion and calamity ; the empire was, at the same time and on every side, attacked by the blind fury of foreign invaders and the wild ambition of domestic usurpers. The Franks crossed the Rhine and ravaged Gaul as far as the Pyrenees. The Alemanni crossed the Danube, and marched across the plains of Lombardy as far as Ravenna. The Goths came down the Euxine and, plundering as they came, ravaged Greece and threatened Italy. The Persians, under the vigorous Sapor, conquered the allied kingdom of Armenia, and spread devastation on either side of the Euphrates. Valerian was taken prisoner by Sapor. Gallienus spent his time in indolent neglect of public affairs, while on all sides the lieutenants of Valerian aspired to the throne, or the mutinous legions forced the pretension upon them. During the eight years of Gallienus' sole reign there were no less than nineteen pretenders to the throne in all parts of the empire, not one of whom enjoyed a life of peace, or died a natural death. Italy, Rome, and the senate constantly adhered to the cause of Gallienus.

To the worthless Gallienus succeeded a series of great princes—CLAUDIUS, AURELIAN, TACITUS, PROBUS, DIOCLETIAN and his colleagues, who during a period of thirty years triumphed over the foreign and domestic foes of the State, re-established military discipline, and restored the prosperity, and to some extent the virtue and dignity, of the Roman world.

DIOCLETIAN (A.D. 284), a statesman of profound and subtle genius, was the founder of a new phase of empire. At the beginning of his reign he recognised that the task was too great for one man, and associated with himself a colleague in MAXIMIAN, giving him equal title (*Augustus*) and power. Diocletian was the brain, Maximian the arm of the monarchy. Six years afterwards Diocletian carried still further this subdivision of power by giving to each of the

Augusti a lieutenant with the title of Cæsar, GALERIUS and CONSTANTIUS. Diocletian adopted Galerius as his son, and gave him his daughter in marriage ; Maximian similarly took Constantius for his son-in-law and adopted son. The empire was distributed among them :—the defence of Gaul, Spain, and Britain was entrusted to Constantius ; Galerius was stationed on the banks of the Danube as the safeguard of the Illyrian provinces ; Italy and Africa were considered the department of Maximian ; while Diocletian reserved as his peculiar portion Thrace, Egypt, and Asia. Each was sovereign in his own jurisdiction, but their united authority extended over the whole monarchy, and each was prepared to assist his colleagues with his counsels or presence. This singular arrangement worked harmoniously, and answered the purpose of the statesman who devised it, so long as he himself presided over it. Rome had virtually ceased to be the capital of the empire. Diocletian had fixed his ordinary residence at Nicomedia, Maximian at Milan ; those two cities rapidly became populous and magnificent, and inferior only to Rome, Alexandria, and Antioch in extent and population. Till his triumph in the twentieth year of his reign, it is doubtful whether Diocletian had ever visited Rome, and then he only remained there two months. It was his policy to lessen the authority of the senate and the power of the ancient Roman families. Diocletian assumed the Eastern titles of Dominus and Basileus, maintained a magnificent appearance, and finally adopted the diadem of royalty, and affected the reserve and state and etiquette of the Eastern kings.

In the twenty-first year of his reign Diocletian laid down his power by a voluntary and public abdication. Maximian on the same day at Milan accomplished a like abdication. The two Cæsars succeeded to the higher title and authority of Augusti, and Galerius filled up the Diocletian scheme of empire by the nomination of two new Cæsars—MAXIMIN, his nephew, for the eastern division of the empire, and SEVERUS, a faithful adherent of his own, for the western.

But the balance of power established by Diocletian could only be maintained by his own political skill and personal authority, and his abdication was succeeded by eighteen years of discord and confusion. The empire was afflicted by five civil wars, into whose details we need not enter, merely glancing at the main outline of events. Constantine the son of Constantius, had been left in the service of Diocletian, and the public voice had designated him as the probable successor to his father's Cæsarship. On the appointment of the new Cæsars, Constantius obtained the tardy and reluctant leave of Galerius that his son should rejoin him. He reached Constantius at the very moment that emperor was embarking at Boulogne for Britain to repel an incursion of the wild tribes of Caledonia. Fifteen months afterwards Constantius died in the imperial palace at Eboracum (York), and the troops saluted Constantine, not as Cæsar, but as Augustus and Emperor. Galerius agreed to accord to him the title of Cæsar and the government of the provinces beyond the Alps, but asserted the authority of the second Augustus for Severus, and Constantine acquiesced in the decision.

In the same year (A.D. 306), MAXENTIUS, son of the retired Emperor Maximian, and son-in-law of Galerius, was set up as emperor by the Romans, and was at once joined by his father. Severus, marching against them, was deserted by his troops, surrendered to Maximian, and was put to death. Maximian conferred on Constantine, the title of Augustus, and gave him his daughter in marriage.

Galerius, marching into Italy against the new emperors, found the obstacles so great, and the fidelity of his troops so doubtful, that he again retreated. To balance the power of his rivals he raised LICINIUS to the dignity of Augustus in place of the dead Severus, passing over Maximin, who however, claimed, and forced Galerius to accord to him the higher title. There were, therefore, now six emperors dividing the empire among them. The number soon began to diminish. Maxentius presently refused to submit to the control of his father Maximian. The ex-emperor fled first to Galerius, and then to his son-in-law Constantine, but by an act of treachery against that emperor brought upon himself a violent death, A.D. 310. Galerius died in the following year of a horrible disease, and Maximin and Licinius divided the whole East between them.

Maxentius, having alienated the Italians by his vices and crimes, made preparations for war against Constantine, but

D

the northern emperor anticipated him and marched into
Italy : in a rapid campaign overcame his troops, and made
himself master of Rome and Italy. It was while on his
march to attack Maxentius, in 311, when he was undecided
as to the truth of Christianity, that a luminous cross is said
to have appeared in the sky at midday in sight of himself
and his army, with this inscription in the Greek language,
" In this conquer."   He had the famous standard (*labarum*)
made, consisting of a cross and the letters XP* surrounded
by a garland. He also, it is said, had the armour of his
soldiers marked with a X, the initial of the name of Christ.
His victory and his conversion followed. The triumphal
arch which he erected in Rome three years afterwards in
honour of his victory still remains.

Secretly Constantine had secured the alliance of Licinius,
while Maximin had been the ally of Maxentius. A war
broke out between these two. Maximin was defeated, fled,
and shortly afterwards died. The world was now divided
between the two surviving emperors, and in little more than
a year (A.D. 314) their arms were turned against one another.
Constantine was victorious, and claimed all Eastern Europe
as the prize of victory, leaving Thrace, Asia Minor, and
Egypt to Licinius. Again (A.D. 323) another war broke out
between them. Licinius was defeated, and the Roman
world was once more united under Constantine, thirty-
seven years after it had been first divided by Diocletian.
This ends an important period both of civil and ecclesiastical
history, and we turn to the history of the Church, of which
this sketch of the empire is intended to form the basis.

* The first two letters—*ch* and *r*—of the name Christ.

CHAPTER V

NERO'S PERSECUTION OF THE CHRISTIANS AT ROME

IN tracing the history of the Church through these early ages we have no contemporary consecutive history to aid us. At intervals some incident is recorded which, like a flash of lightning, reveals the scene and the actors for a few moments, then all is dark, till the next flash again lights up the scene, and we have to infer as well as we can the intervening history.

The first of these incidents occurs A.D. 64, the seventh year of the reign of Nero, the year after St. Paul's first imprisonment at Rome, and we find it in the pages of the great Roman historian Tacitus. In that year a great fire broke out, which burnt three parts of the city. The character of the emperor led to the suspicion that he himself had wantonly set fire to his capital ; and the murmurs of the multitude who had been burnt out of their houses began to assume a threatening tone. The emperor endeavoured to evade the danger by diverting the popular suspicions. " With this view," says the historian, " he accused those men who, under the appellation of Christians, were already branded with deserved infamy. They derived their name and origin from Christ, who in the reign of Tiberius had suffered death by the sentence of the procurator, Pontius Pilate. For a while this dire superstition was checked, but it again burst forth, and not only spread itself over Judea, the first seat of this mischievous sect, but was even introduced into Rome, the common asylum which receives and protects whatever is impure, whatever is atrocious. The confessions of those who were seized discovered a great multitude of their accomplices, and they were all convicted, not so much for the crime of setting fire to the city as for their hatred of humankind. They died in torments, and their torments were embittered by insult and derision.   Some were nailed on crosses ; others sewn up in the skins of wild beasts and exposed to the fury of dogs ; others, again, smeared over with combustible materials, were used as torches to illuminate the darkness of the night. The gardens of Nero * were destined for the melancholy spectacle, which was accompanied with a horse-race, and honoured with the presence of the emperor, who mingled with the populace in the dress and attitude of a charioteer. The guilt of the Christians deserved indeed the most exemplary punishment, but the public abhorrence was changed into commiseration, from the opinion that those unhappy wretches were sacrificed not so much to the public welfare as to the cruelty of a jealous tyrant."

In this brief narrative we observe that the Christians had become numerous, and had attracted general attention, and that the prejudice against them was such as to make people believe them capable of a monstrous crime.   If we examine the causes which led to this prejudice—which continued through the whole of the period under our consideration—we shall have the clue to the reasons of the long series of acts of violence against them, of which this is the first recorded instance.

Christianity sprang out of Judaism.   At first the Christians appeared to outsiders to be nothing more than a Jewish sect.   Early opposition to the Gospel down to the time of Nero came entirely from the Jews.   From the heathen it had nothing to fear, except what its professors might suffer from any legal action or popular violence directed against the Jews, with whom they would be confounded.   For example, when Claudius banished all Jews from Rome, probably the Christians would be expelled among them.

But as the number of Gentile converts increased, and the Jewish converts were absorbed into the body of believers, the Christian Church began to assume a new appearance in the eyes of the world, and several features were liable to animadversion.

First, it was not a national religion.   The ancient heathens believed that different nations had different gods.

* The gardens of Nero covered the present site of the Vatican.   The obelisk which now stands in the esplanade in front of St. Peter's ornamented the spina of the circus of Nero's gardens.

Egypt worshipped Isis, the Persians the sun ; and Rome
freely allowed the conquered nations the use of their
national religions, and even tolerated in Rome itself the
erection of temples of foreign deities beside the temples of
the gods of Rome.   But Christianity had not the prestige of
an ancient national religion.   It was not the acknowledged
religion of any country.   It was a " new superstition,"
which seemed to have suddenly sprung up sporadically all
over the empire, chiefly among the lower classes.

Again, such a religion was unintelligible to the pagan ;
it was contrary to all his ideas of a religion.   All ancient
religions had temples, statues, altars, sacrifices, and grand
ceremonials ; and religion had come to mean the mechanical
observance of external rites.   The Christians meeting (at
first) in private houses, with rites needing little apparatus,
presented the spectacle of a sect destitute of the usual
appliances of religion.   People who had no temples and
statues seemed to popular apprehension to have no god ;
and the commonest accusation which the mob flung at
Christians was, that they were Atheists—godless.   Those
better informed reported that the Christians worshipped as
a god a certain Jew who had been crucified in Judea for
sedition, under the procurator Pilate, in the time of
Tiberius, which to the Greeks was foolishness.

The exclusion of strangers from their principal act of
worship gave an air of secrecy to their meetings, and not
unnaturally excited suspicions ; and incorrect reports of
their worship afforded a foundation for most horrible
misconceptions.   Some vague report of the Eucharistic
sacrifice led to the story that Christians offered human sacrifice ; and the doctrine that the faithful communicants par-
took of the body and blood of Christ led to the horrible
belief that they ate of human victims : while a similar
misrepresentation of the love feast and kiss of peace gave
rise to the belief among the mob, always credulous of
horrors, that they indulged in luxurious orgies and horrible
lusts.

Moreover, these Christians seemed to shun the ordinary
intercourse of men.   The fact that heathen religious
ceremonies were mixed up with all the business, public
amusements, and social customs of the pagan world, made

the Christian hold aloof from them.   An altar was placed
before the magistrate's chair ;   the games of the amphitheatre were celebrated in honour of the gods; the standards
of the legions were idols ;   at the public festivities of the
imperial birthday sacrifice had to be made to the divinity
of the emperor ;   even at a neighbour's supper-table the
first cup was a libation to the gods.   This reserve gave to
the Christians the appearance of men of secret habits and
unknown designs ;   morose neighbours, bad citizens, hostile
to the gods, and " enemies of mankind."

A circumstance calculated to excite the jealousy of the
Roman authorities was that these Christians formed all over
the empire associations unrecognised by the law, bound by
their own rules, obedient to their own officers, all united
together in a great confederation.   The Church might not
unreasonably appear to a Roman statesman as a network
of secret societies, capable at least of being employed as a
political engine.   Here was matter enough, on the whole, to
account for popular prejudice against the Christians, and
for the jealousy of the authorities of their unlawful religion
and their dangerous association.

The schools of philosophy had some points of resemblance
with Christianity, but were not liable to the same objections.
The philosophies were intellectual speculations, entertained
chiefly by the educated classes ;   they did not oppose the
popular superstitions, on the contrary it was a maxim of the
philosophers that it was wise to pay a decent respect to the
national religion.

CHAPTER VI

PLINY'S LETTER TO TRAJAN. MARTYRDOM OF IGNATIUS

THIRTY years later, in the time of the Emperor Trajan, secular history again gives us a view of the condition of the Church, and the impression it was making upon the world, in a distant province of the empire.

Pliny the Younger, well known to the student of Roman history as a highly educated, amiable man, and an experienced statesman, was proconsul of Bithynia and Pontus. We have an official letter written A.D. 112, in which he makes a report to the emperor, and asks for instructions in the novel circumstances in which he finds himself.

Here are the very words of this important document. " C. Pliny to Trajan, emperor, health. It is my usual custom, sir, to refer all things of which I harbour any doubts to you . . . It has never been my lot to be present at any examination of Christians before. I am therefore at a loss to determine what is the usual object either of inquiry or of punishment, and to what length either of them is to be carried. It has also been with me a question very problematical whether any distinction should be made between the young and the old, the tender and the robust; whether pardon should be given on repentance, or whether retraction is not to be allowed to profit the man who has been a Christian ; whether the name itself abstracted from flagitiousness of conduct, or the crimes connected with the name, be the object of punishment. In the meantime this has been my method with respect to those who were brought before me as Christians. I asked them whether they were Christians ; if they pleaded guilty I interrogated them a second and a third time with a menace of capital punishment. In case of obstinate perseverance I ordered them to be executed. For of this I had no doubt, whatever was the nature of their religion, that stubbornness and inflexible obstinacy ought to be punished. Some infected with the same madness, on account of their privilege of citizenship, I reserved to be sent to Rome, to be referred to your tribunal. But this crime spreading (as is usually the case) while it was actually under persecution, more cases soon occurred. An anonymous libel was exhibited with a catalogue of names of persons, who yet declared that they were not Christians then, and never had been, and they repeated after me an invocation of the gods, and offered worship with wine and frankincense to your image, which, for this purpose, I had ordered to be brought with the images of the deities ; and they likewise reviled Christ ; none of which things, I am told, a real Christian can ever be compelled to do. On this account I dismissed them. Others named by an informer, first affirmed and then denied the charge of Christianity, declaring that they had been Christians, but had ceased to be so some three years ago, others still longer, some even twenty years ago. All of them worshipped your image and the statues of the gods, and also reviled Christ. And this was the account they gave of the nature of the religion they once had professed, whether it deserves the name of crime or error, namely, that they were accustomed on a stated day to meet before daylight, and to say in turns a hymn to Christ as to a god, and to bind themselves by an oath (*sacramentum*) not to commit any wickedness, but, on the contrary, to abstain from thefts, robberies, and adulteries ; also not to violate their promise or deny a pledge ; after which it was their custom to separate, and to meet again at a promiscuous harmless meal, from which last practice they, however, desisted after the publication of my edict, in which, agreeably to your orders, I forbade any associations of that sort. On which account I judged it the more necessary to inquire by torture from two females, who were said to be deaconesses (*ministræ*), what was the real truth. But nothing could I collect except a depraved and excessive superstition. Deferring, therefore, any further investigation I determined to consult you ; for the number of culprits is so great as to call for serious consultation. Many persons are informed against of every age and rank and of both sexes : more still will be in the same situation. The contagion of the superstition has spread not only through cities, but even villages and the country."

This is a very striking testimony to the all but universal prevalence of Christianity in the province of Bithynia at this early period, and there is other reason to believe that the whole of Asia Minor was more thoroughly evangelised in this earliest period than any other part. The Christian customs spoken of seem to have been the Eucharistic service early in the morning, and the love feast in the evening, the latter being given up in obedience to Trajan's edict against unlawful meetings. These people seemed to Pliny to be harmless enthusiasts rather than criminals or political intriguers, and he shrank from the wholesale cruelties which a general enforcement of the law would have occasioned. We give the emperor's rescript also in its very words. " Trajan to Pliny. You have done perfectly right, my dear Pliny, in the inquiry which you have made concerning Christians. For truly no one general rule can be laid down which will apply to all such cases. These people must not be sought after. If they are brought before you and convicted, let them be capitally punished, yet with this restriction, that if any one renounce Christianity and prove his sincerity by supplicating our gods, however suspected he may be for the past, let him on his repentance obtain pardon. But anonymous libels ought in no case to be attended to ; for it is a very dangerous precedent, and perfectly incongruous with the maxims of our age."

Trajan himself, a little later, was brought into contact with the Christians of the East, and treated them in the spirit of his rescript to Pliny. He had arrived at Antioch, the capital of the East, on his way to take command of the war against the Parthians. At the time the people were greatly excited by a series of public disasters, and were clamorous against the Christians as the cause of the anger of the gods. The venerable Ignatius, Bishop of Antioch, was denounced to the emperor as one of the leaders of the sect. We learn from the sequel the veneration in which he was everywhere held, and the vigour with which he exercised his influence in the churches. The emperor thought it politic to fall in with the popular superstition; a blow struck at this eminent leader of the Christians would satisfy the public mind. Accordingly Ignatius was arrested and brought before the emperor's tribunal.

The account of his trial and of the subsequent proceedings was compiled by eye-witnesses of his sufferings. Being introduced into Trajan's presence he was thus addressed by him : " What an impious spirit art thou, both to transgress our commands and to inveigle others into the same folly to their ruin." Ignatius answered, " Theophorus ought not be called so, forasmuch as all wicked spirits are departed far from the servants of God. But if you call me impious because I am hostile to evil spirits, I own the charge in that respect, for I dissolve all their snares through the inward support of Christ the heavenly King." *Trajan*— " Pray, who is Theophorus ? " *Ignatius*—" He who has Christ in his breast." *Traj.*—" And thinkest thou not that gods reside in us, who fight for us against our enemies ? " *Ign.*—" You mistake in calling the dæmons of the nations by the name of gods ; for there is only one God, Who made heaven and earth, the sea and all that is in them ; and one Jesus Christ, His only-begotten Son, Whose kingdom be my portion." *Traj.*—" His kingdom, do you say, Who was crucified under Pilate ? " *Ign.*—" His, Who crucified my sin with its author, and has put all the fraud and malice of Satan under the feet of those who carry Him in their heart." *Traj.*—" Dost thou then carry Him Who was crucified within thee ? " *Ing.*—" I do ; for it is written, I dwell in them and walk in them." Then Trajan pronounced sentence : " Since Ignatius confesses that he carries within himself Him that was crucified, we command that he be carried bound by soldiers to great Rome, there to be thrown to the wild beasts for the entertainment of the people."

The venerable bishop was at once sent off under the care of a military escort, but was treated with consideration. From Antioch he was carried to Seleucia, and sailed thence to Smyrna. While waiting for a ship he was allowed free intercourse with his friends. Foremost among them was the venerated Polycarp, who had been his fellow-disciple under St. John, and who for many years had been " the

angel of the Church in Smyrna." Deputations, consisting
of bishops, presbyters, deacons, and lay people, came from
the churches of Asia to express sympathy and confer with
him.   After some stay they sailed for Troas, thence to
Neapolis, across Macedonia to the coast of Epirus, across
the Adriatic, and so round to Puteoli, Ostia, and Rome.
It was a kind of triumphal procession.   Everywhere the
churches sent their bishops and others to meet him and
sympathise with him.   From several places he sent back
letters to the churches of Asia, to Polycarp, and lastly he
sent forward a letter to the Christians of Rome, begging
them not to endeavour to obtain a remission of his sentence,
and so deprive him of the crown of martyrdom.*   They
reached Rome when the games were almost over ; he was
hurried to the amphitheatre and the wild beasts let loose
upon him.   A few of the larger bones only were left, which
the Christians gathered together as relics, and afterwards
buried at his own city of Antioch.

* These letters still remain to us, and are among the most valuable
evidences of the sub-Apostolic Church.   Three editions have descended
to us.   Until the middle of the seventeenth century there were twelve
epistles in Greek, which laboured under great suspicion of forgery or
interpolation, besides some others which existed in Latin only, and were
undoubtedly spurious.   About 1644 a MS. was discovered at Florence
which contained seven of the epistles in a shorter form.   The learned
generally accepted these seven (Eph., Magn., Trall., Rom., Phil., Smyr.,
and Polyc.) in their shorter form as genuine ; but a few years ago, among
some Syrian MSS. procured for the British Museum, one was found to be
a translation in Syriac of three (Polyc., Eph., and Rom.) of these
epistles in a still more abbreviated form.   These are decided, by the
majority of those competent to form an opinion, to be abridgments of
the Greek ; and the seven epistles of the Florentine MS. are still
generally accepted as the genuine work of Ignatius.

CHAPTER VIII

THE RESCRIPT OF HADRIAN. THE MARTYRDOM OF
POLYCARP

WHEN the name of " the Age of Persecution " is
given to the first three centuries of the Christian
era, it does not mean that persecution was continuous against the Church of Christ throughout the Roman
empire.   Christians were liable to persecution at any time,
in any province, but hostile action against them was very
fitful.   Sometimes a private enemy would seek to get rid of
a rival or to wreak his revenge, by putting the law in motion
against a Christian.

An example of this is the story told by Eusebius about
Marinus (A.D. 259), a martyr of the time of Gallienus :
" Marinus being a candidate for a Roman office at Cæsarea
was informed against as a Christian by an antagonist, who
pleaded that, upon that account, he ought not to have the
office.   The judge, upon examination finding it to be so,
gave him three hours' time to consider whether he would quit
his religion or his life.   During this space Theotecnus,
Bishop of Cæsarea, met him, and taking him by the hand,
led him to the church, and set him by the Holy Table, then
offered him a Bible and a sword, and bade him take his
choice.   He readily without any demur laid his hand upon
the Bible.   Whereupon the Bishop thus addressed him :
' Adhere,' said he, ' to God, and in His strength enjoy what
thou hast chosen, and go in peace.'   He immediately
returned from the church to the judge, made his profession
of faith, received sentence, and died a martyr."

If anything went wrong—a bad harvest or a military
reverse—the superstitious were always ready to attribute it
to the anger of the gods against the Christians, and a

popular clamour for their death arose. If the Tiber
rose, says Tertullian (*Apol.* xl), if famine or pestilence
threatened Rome, the cry was, " The Christians to the
lion ! " This popular cry was more dangerous than might
be supposed : for when the people, assembled in the amphitheatre at the celebration of any festival, demanded anything with tolerable unanimity, this was accepted as a
declaration of the will of the people, and the magistrate was
bound by the prescription of ancient usage to defer to it, and
thus might send his officers at once to arrest the prominent
members of the Christian body, bring them before his seat
in the amphitheatre, and on their refusal to sacrifice to the
emperor and the gods they might be cast into the arena to
the wild beasts as an exciting *finale* to the exhibition.
Magistrates, no doubt, acted very variously. One would
turn a deaf ear to the loudest mob clamour : another would
make a slight demonstration a pretext for action against the
Christians. A humane prefect discouraged informers, and
sometimes made a way for the accused to evade the
customary tests ; while some wicked magistrates used the
law against Christians to gratify their own greed or lust.

Hadrian issued an edict which restrained the outbursts of
popular prejudice against the Christians. Serenus Graiianus, Proconsul of Asia, applied for instructions. He says
" that it seems to him unreasonable that the Christians
should be put to death merely to gratify the clamours of the
people, without trial and without any crime proved against
them," and asks what course should be taken. Hadrian's
reply is addressed to Minucius Fundanus, who had meantime succeeded Graiianus in the government of the province.
He desires " that men may not be disturbed without cause,
and that base informers may not be encouraged in their
odious practices. If the people of the province will appear
publicly and make open charges against the Christians, so as
to give them an opportunity of answering for themselves,
let them proceed in that manner only, and not by rude
demands and mere clamours. But it is very proper, if any
person will accuse them, that you should take cognisance of
these matters. If any then accuse them, and show that they
actually break the laws, do you determine according to the
nature of the crime. But, by Hercules, if the charge be a

mere calumny, do you estimate the enormity of such calumny, and punish it as it deserves." The rescript seems intended to declare that Christians are not to be punished merely for being Christians.

Hadrian was specially curious about all the religions of the empire, and was not ignorant of Christianity. Two of the early Defences of Christianity—one by Quadratus, the other by Aristides—were dedicated, and no doubt presented, to him. There is extant, moreover, one of Hadrian's letters, which shows the progress which Christianity had made in Egypt, and makes it clear that its chief officials were conspicuous in the world of Alexandria. On the whole the long and peaceful reigns of Hadrian and Antoninus Pius were favourable to Christianity, which was rapidly growing in numbers and assuming a more important position in the world. The philosophers were joining its ranks, its professors affected no disguise, its clergy were well-known, its apologies were no longer mere defences of Christianity against prejudice and misrepresentation : they boldly attacked the folly and wickedness of the established polytheism.

Marcus Aurelius, who commands our admiration for his philosophic spirit and many virtues, was nevertheless the first emperor who encouraged a general persecution of the Christians. There were probably three causes for this : 1. The growth of Christianity and the aggressive tone which it assumed more and more against the religion of the State, with which the institutions of the State appeared to be bound up. 2. The temper of the emperor, who believed that philosophy would elevate the soul of man to higher dignity, and human life to its greatest possible happiness and was himself, as a writer and teacher of this philosophy, a competitor with Christianity for the ear of mankind. It was not incompatible with his philosophy to support the established polytheism, whether, with the earlier philosophers, he regarded the ancient religion as so interwoven with the constitution of the State and with the customs of the people that it could not be destroyed without danger to the whole social fabric, or as a set of superstitions adapted to the gross minds of the ignorant, and useful in controlling them. 3. At this period the superstitious fears of the people were deeply stirred. A series of misfortunes happened in various parts of the empire—inundations, famines, a new and virulent plague (so described by the great physician Galen) swept from east to west of the empire, earthquakes, irruptions of barbarians all along the northern frontier, defeats of the armies. Such visitations naturally turn men's thoughts to the unseen powers which rule the world. What met their gaze? The temples everywhere half deserted; the majority of the people no longer worshipping the ancient gods to whose favour they were wont to attribute fruitful seasons or the lesser tutelar deities, to whose special favour they had consigned the protection of this or that nation, city, guild, or family. Everywhere was found this sect of Christians, to whom the decay of the ancient faith was owing, and, who, growing daily bolder, openly blasphemed the gods, and were drawing all men into the same impiety. A general revival of the worship of these gods was accompanied by a general demand for the suppression of Christianity, and the emperor, falling in with the popular feeling, ordered the most solemn and costly religious ceremonies, offered great numbers of sacrifices, and repealed the edicts which had hitherto protected the Christians from persecution, and issued new edicts, encouraging informers by the offer of half the forfeited goods of the convicted Christians, and authorising for the first time the use of torture to force them into recantation. The leaders of Christianity were sought out. Among them Justin the Philosopher, of whom we shall speak presently, suffered at Rome, and acquired his honourable title of Justin Martyr. A still more distinguished victim was Polycarp, whose death is minutely recorded in a letter from the Church of Smyrna to that of Philadelphia, which bears every mark of authenticity. He was now at least one hundred years old; one of the last links which united the present with the apostolic age. Many Christians had already suffered at Smyrna. Polycarp, at the solicitation of his friends, had removed from the city; but his retreat having been betrayed by two slaves under torture, he was at length seized by the soldiers sent in search of him. " The will of God be done," said he, and bade food be prepared for his captors while he spent in prayer the two hours during which they refreshed themselves. He was carried straight to the arena, where a great concourse was assembled for the games As he entered the place a voice was heard—from heaven the Christians among the spectators thought—saying, " Be strong, Polycarp, and play the man." He was brought before the proconsul, Status Quadratus, who, whether moved to compassion by his venerable age, or anxious to obtain his recantation for the effect it would have on his followers, urged him to save his life, " to have respect to his old age "; the multitude joined in the scene with their clamour. " Swear by the genius of Cæsar ; retract ; away with the Atheists." Polycarp repeated the words, with a gesture which gave them a different application, " Away with the Atheists." " Swear," said the proconsul, " and I release thee ; blaspheme Christ." " Eighty and six years," he replied, " have I served Christ, and He has never done me wrong ; how can I now blaspheme my King and my Saviour ? " The proconsul continued in vain to urge him with threats to retract and to address the people against Christianity. At length he condemned him ; and the herald, in the midst of the amphitheatre proclaimed thrice, " Polycarp has professed himself a Christian." Jews and heathens replied with loud shouts, " This is the teacher of all Asia, the overthrower of our gods, who has perverted so many from sacrifice and the adoration of the gods." They demanded of the Asiarch who presided over the games that a lion should be let loose upon him. The Asiarch pleaded that the games were over. A general cry arose that he should be burned. A quantity of wood was soon collected from the neighbouring baths ; the Jews, we are told, " as was their custom," being specially zealous in the work. Polycarp was unrobed, bound to the stake in the midst of the arena, and the fuel piled up about him. His prayer at the stake doubtless embodied the sentiments of the Christians of that period : " O Lord God Almighty, the Father of Thy well-beloved and ever-blessed Son Jesus Christ, by Whom we have received the knowledge of Thee ; the God of angels, powers, and of every creature, and of the whole race of the righteous who live before Thee, I thank Thee that Thou hast graciously thought me worthy of this day and this hour, that I may receive a portion in the number of Thy martyrs, and drink of Christ's cup, for the resurrection to eternal life, both of body and soul, in the incorruptibleness of the Holy Spirit : among whom may I be admitted this day, as a rich and acceptable sacrifice, as Thou, O true and faithful God, hast prepared and fore-shown and accomplished. Wherefore I praise Thee for all Thy mercies ; I bless Thee, I glorify Thee, with the eternal and heavenly Jesus Christ, Thy beloved Son, to Whom with Thee and the Holy Spirit be glory now and for ever."

The pile was kindled, but the flame swept round him " like the sail of a ship filled with wind," while his body appeared in the midst, not like flesh that is burnt, but like bread that is baked, or like gold and silver glowing in the furnace, " and a perfume as of spices and frankincense filled the air." The confector (the man whose duty at the games it was to dispatch any beast that was dangerous) was ordered to plunge his sword into his body, whereupon the blood gushed forth so that the fire was extinguished. The body was then placed in the midst of the fire and burnt. "Then we gathered up his bones, more precious than gold and jewels, and deposited them in a proper place, where if it be possible we shall meet, and the Lord will grant us, in glad-ness and joy, to celebrate the birthday of his martyrdom, both in commemoration of those who have wrestled before us, and for the instruction and confirmation of those who may hereafter be called upon to suffer."

CHAPTER VIII

THE MERCHANTMAN SEEKING GOODLY PEARLS

THE early Christian writings show how Christianity was then presented to the minds of men. The arguments *pro* and *con*—between the Christian teacher on one side, and the learned Jew, the Greek philosopher, the Eastern religionist, and the Christian heretic on the other—are recorded with great fulness, and are of the profoundest interest. A couple of brief extracts will lay before the reader in an interesting and graphic way some general notion of the mental process by which thousands of thoughtful men found their way out of the philosophical scepticism of educated Roman society into the faith of Christ.

The Recognitions of Clement is a kind of philosophical and theological romance. It has a plot whose gradual development is just enough to interest the reader, and into the mouths of the characters the author puts the arguments *pro* and *con* on a multitude of religious and philosophical questions. The characters of the story are apostles and the companions of apostles ; Peter is the most prominent person. Clement of Rome is supposed to be the relater of the story : and the plot turns on the adventures of Clement's family ; and is just such a story of love and intrigue, adventures and escapes, with a final re-union of the characters, and clearing up of their perplexities, as a modern novelist might weave. We condense the account which Clement gives of his early training, and of the motives which led him to Christianity, which represents no doubt the spiritual history of thousands of educated thoughtful heathens.

Chapter I.—Clement's Early History and Doubts

" I, Clement, born in the city of Rome, was from my earliest age a lover of chastity, while the bent of my mind held me bound as with chains of anxiety and sorrow. For a thought that was in me constantly led me to discuss such questions as these : whether there be for me any life after death, or whether I am to be wholly annihilated ; whether I did not exist before I was born ; and whether there shall be no remembrance of this life after death, and so the boundlessness of time shall consign all things to oblivion and silence, so that not only we shall cease to be, but there shall be no remembrance that we have ever been. This also I revolved in my mind : when the world was made, or what was before it was made, or whether it has existed from eternity."

Chapter III.—His Dissatisfaction with the Schools of the Philosophers

" Having therefore such a bent of mind from my earliest years, the desire of learning led me to frequent the schools of the philosophers. There I saw that nought else was done, save that doctrines were asserted and controverted without end, contests waged, and the arts of syllogisms and the subtleties of conclusions discussed. If at any time the doctrine of the immortality of the soul prevailed, I was thankful ; if at any time it was impugned, I went away sorrowful. Still, neither doctrine had the power of truth over my heart. This only I understood, that opinions and definitions of things were accounted true or false, not in accordance with their nature and the truths of the arguments, but in proportion to the talents of those who supported them. I was neither able to lay hold on any of those things which were spoken of as firmly established, nor was I able to lay aside the desire of inquiry."

Chapter IV.—His Increasing Disquiet

" Being therefore straitened in the discovery of things, I said to myself, Why do we labour in vain since, if after death I shall be no more, my present torture is useless ; but if there is to be for me a life after death, let us keep for that life the excitements that belong to it, lest, perhaps, some sadder things befall me than those which I now suffer, unless I shall have lived piously and soberly, and, according to the opinions of some philosophers, I be consigned to the stream of dark-rolling Phlegethon or to Tartarus, like Sisyphus and Tityus, and to eternal punishment in the infernal regions, like Ixion and Tantalus. Again I would answer to myself, But these things are fables ; or if it be so, since the matter is in doubt, it is better to live piously. But I would ponder with myself, How shall I restrain myself from the lust of sin, while uncertain as to the reward of the righteous ?—and all the more when I have no certainty what righteousness is or what is pleasing to God ; and when I cannot ascertain whether the soul be immortal, and as such has anything to hope for ; nor do I know what the future is certainly to be. Yet I cannot rest from thoughts of this sort."

Chapter V.—His Design to Test the Immortality of the Soul

" What, then, shall I do ? This I shall do. I shall proceed to Egypt, and there cultivate the friendship of the necrophants or prophets who preside at the shrines. Then I shall win over a magician by money, and entreat him by what they call their necromantic art to bring me a soul from the infernal regions. But this shall be my consultation, whether the soul be immortal. Now, the proof that the soul is immortal will be put past doubt, not from what it says, or from what I hear, but from what I see ; for seeing it with my eyes I shall ever afterwards hold the surest conviction of its immortality, and no fallacy of words or uncertainty of hearing shall ever be able to disturb the persuasion produced by sight. However, a certain philosopher with whom I was intimate counselled me not to venture upon it : ' For,' said he, ' if the soul should not obey the call of the magician, you henceforth will live more hopelessly, as thinking that there is nothing after death, and also as having tried things unlawful. If, however, you seem to see anything, what religion or what piety can arise to you from

things unlawful or impious ? For they say that trans-
actions of this sort are hateful to the Divinity, and that God
sets Himself in opposition to those who trouble souls after
their release from the body.' When I heard this I was
indeed staggered in my purpose, yet could not lay aside my
longing or cast off the distressing thought."

Chapter VI.—Hears of Christ

" Whilst I was tossed upon these billows of my thought, a
certain report, which took its rise in the regions of the East
in the reign of Tiberius Cæsar, gradually reached us ; and
gaining strength as it passed through every place, like some
good message sent from God, was filling the whole world,
and suffered not the Divine will to be concealed in silence.
For it was spread over all places, announcing that there was
a certain person in Judea, who, beginning in the spring-
time, was preaching the kingdom of God to the Jews, and
saying that those should receive it who should observe the
ordinances of His commandments and His doctrine.   That
His speech might be believed worthy of credit and full of
Divinity, He was used to perform many mighty works,
and wonderful signs and prodigies by His mere word, so
that, as one having power from God, He made the deaf to
hear, the blind to see, and the lame to stand erect, and
expelled every infirmity and all demons from men ; yea,
that He even raised dead persons who were brought to Him ;
that He cured lepers also, looking at them from a distance,
and that there was absolutely nothing which seemed impossible to Him.   These and like things were confirmed in
process of time, not now by frequent rumours, but by
plain statements of persons coming from those quarters ;
and day by day the truth was further disclosed."

Chapter VII.—Arrival of Barnabas at Rome

" At length meetings began to be held in various places in
the city, and this subject to be discussed in conversation,
and be a matter of wonder Who this might be Who had appeared, and what message He had brought from God to
men ; until about the same year a certain man, standing in

a most crowded place in the city, made proclamation to the people, saying, ' Hear me, O ye citizens of Rome ! The Son of God is now in the regions of Judea, promising eternal life to every one who will hear Him, but upon condition that he should regulate his actions according to the will of Him by Whom He hath been sent, even of God the Father. Wherefore turn ye from evil things to good, from things temporal to things eternal. Acknowledge that there is one God, ruler of heaven and earth, in whose righteous sight ye unrighteous inhabit His world. But if ye be converted, and act according to His will, then in the world to come, being made immortal, ye shall enjoy His unspeakable blessings and rewards.' Now, the man who spake these things to the people was from the regions of the East, by nation a Hebrew, by name Barnabas, who said that he was one of His disciples, and was sent to declare these things to those who would hear them."

The story tells how some put puzzling questions, and the crowd raised a shout of derision. But Clement took his part ; and brought Barnabas to his house. Next day Barnabas departs for Cæsarea ; after a little while Clement follows him, is introduced to Peter, and by Peter's instruction is converted.

Our next extract is condensed from Justin Martyr's " Dialogue with Trypho the Jew." Justin, a philosopher by profession, was a native of Flavia Neapolis, a Greek town, on the site of the ancient Sychem, in Samaria. After his conversion he wrote a defence of Christianity, addressed to the Emperor Antoninus and the senate and people of Rome, which is still extant, and is one of our authorities for the condition of the Church at that early period.*

His Dialogue with Trypho is an elaborate work on the Judeo-Christian controversy, thrown into the form of a dialogue to bring out the argument in a more pointed and lively manner. It opens with a little adventure which at once interests the reader, and affords opportunity to the author to give an account of his own early studies and conversion.

---

* Its date is usually fixed at about 138 or 140.

Chapter I.—Introduction

" While I was going about one morning on the walks of the Xystus,* a certain man, with others in his company, having met me, said, ' Hail, O philosopher ! ' †   I in turn, said, ' What is there important ? '

" He replied that he had been taught to respect philosophers : ' therefore whenever I see one in such costume I gladly approach him, and for that reason have willingly accosted you ; and these accompany me in the expectation of hearing for themselves something profitable from you.'

——" ' Tell us,' says Trypho, smiling gently, ' your opinion of these matters, and what ideas you entertain respecting God, and what your philosophy is.' "

Chapter II.—Justin Describes his Studies in Philosophy

" ' I will tell you,' said I, ' for philosophy is in fact the greatest possession and most honourable before God, to Whom it leads us and alone commends us ; and there are truly holy men who have bestowed attention on philosophy. What philosophy is, however, and the reason why it has been sent down to men, have escaped the observation of most . . . Being desirous of personally conversing with one of these men, I surrendered myself to a certain Stoic ; and having spent a considerable time with him, and when I had not acquired any further knowledge of God (for he did not know himself, and said such knowledge was unnecessary), I left him, and betook myself to another, who was called a Peripatetic, and, as he fancied, shrewd. This man, after having entertained me for the first few days, requested me to settle the fee, in order that our intercourse might not be unprofitable. Him, too, for this reason I abandoned, believing him to be no philosopher at all. I came to a Pythagorean, very celebrated, a man who thought much of his own wisdom. When I had an interview with him, willing to become his hearer and disciple, he said, " What then ?   Are you acquainted with music, astronomy, and geometry ?   Do you expect to perceive any of those

* Eusebius says this was at Ephesus.
† Justin retained the garb after his conversion. Eusebius says, " Justin, in philosopher's garb, preached the Word of God."

things which conduce to a happy life if you have not first, etc."—he dismissed me when I confessed to him my ignorance. . . . In my helpless condition it occurred to me to have a meeting with the Platonists, for their fame was great. I therefore spent as much of my time as possible with one who had lately settled in our city—a sagacious man, holding a high position among the Platonists—and I progressed and made the greatest improvements daily. The perception of immaterial things quite overpowered me, and the contemplation of ideas furnished my mind with wings, so that in a little while I supposed that I had become wise ; and such was my stupidity, I expected forthwith to look upon God, for this is the end of Plato's philosophy.' "

Chapter III.—Justin Narrates the Manner of his Conversion

" While I was thus disposed, when I wished to be filled with great quietness and shun the path of men, I used to go into a certain field not far from the sea. When near that spot one day a certain old man, by no means contemptible in appearance, exhibiting meek and venerable manners, followed me at a little distance. Having halted, I fixed my eyes rather keenly on him." A long conversation ensues about God and the human soul, in which the stranger shows Justin that his philosophy gives no satisfactory conclusions. He concludes thus :—

" ' There existed long before this time certain men more ancient than all who are esteemed philosophers, both righteous and beloved by God, who spoke by the Divine Spirit, and foretold events which would take place, and which are now taking place. They are called prophets. These alone both saw and announced the truth to men, neither reverencing nor fearing any man, not influenced by a desire for glory, but speaking those things alone which they saw and heard, being filled with the Holy Spirit. Their writings are still extant, and he who has read them is much helped in his knowledge of the beginning and end of things, and of those things which the philosopher ought to know, provided he has believed them. For those events which have happened, and those which are happening, compel you to assent to the utterances made by them, although indeed they were entitled to credit on account of the miracles which they performed, since they both glorified the Creator, the God and Father of all things, and proclaimed His Son the Christ [sent] by Him, which, indeed, the false prophets, who are filled with the lying, unclean spirit, neither have done nor do, but venture to work certain wonderful deeds for the purpose of astonishing men, and glorify the spirits and demons of error. But pray that, above all things, the gates of light may be opened to you ; for these things cannot be perceived or understood by all, but only by the man to whom God and His Christ have imparted wisdom.'

" When he had spoken these and many other things he went away, bidding me attend to them ; and I have not seen him since. But straightway a flame was kindled in my soul, and a love of the prophets, and of those men who are friends of Christ, possessed me ; and whilst revolving his words in my mind I found this philosophy alone to be safe and profitable. Moreover, I wish that all making a resolution similar to my own do not keep themselves away from the words of the Saviour, for they possess a terrible power in themselves, and are sufficient to inspire them who turn aside from the path of rectitude with awe, while the sweetest rest is afforded those who make a diligent practice of them. If, then, you have any concern for yourself and are eagerly looking for salvation, and if you believe in God, you may— since you are not indifferent—become acquainted with the Christ of God, and, after being initiated,* live a happy life."

This account of Justin's conversion is the more interesting because of our knowledge of his subsequent history. Having thus found the true philosophy he devoted himself to its defence and propagation. Still retaining his philosopher's garb and character, he established a school of Christian philosophy in Rome. He also wrote two Apologies (or Defences) of Christianity, the first dedicated to the Emperor Antoninus, the second to the Emperor Marcus Aurelius. During the reign of the latter emperor, probably on the accusation of Crescens, a Cynic philosopher who had been his bitter opponent, he was condemned as a Christian, behaved with great firmness and dignity, and earned the honourable title of " the Martyr," which is usually appended to his name.

* *i.e.*, Baptized.

CHAPTER IX

THE MARTYRS OF VIENNE

THE story of the martyrs of Vienne and Lyons, in the latter part of the reign of Marcus Aurelius, may be given as an example of the more general persecutions in which the whole body of Christians in a city was occasionally involved. The history is further interesting as giving the first distinct glimpse of the state of the Church in Gaul. Vienne was an ancient Roman colony; Lyons was a town of more recent foundation, planted by merchants from Asia Minor, as an emporium of commerce, at the junction of the great rivers which were then the commercial highways of the continent; and the two churches seem to have been planted not very long before by Christians coming from Asia Minor. We notice all the features of a settled church. Pothinus is the Bishop of Lyons; Irenæus, the pupil of Polycarp, was a presbyter of Lyons, but, being absent on a deputation to Rome, escaped the persecution, and on his return was elected bishop in place of Pothinus, and became one of the great lights of the Church; Sanctus was a deacon of the Church of Vienne. The history is told in a letter from the churches of Vienne and Lyons to those of Asia and Phrygia, with such circumstantiality and absence of exaggeration as to carry conviction of its truth. We abbreviate it, but give it mostly in the words of the original.

A popular clamour had been raised against the Christians. The mob assailed them with shouts and blows, dragging them about and plundering their goods. The magistrates, to prevent the tumults, prohibited the Christians from appearing in any houses except their own, in the baths, the market, or any public place. Then they were apprehended and led to the Forum by the tribune and the magistrates, and

examined before all the people whether they were Christians.
On pleading guilty they were committed to prison till the
arrival of the governor, who was then absent. The prefect,
when they were brought before him, treated them with great
savageness of manner. The spirit of Vettius Epagathus,
a young man of rank, was roused ; he could not bear to see
so manifest a perversion of justice, and demanded to be
heard in behalf of the brethren, and pledged himself to
prove that there was nothing atheistic or impious among
them. Those about the tribunal shouted against him ; the
governor, irritated at his interference, only asked if he were
a Christian, and on his admitting it, he also was put among
the accused. Ten of them, when questioned, lapsed,* in
fear of what was to come. Persons were now apprehended
daily, so there were selected from the two churches those by
whose labour they had been founded and established (which
seems to imply that these churches had existed only a very
short time). Some of the heathen servants of the accused
were also seized, and, under threat of torture, at the
suggestion of the soldiers, accused the Christians of eating
human flesh, and of various abominable crimes (the old
vulgar stories, as old as Nero, which were revived again from
time to time as late as Gallienus). These things being
commonly reported, all were incensed even to madness
against them ; so that some, formerly more moderate on
account of relationship or friendship, were now transported
beyond all bounds with indignation, and our Lord's word
was fulfilled, " The time will come when whoso killeth you
will think that he doeth God service " (John xvi. 2). The
holy martyrs now sustained tortures which exceed the power
of description, Satan labouring by means of these tortures
to extort something slanderous against Christianity. The
whole fury of the multitude, the governor, and the soldiers,
was particularly spent on Sanctus of Vienne, a deacon ; and
on Maturus, a late convert indeed, but a magnanimous
wrestler in spiritual things, son of Attalus of Pergamus, a
man who had ever been the pillar and support of our
Church ; and, lastly, on Blandina, through whom Christ
showed that those things that appear unsightly and contemptible among men are most honourable in the presence

* *i.e.*, denied that they were Christians.

of God on account of love to His name, exhibited in real energy, and not in boasting and pompous pretences.

While we all feared, and, among the rest, while her mistress, who herself was one of the noble army of martyrs, dreaded that she would not be able to witness a good confession because of the weakness of her body, Blandina was endued with so much fortitude that those who successively tortured her from morning to night were quite worn out with fatigue, and owned themselves conquered, and were amazed to see her still breathing while her body was torn and laid open; they confessed that any single species of the torture would have been sufficient to dispatch her, much more so great a variety as had been applied. But the blessed woman, as a generous wrestler, received fresh vigour in the act of confessing Christ, and it was an evident refreshment, support, and annihilation of all her pains to say, "I am a Christian, and no evil is committed among us." Sanctus also, through long and intense tortures, resisted so firmly that he would neither tell his own name nor that of his nation or state, nor whether he was a freeman or slave; but to every interrogation answered, "*I am a Christian.*" This, he used to say, was to him both name and state and race and everything; and nothing else did the heathen draw from him. They were so exasperated that, having exhausted the usual tortures, they applied hot brazen plates to the most tender parts of his body, so that at length his body "was one continued wound and bruise, and contracted together, and no longer retaining the form of a human creature." Some young persons died in prison. The blessed Pothinus, Bishop of Lyons, upwards of ninety years of age, and very infirm and asthmatic, yet strong in spirit and panting after martyrdom, was dragged before the tribunal; his body was worn out with age and disease, yet he retained a soul through which Christ might triumph. The magistrates and all the multitude shouting against him as if he were Christ himself, he made a good confession. Being asked by the governor who was the God of the Christians? he answered, "If ye be worthy ye shall know." He was then unmercifully dragged about and suffered a variety of ill-treatment. Those who were near insulted him with their hands and feet without the least respect to his age, and those at a distance threw at him whatever came to hand ; every one looked upon himself as deficient in zeal if he did not insult him. For thus they imagined they revenged the cause of their gods. He was thrown into prison almost breathless, and after two days expired.

Many who had denied their Saviour had nevertheless been thrown into prison ; these were dejected and spiritless, forlorn, and in every way disgraced, even insulted by the heathen as cowards ; while they who had been faithful, the joy of martyrdom, and the hope of the promises, and the love of Christ, and the Spirit of the Father, supported them, so that their countenances shone with grace and glory.

An extra day having been added to the shows of the amphitheatre on account of these Christians, Maturus and Sanctus again underwent various tortures in the amphitheatre ; they were beaten with stripes, dragged and torn by the wild beasts, then made to sit in a hot iron chair, in which their bodies were roasted and emitted a disgusting smell, and at length died under the tortures, not a word having been extracted from Sanctus beyond what he had at first uttered—" I am a Christian." Blandina was all the while suspended from a stake in the amphitheatre, but none of the wild beasts at that time touched her, and at the end of the day she was again thrown into prison and reserved for another contest. Attalus was vehemently demanded by the multitude, and was led round the amphitheatre, cheerful and serene, with a tablet carried before him with an inscription, " This is Attalus, a Christian " ; but, being a Roman citizen, he was remanded to prison till instructions should arrive from the emperor.

Cæsar sent orders that the confessors of Christ should be put to death, and those who denied Him should be liberated. They were again brought before the tribunal in the presence of the people. Some who had apostatised now withdrew their denial of Christ, and were added to the list of martyrs. During this re-examination a man who had lived many years in Gaul, and was generally known for his love of God and zealous regard for Divine truth—a person of apostolical endowments, a physician by profession, a Phrygian by nation—stood near the tribunal, and by his gestures encouraged them to confess the truth. The multitude clamoured against him as the cause of the recovered firmness of the lapsed. The governor ordered him to be placed before him, and asked him who he was, when he declared that he was a Christian, and was at once condemned to the wild beasts ; and the next day he and Attalus underwent all the usual tortures in the amphitheatre.

On the last day of the spectacles Blandina was again introduced, with Ponticus, a youth of fifteen. They had been daily brought in to see the punishment of the rest, in hope of intimidating them ; but on their refusing to swear by the idols, and treating the menaces with contempt, the people were incensed, and no pity was shown to the youth of the one or the sex of the other. The tortures were aggravated, and the whole round of barbarities inflicted. Ponticus, animated by his sister, who was observed to strengthen and confirm him, after a magnanimous exertion of patience, yielded up the ghost. The blessed Blandina, last of all, as a generous mother, having exhorted her children and sent them before her victorious to the King, hastened to undergo the same sufferings herself, rejoicing and triumphing in her exit, as if invited to a marriage supper, not going to be exposed to wild beasts. After she had endured stripes, the tearing of the beasts, and the iron chair, she was enclosed in a net and thrown to a bull, and having been tossed by it some time, and proving quite superior to her pains, through the influence of hope and the realising view of the objects of her faith and fellowship with Christ, at length breathed out her soul. Even her enemies confessed that no woman had ever suffered such and so great things. The bodies of those who had died in prison were cast to the dogs. All the relics of the dead were exposed for some days *in terrorem*, and at length were burnt and the ashes cast into the Rhone, that the Christians might not honour them, according to their custom.

CHAPTER X

THE CHURCHES OF EGYPT AND NORTH AFRICA

FROM the death of Marcus Aurelius to the death of Severus there is little of importance in the external history of the Church to demand notice. Severus in the earlier part of his reign was not unfavourable to Christianity. When ill he had been anointed with oil by a Christian named Proculus Torpacion, and attributed his recovery to this unction. In gratitude he took Proculus into his household, and perhaps it was through his influence that a Christian nurse and a Christian preceptor were provided for his son Caracalla.

Towards the end of his reign, however (A.D. 202), Severus issued an edict forbidding any of his subjects to embrace Judaism or Christianity. The edict did not command, and did not lead to, any general persecution of those who were already Christians but a persecution broke out against the Christians in Egypt and Proconsular Africa.

The history of the Church in these countries is of special interest and importance. The city of Alexandria was the Greek and subsequently the Roman capital of Egypt. Founded by Alexander the Great, it became the capital of the Ptolemies, who succeeded to that part of his conquests ; the inhabitants, claiming descent from the first colonists, proudly called themselves Macedonians ; their language and civilisation were Greek ; and under the patronage of an enlightened dynasty the city had become one of the great centres of learning and philosophy.

The philosophy of Alexandria was not merely Greek, it was a combination of all the learning of all the great schools of human thought. A great colony of Jews, attracted by the offer of special privileges, had settled there under the early Ptolemies, and the rabbis of Alexandria were famous for their Jewish learning, and had also diligently cultivated the philosophy of the Greeks.   The mysterious monuments of Egypt pressed upon every intelligent mind within their influence the study of that most ancient civilisation and religion : while in this emporium of the commerce of the East the curious inquirer came in contact with the religions of Persia and Chaldea, themselves affected by the systems of India and the further East.

The Christian Church was early planted here.   St. Peter is said to have founded the Alexandrian Church and appointed St. Mark its first bishop.   The new religion, from the philosophic point of view, attracted the attention of the learned of Alexandria.   It exercised a considerable influence on the existing philosophies, and was itself influenced in return.   It gave rise to a new philosophy, the Neoplatonic.   Platonism was its basis ; some of its profound but vague shadowings forth of great truths were interpreted by the light of Christianity, and other truths of the Christian revelation were incorporated into it.

On the other hand, the philosophic side of Christianity was rapidly developed by its Alexandrian professors.   They found in the language of Plato a vehicle which enabled them to present Christian truth acceptably to minds trained in philosophy : they did not hesitate to adopt from philosophy, all which was in harmony with revelation.   A famous school of Christian learning thus arose which exercised considerable influence on the mind of the Church.

The Catechetical school of Alexandria is said indeed to have existed from the time of St. Mark, but about the middle of the second century it assumed the shape of a great school of thought, in which the clergy and the educated converts were trained, and even heathen disciples came to learn the Christian philosophy.   The first famous master of the school known by name to us was Pantænus, a convert from the Stoic philosophy, described by his successor, Clement, as superior in learning and ability to all his contemporaries.   Clement, a native of Athens, had (like so many inquirers of the time) travelled through various countries in search of wisdom till he found satisfaction in the teaching of Pantænus.

Clement of Alexandria, as he is called, to distinguish him from Clement of Rome, was master of the Catechetical school when the persecution broke out in the end of the reign of Severus. One of its most distinguished pupils was Origen, a young man of seventeen or eighteen. He was born at Alexandria *c*. A.D. 185, and from his childhood had been carefully trained in literature and in the Christian religion by his father Leonidas, a teacher of rhetoric by profession, and a Christian. When the persecution broke out it was thought right that Clement should take refuge elsewhere. Some priests were burned. Leonidas was one of the victims ; his property was seized and his widow and her seven children were in deep distress. Origen, the eldest, was compassionately received into the house of a wealthy Christian lady. Some educated heathen applied for instruction in Christian philosophy to Origen, whose extraordinary learning and abilities were known ; and thus at the age of eighteen he became a public lecturer, and soon afterwards was appointed by the Bishop Demetrius, the master of the Catechetical school. When the persecution broke out afresh on the arrival of a new governor, and priests were burnt and virgins tortured, Origen encouraged his disciples in their sufferings, not without himself enduring some violence from the mob. We cannot here follow the subsequent life and labours of Origen, but content ourselves with this glance at the state of the Christian Church in Alexandria at the end of the reign of Severus.

The persecution extended to the neighbouring province of Africa. The north of Africa was then crowded with rich and populous cities, and formed the granary of the Western world. Carthage, its capital, and most of its towns, had inherited from the conquests of Scipio and the victories of Cæsar the Roman language and civilisation. In no part of the empire had Christianity taken more deep and permanent root. Its Christianity had a special tone—severe, simple, and practical in its creed, earnest and fervent in its spirit. Africa rather than Rome was the parent of Latin Christianity. Tertullian was at this period the chief representative of African Christianity, and Tertullian is the first of the great writers of the Church who wrote in Latin. Still later Cyprian, and later still Augustine, are the representatives of the ecclesiastical organisation and the grand theology of this Latin Church. No churches in the world have been so influential as the Greek Church of Alexandria and the Latin Church of Africa—one the mother of Eastern, the other of Western theology—and no churches have so utterly passed away.   To-day it requires an effort of the mind to realise that Alexandria was once the second largest city in the world and the second greatest patriarchate of the Church—the Church of Clement, Origen, Athanasius, and Cyril, and to recall that the land of Tertullian, Cyprian, and Augustine is the modern Tunisia and Algeria.

Tertullian's first Apology was written at the time of the persecution of Severus.   He urges with characteristic force most of the arguments of the earlier apologists and adds many new ones in favour of Christianity and in refutation of heathenism.   He also incidentally gives much interesting information as to the history and circumstances of the Church, and its extension at that time.   He says : " We are a people of yesterday, and yet we have filled every place belonging to you—cities, islands, castles, towns, assemblies, your very camp, your tribes, companies, palace, senate, forum.   We leave you your temples only.   We can count your armies : our numbers, in a single province, are greater."   In a second Defence, a few years later, he says to Scapula the prefect : " Thousands of both sexes, of every rank, will eagerly crowd to martyrdom, exhaust your fires, and weary your swords.   Carthage must be decimated ; the principal persons in the city, even perhaps your own most intimate friends and kindred, must be sacrificed."   Even if we make allowance for rhetorical exaggeration, there remains a general assertion that Christianity was widely spread in Africa in this early part of the third century, an assertion corroborated by independent evidence.

The year after the death of Severus, apparently as an isolated outbreak of the persecuting spirit, there occurred in this African province the martyrdom of Perpetua and Felicitas.   " Of all the histories of martyrdom none is so unexaggerated in its tone and language, none abounds in such exquisite touches of nature, or on the whole breathes such an air of truth and reality as that of Perpetua and Felicitas." *   We give it for its value in helping us to

* Milman.   The place of martyrdom has, since he wrote, been established as Carthage.

Severus was (a non Roman) Emperor 192-211 (born 146)
Perpetua martyred 203.

realise the actual Christian life of the time.   The youthful catechumens, Revocatus and Felicitas, Saturninus and Secundulus, were apprehended, and with them Vivia Perpetua, a woman of good family and liberal education. Perpetua was about twenty-two years old, married, with an infant at the breast.   Her father and mother were living ; she had two brothers, one, like herself, a catechumen.   The history is related by Perpetua herself, and is said to have been written by her own hand.   " When we were in the hands of the persecutors, my father, in his tender affection, persevered in his endeavours to pervert me from the faith. ' My father, this vessel—be it a pitcher, or whatever it is— can we call it anything else than what it is ? '   ' Certainly not,' he replied.   ' Nor can I call myself by any other name than that of a Christian.'   My father looked as if he could have plucked my eyes out : but he only harassed me, and departed, persuaded by the arguments of the devil . . . After a few days we were baptized, and the waters of baptism seemed to give power of endurance to my body. Again a few days and we were cast into prison.   I was terrified, for I had never before seen such total darkness. O miserable day ! from the dreadful heat of the prisoners crowded together and the insults of the soldiers.   But I was wrung with solicitude for my infant.   Two of our deacons, however, by the payment of money, obtained our removal for some hours in the day to a more open part of the prison.   Each of the captives there pursued his usual occupation : but I suckled my infant, who was wasting away with hunger.   In my anxiety I addressed and consoled my mother, and commended my child to my brother : and I began to pine away at seeing them pine away on my account. For many days I suffered this anxiety, and accustomed my child to remain in the prison with me, and I immediately recovered my strength, and was relieved from my toil and trouble for my infant, and the prison became to me like a palace ; and I was happier there than I should have been anywhere else.

" My brother then said to me, ' Perpetua, you are exalted to such dignity that you may pray for a vision, and it shall be shown you whether our doom is martyrdom or release.' Accordingly I had a vision.   I saw a lofty ladder of gold ascending to heaven; around it were swords, lances, hooks, and a great dragon lay at its foot to seize those who would ascend. Saturus, a distinguished Christian, went up first, beckoned me to follow, and controlled the dragon by the name of Jesus Christ. I ascended, and found myself in a spacious garden, in which sat a man with white hair, in the garb of a shepherd, milking his sheep, with many myriads round him. He welcomed me, and gave me a morsel of cheese; and I received it with folded hands, and ate it; and all the saints around exclaimed, ' Amen.' I awoke at the sound, with the sweet taste in my mouth, and I related it to my brother; and we knew that our martyrdom was at hand, and we began to have no hope in this world.

" After a few days there was a rumour that we were to be heard. My father came from the city, wasted away with anxiety, to pervert me. He said, ' Have compassion, O my daughter! on my grey hairs; have compassion on thy father, if he is worthy of the name of father. If I have thus brought thee up to the flower of thine age, if I have preferred thee to all thy brothers, do not expose me to this disgrace. Look on thy brother, thy mother, and thy aunt; look on thy child, who cannot live without thee. Do not destroy us all!' Thus spake my father, kissing my hands in his fondness, and throwing himself at my feet; and in his tears he called me not his daughter, but his lady (*domina*). I was grieved for his grey hairs, because he alone of all my family did not rejoice in my martyrdom; and I consoled him, saying, ' In this trial what God wills will take place. Know that we are not in our own power, but in that of God.' He went away sorrowing. Another day, while we were at dinner, we were suddenly seized and carried off to trial, and we came to the town. The report spread rapidly, and an immense multitude assembled. We were placed at the bar; the rest were interrogated and made their confession. It came to my turn; my father at that moment appeared with my child, drew me down the step, and said in a beseeching tone, ' Have compassion on your infant '; and Hilarianus the Procurator, who exercised the power of life and death, said, ' Spare the grey hairs of your parent; spare your infant; offer sacrifice for the welfare of the emperor.' I answered, ' I will not sacrifice.' ' Art thou a Christian ? ' said Hilarianus. I answered, ' I am a Christian '; and while my father stood there to persuade me, Hilarianus ordered him to be beaten with rods. The misfortune of my father grieved me, I was as much grieved for his old age as if I had been scourged myself. He then passed sentence on us all, and condemned us to the wild beasts; and we went back in cheerfulness to the prison. Because I was accustomed to suckle my infant, and to keep it with me in prison, I sent Pomponius the deacon to seek it from my father; but he would not send it. But by the will of God the child no longer desired the breast, and I suffered no uneasiness, that at such a time I should not be afflicted by the sufferings of my child or by pains in my breasts."

The keeper of the prison, profoundly impressed by their conduct, and beginning to discern " the power of God within them," admitted many to visit them, for mutual consolation.

" As the day of the games approached, my father entered, worn out with affliction, and began to pluck his beard and throw himself down with his face upon the ground, and to wish that he could hasten his death, and to speak words which might have moved any living creature, and I was grieved for the sorrows of his old age." The night before they were exposed in the arena she dreamed that she was changed to a man; fought and triumphed over a huge and terrible Egyptian gladiator, put her foot upon his head, received the crown, passed out of the Vivarian Gate, and knew that she had triumphed not over man, but over the devil. The vision of Saturninus, related for their consolation, was more splendid. He ascended into the Realms of Light, into a beautiful garden and palace, the walls of which were light, and there was welcomed, not only by angels, but by all the friends who had preceded him in the glorious career. Among them he saw a bishop and a priest, between whom there had been dissensions; and while Perpetua was conversing with them the angels interfered, and insisted on their reconciliation.

Felicitas was in the eighth month of her pregnancy. She and her friends feared that on that account her martyrdom might be delayed. They prayed together, and her travail came on. In her agony she gave way to expressions of her suffering. " How then," said one of the servants of the prison, " if you cannot endure these pains, will you endure exposure to the wild beasts ? " She replied, " I bear now my own sufferings ; then there will be One within me Who will bear my sufferings for me, because I shall suffer for His sake." She brought forth a girl, of whom a Christian sister took charge.

Perpetua maintained her calmness to the end. While they were treated with severity by a tribune, who feared lest they should be delivered from the prison by enchantment, Perpetua remonstrated with a kind of mournful pleasantry, and said that if ill-used they would do no credit to the birthday of Cæsar ; the victims ought to be fattened for the sacrifice. But their language and demeanour were not always so calm and gentle ; to the people who gazed in importunate curiosity at their Agape, they said, " Is not to-morrow's spectacle enough to satiate your hate ? To-day you look on us with friendly faces, to-morrow you will be our deadly enemies. Mark well our countenances, that you may know them again on the day of judgment." To Hilarianus on his tribunal they said, " Thou judgest us, but God will judge thee." At this language the exasperated people demanded that they should be scourged. When taken out to the execution they declined, and were permitted to decline, to wear the profane dress offered them —the men that of priests of Saturn, the women that of priestesses of Ceres. They came forward in their simple attire, Perpetua singing psalms. The men were exposed to leopards and bears ; the women were hung up naked in nets, to be gored by a furious cow. But even the excited populace shrank with horror at the spectacle of two young and delicate women in this state. They were recalled by acclamation, and in mercy brought forward again clad in loose robes. Perpetua was tossed, her garment was rent, and more conscious of her wounded modesty than of pain, she drew the robe over her person. She calmly clasped up her hair, because it did not become a martyr to suffer with dishevelled locks—the sign of sorrow. She then raised up the fainting and mortally wounded Felicitas, and they were permitted to retire. Perpetua seemed rapt in ecstasy, and, as if awaking from sleep, inquired when she was to be exposed to the beast. She could scarcely be made to believe what had taken place. Her last words tenderly admonished her brother to be steadfast in the faith. Perpetua guided with her own hand the merciful sword of the gladiator which terminated her sufferings.

CHAPTER XI

PROGRESS OF THE CHURCH—MARTYRDOM OF CYPRIAN

FROM the close of the African persecution, which lasted till the second year of Caracalla (212 A.D.), the Church enjoyed uninterrupted peace till the reign of Decius (249 A.D.).

In the reign of Alexander Severus it was even protected and encouraged. His mother, Mammæa, had at least taken so much interest in Christianity as to seek an interview with Origen when he was living at Cæsarea, and to converse with him on the subject. The emperor was acquainted with its doctrines, and had a favourable opinion of them, but he was not a Christian. He seems to have been in the state of mind in which were many educated and inquiring minds at the time. He had a good deal of religious sentiment : his first daily duty was to offer adoration to the Deity ; but he believed all religions to be worthy of respect. He paid the customary honours to the ancient gods of Rome, and at the same time held the Egyptian worship in respect, and enlarged the temples of Isis and Serapis. In his own chamber he had statues of those whom he specially honoured as the great religious teachers of mankind—viz., Orpheus and Abraham, Christ and Apollonius of Tyana. In his reign Christian bishops were received at the imperial court in a recognised official position. Churches were built in different parts of the empire. In the case of a disputed title to a piece of ground in Rome, which was claimed by the Christians as the site of a church, and claimed also by the guild of victuallers, the emperor gave his decision in favour of the Christians, upon the principle that it was better that the land should be devoted to the worship of God in any form than applied to an unworthy use. It is clear that the Church transacted her affairs in the light of day.

Indeed a striking, though indirect, indication of the spread of Christian doctrine is the change in the tone of the prevalent paganism and its whole attitude towards Christianity. The old speculative philosophy had become a religion. It had come to acknowledge the being of one Supreme God, and either to look upon the gods of the nations as created beings, or emanations, employed by the Supreme Deity in the affairs of the world, or to explain them away as myths and symbols. It had joined philosophy with morality. It had begun to preach its belief as a means of ameliorating the condition of mankind. It no longer despised Christianity, but seriously argued against it, and defended itself against the Christian attack.

The persecution under Decius was deliberate and general. That able sovereign desired to revive the ancient virtue of the Roman character. He procured the revival in Valerian of the long obsolete office of censor, and his measures against Christianity were part of his design to restore the ancient religion and manners of Rome. Fabian, Bishop of Rome, was one of the first victims. Origen suffered cruel torments, but escaped with life. Antioch saw the martyrdom of its bishop, Babylas. Cyprian, Bishop of Carthage, escaped the same fate by a timely retreat. The persecution was general, its effect upon the Church great. The prosperity of the Church for many years had made it easy to embrace the faith. With many it was an hereditary faith, not one adopted with mature convictions, and many shrank from the painful honour of martyrdom. In the African Church especially many lapsed : among them some bishops and clergy. Many obtained from the officers, by bribes, certificates (*libelli*) that they had complied with the required tests when they had not. The former were called Lapsi, the latter Libellatici ; and the question of their subsequent treatment by the Church raised a great controversy when the persecution was over. The death of Decius, after two years' reign, put an end to the persecution. Valerian, in the early part of his reign, was favourable to the Christians. In the latter part of his reign, however, he issued an edict, by which all bishops who refused to conform were subject to death, and the church endowments were confiscated. Under this edict died Cyprian, Bishop of Carthage, whose life is so bound up with the history of the Church.

Cyprian was a teacher of rhetoric at Carthage, a man of talent and wealth, when in mature age he embraced the faith of Christ. He passed rapidly through the steps of initiation, almost as rapidly through the first orders of the Christian ministry ; and on the occurrence of a vacancy in the bishopric the people of the city surrounded his house, and by acclamation forced on him the honourable office of bishop. At the time of the Decian persecution he acted on the prudent policy which was considered right for the rulers of the Church at such crises—he retreated from the city, and took refuge among the recluses of the desert, whence, by frequent letters, he directed the affairs of his Church, and animated and consoled the sufferers. His letters afford an authentic contemporary authority for the cruelty of the tortures to which the Christians were put, and for the number of the sufferers in this persecution.

At the commencement of Valerian's reign a plague, which the armies brought back from the East, ravaged the whole western world. It was specially destructive in Carthage. Panic seized the inhabitants, and the usual paralysis of all natural affection was exhibited. The sick were left untended or thrust out of doors ; the dead unburied in the houses and the streets. Cyprian exhorted his flock to show the sincerity of their belief in the doctrines of their Master, by not confining their acts of Christian charity to their own relations, or to the Christian brotherhood, but by showing like love to their enemies. The rich gave their money, the poor gave their labour ; the dead were buried, the sick nursed. Confessors,* just released from the prisons and mines, with the scars of their tortures yet upon them, risked their lives anew in these acts of love to their enemies.

When the Valerian edict appeared Cyprian declined to seek safety again in concealment. He was arrested and carried about four miles from the city to where the proconsul was residing. Here he was treated with great respect, and allowed to enjoy the society of his friends at supper. The news of his arrest drew the whole population of the city

---

* A Confessor was one who, during a persecution, risked his life by confessing Christ before the Magistrate.

together ; many spent the night in the open air around the house. A great multitude crowded the place of judgment the next day. There is a notable difference between the passionate fury with which the magistrates and the mob tore and burned the martyrs of Vienne, and the respect and courtesy with which the proprætor treats Cyprian and the reluctance with which he sentences him. The examination was brief. The report of it is from the pen of one of Cyprian's clergy : " Art thou Thascius Cyprian, the bishop of so many impious men ? The most sacred emperor commands thee to sacrifice." " I will not sacrifice." " Consider well what thou dost." " There is no need of consideration ; do as thou art commanded." The proconsul consulted with his council, and reluctantly delivered the inevitable sentence of condemnation : " Thascius Cyprian, thou hast lived long in thy impiety, and assembled around thee many men involved in the same wicked conspiracy. Thou hast shown thyself an enemy alike to the gods and the laws of the empire ; the pious and sacred emperors have in vain endeavoured to recall thee to the worship of thy ancestors. Since, then, thou hast been the chief author and leader of those most guilty practices, thou shalt be an example to those whom thou hast deluded to thy unlawful assemblies. Thou must expiate thy crime with thy blood." Cyprian replied : " God be thanked." The multitude of Christians cried : " Let us go and be beheaded with him." He was removed at once to a neighbouring field, surrounded by trees, whose branches were soon crowded with spectators. He spent a short time in prayer, bound his own eyes, ordered a considerable present to be given to the executioner, and submitted to the stroke. His blood was caught by the Christians in cloths and handkerchiefs to be preserved as relics. His body was buried close by, but was afterwards removed by torchlight with great solemnity and honourably sepultured.

Gallienus, when left sole emperor by the captivity of Valerian, rescinded the persecuting edict. Bishops were allowed to return to their sees, churches, cemeteries, and endowments restored, and the free exercise of their religion for the first time expressly granted to Christians.

CHAPTER XII

THE DIOCLETIAN PERSECUTION—THE CONVERSION OF CONSTANTINE

FROM the conclusion of the Valerian persecution to the latter years of Diocletian (A.D. 260 to 302) the Church enjoyed half a century of uninterrupted prosperity. The Christians became a numerous and influential body. Eusebius says : " The number so grew and multiplied in these fifty years that their ancient churches were not large enough to receive them, and therefore they erected from the foundations more ample and spacious ones in every city." There were more than forty churches in Rome at the time of the Diocletian persecution. Some displayed a degree of architectural splendour, and were furnished with chalices, lamps, and chandeliers of gold and silver. Christians were found in the highest ranks of society and the highest offices of army and State. Prisca the wife of Diocletian, and Valeria, his daughter and wife of the Cæsar Galerius, were believed to be Christians, as were some of the chief officials of the imperial household. Provincial governments were conferred on Christians, with an exemption from all duties which might interfere with their religion. The two co-emperors—Diocletian and Maximian—tolerated Christianity ; of the two Cæsars, Constantius favoured and protected it, Galerius was bitterly opposed to it. In the years 302 and 303 Diocletian was induced by Galerius, his colleague in the East, to adopt a different policy, and to endeavour to suppress the Christian religion.

A series of edicts was issued. The first ordered that all who refused to sacrifice should lose their offices, property, rank, and civil privileges ; that all ranks of Christians should be liable to torture ; that churches should be razed to the ground, the sacred books burned, the endowments confiscated. A second edict ordered the arrest of the clergy. A third edict required them to sacrifice or be tortured. A fourth edict in the next year extended this to all Christians. Since the constancy of Christians under torture was well known, the judges were charged to invent new and more exquisite torments. No edict expressly enacted the punishment of death, but it must often have resulted from torture, and was in many cases actually inflicted.

Constantius, in the provinces under his government, ordered the destruction of churches, but discountenanced violence against the persons of the Christians : * and on his death Constantine still more avowedly favoured Christianity, and promoted Christians to office. In the rest of the empire the persecution raged with great severity. Thousands were tortured, sent to the mines, mutilated, killed.

After the first two years the persecuting edicts were not pressed in the western provinces, but Galerius continued his endeavours to root out Christianity in the East until A.D. 311. In that year, sinking under a horrible disease, and impressed probably with the idea that it was a punishment for his persecution of the Christians, he published an edict of toleration. He allowed Christians to rebuild their churches and freely exercise their religion, and made so much admission of the truth of their religion as is implied in asking their prayers for his own health and safety. The prisons and mines released their victims. Long trains of Christians were seen hastening to the ruined churches ; the public roads and market-places were crowded with long processions singing psalms of thanksgiving. The confessors were received with honour ; the lapsed hastened to reconcile themselves to the Church.

Maximin's † name had not been appended to the edict of toleration, and he now desisted from open persecution, but continued to oppose Christianity by other weapons. Old stories to the prejudice of the faith were revived, new ones invented and disseminated. Paganism was reorganised as

* To this persecution is attributed the death of St. Alban, the protomartyr of Britain.   † P. 32.

a rival religion ; a complete hierarchy was established after the model of the Christian episcopacy.   Men of rank and wealth in different towns were appointed pontiffs, the sacrifices were performed with great splendour, the people required to attend them ; Christians were forbidden to meet for worship and harassed by petty persecutions, which sometimes rose to the dignity of torture and death.

As Constantine extended his power first over one then over another part of the empire, the cause of Christianity triumphed with him.   In his contest with Maxentius the strife for empire assumed also the aspect of a religious war. Maxentius at Rome had ostentatiously displayed his belief in the ancient gods, and promised, if victorious, to restore their worship throughout the empire.   Constantine, on his march against him, had seen the famous vision of the cross in the sky with the words, " IN THIS CONQUER," had definitely embraced Christianity, and resolved to establish it as the religion of the empire, should God give him the victory. After his victory over Maxentius, in October 312, he at once published an edict in favour of the Christians.   In the following June, after the overthrow of Maximin by Licinius, another edict was issued from Milan, in the joint names of Constantine and Licinius, giving complete religious tolera- tion to the Christians, ordering churches and other property to be restored to them, giving compensation out of the public purse to those who might be losers by the restitution, and ordering the prefects to see the restitution carried into effect without delay or chicanery.   It was the great charter of the liberties of Christianity.

The emperor also made a considerable donation to the Christians of Africa towards rebuilding their destroyed churches.   He gave the Church the right to hold property and to receive it by bequest.   This was the legal ground of the vast property afterwards acquired by the Church.

When the rivalry between Constantine and Licinius sprang up, the favour shown by Constantine to Christianity led Licinius to favour the pagan party.   He would retain none in the ranks of his household troops who would not sacrifice.   He confined the bishops to the care of their own dioceses, and forbad the holding of synods.   At length he closed the churches in Pontus, and there was widespread

apprehension of a general persecution, when Constantine
again took up arms against Licinius.   The defeat of Licinius
(A.D. 323) made Constantine sole emperor, and assured the
triumph of Christianity.   Among Constantine's first acts
was the extension to the East of the favours accorded to
Christians in the West.   In an edict he exhorted all his
subjects to embrace the Christian religion, but professed to
wish that it should be advanced by persuasion only.   He
ordered that churches should be built everywhere of a size
to contain the whole population.   He withdrew the State
sanction of paganism by discontinuing all sacrifices hitherto
celebrated at the expense of the State, but allowed other
sacrifices to continue.   For himself, though he continued
only a catechumen, according to a custom unhappily prevalent then and long subsequently, he regularly attended
the services of the Church, read the Scriptures, heard
sermons, in his journeys was attended by a travelling
chaplain, and received bishops among his chosen associates.

The foundation of a new capital on the Bosphorus
marked the establishment of Christianity as the religion of
the empire.   The genius of paganism continued for many
years to influence the men who were born and lived beneath
the shadow of the ancient temples and the great prestige of
Rome ; but from the first Constantinople was a Christian
city.   Several temples of the ancient Byzantine town were
allowed to remain, but the new temples which rose in it were
Christian churches.

Next to the adoption of the Christian symbol of the
Labarum as the standard of his armies and on the coinage
of the empire, the numerous and magnificent churches he
built were perhaps the most conspicuous evidences to the
world that the emperor had embraced the Christian religion.
He built a grand church at Jerusalem, near where his mother
Helena believed that she had identified the site of the holy
sepulchre ; the emperor himself was present with a great
concourse of bishops at the dedication of it.   He built
another at Antioch, called for its splendour the Golden
Church : and others at Mamre and Bethlehem, at Heliopolis
in Phœnicia, and at Nicomedia.   Especially in his new
capital at Constantinople he built the noble church called,
after his name, *Ecclesia Constantiniana*, to the memory of

the twelve apostles, which, as Eusebius says, " was vastly high, yet had all its walls covered with marble, its roof overlaid with gold, and the outside, instead of tiles, covered with gilded brass." He also laid the foundations of a second church in the capital dedicated to the Holy Wisdom, *Sancta Sophia*, which was finished by Constantius, and, after its destruction by fire, was rebuilt by Justinian as it stands to this day, though now a mosque.

The emperor's mother was also a great encourager of devotion. Our early historians used to tell us that Helena was a Christian princess, the daughter of a British king, who was married by Constantius, and that their son Constantine was born in Britain. But we must be content to abandon the distinction. There is no trace of Constantius having been in Britain at all before A.D. 296, at which time his son was twenty-four years old ; the most credible writers assert that his consort was not a Briton but a Bithynian, and that Constantine was born at Naissus in Upper Mœsia ; and there is no evidence that Helena was a Christian before the conversion of her son. She was, however, a devout Christian and a liberal benefactress to the Church, building many churches and monasteries. She took special interest in the holy places of Palestine ; and probably the passion for pilgrimages, which sprang up in that age, was largely due to her example. She endeavoured to identify the scenes of the great events of our Lord's life, and to recover relics of the Gospel age. The finding of the cross upon which our Lord suffered, buried in the place of execution, is credited to her ; and many other relics venerated in the middle ages are due to her zeal and munificence.

CHAPTER XIII

THE CONSTITUTION OF THE CHURCH

THREE theories of Church constitution claim to be primitive—the Congregational, the Presbyterian, and the Episcopal.

The Congregational theory is that any number of Christian people agreeing to form an organised congregation constitute a Church with the right to elect their own ministers ; that every such Church is complete and independent ; that no one has a right to interfere with it in doctrine or discipline ; and that it has a right to claim recognition and be received into full communion by all other churches.

There is no example in the New Testament of any community of Christians organising itself and electing its ministers ; nor any example of it until the sixteenth century of the Christian era.

The Congregationalists point to two facts in the history of the Apostolic Church—the election of Matthias to the apostolate, and the election by the people of the deacons of Jerusalem—in favour of their theory. They refer also to the popular nomination of bishops—as of Cyprian, Ambrose, and others—as illustrations of their theory in the later history of the Church. The reply is that, however the designation of men to be raised to the sacred ministry may have been effected, yet their ordination—the actual conferring of the ministerial character and office—has always been by the laying on of hands of the bishop and presbytery.

When the Congregationalists boldly urge that though the constitution of the Church in primitive times may have been monarchical or aristocratical, yet this is not of Divine obligation, and that Christian men are at liberty to adopt the

81   G

democratic form of Church constitution and government :
that the clergy have no Divine right to rule, teach, or administer sacraments ; we reply that Christ, by His apostles,
organised the Church, and that no body of men can give one
of their number the character and authority of one of
Christ's ministers independently of Christ's appointment.

When a man claims to exercise this office on the ground
of an inward call, those whose duty in the Church it is must
examine his call, and, if it appear to be real, confer ordina
tion upon him ; but we decline to accept his assertion of an
inward call as a valid title to assume the office, independently of Christ's ordinary appointment and regular ordination.

The Presbyterian theory of Church government admits
that the ministry is of Divine appointment, and has a
Divine right to rule, teach, and administer sacraments ; but
asserts that the ministry is of only one order—the pres-
byterate—that deacons are only lay assistants, and that
bishops are an usurpation. They point out that elders
were also called bishops in primitive times. They grant
that the apostles exercised authority over these elders, but
assert that this authority was exceptional and that when the
apostles died the elders remained the sole order of the
ministry, without any superior under Christ. They admit
that at a very early period churches were governed by
bishops, but account for it in this way, that the affairs of
each church were at first ruled by a college of presbyters and
that one of these, ordinarily presiding at their meetings,
gradually assumed a superior function and authority.

We admit that the names of the various orders of the
clergy were not at first settled, and that during the days of
the apostles the title bishop was often applied to the second
order. Theodoret, in the beginning of the fifth century,
explains this point so clearly that we need not add a word to
it : " The same persons," he says, " were anciently called
bishops and presbyters ; they whom we now call bishops
were then called apostles. But in process of time the name
of apostles was appropriated to those who were apostles in
the strict sense ; and the rest, who had formerly the name of
apostles, were styled bishops. In this sense Epaphroditus
is called the Apostle of the Philippians ; Titus was the

Apostle of the Cretans; and Timothy of Asia." But we
claim that the apostles ordained an order superior to that
of the elders, to whom they committed the supreme rule of
the several churches and the power of ordination.

For the assumption that a presiding presbyter gradually
usurped authority there is no evidence in the history of
the primitive Church. It is impossible to believe that
this usurpation should have taken place universally in
all the churches of the world, without an exception here
and there, and without any trace or tradition of such a
revolution.

On the other hand, we have the scriptural examples of
Episcopal constitution in Ephesus and Crete, and in the
seven churches of Asia. When the Church emerged out of
the obscurity which enveloped it, for thirty years or there-
abouts, in the latter part of the first century, the Episcopal
constitution was absolutely universal throughout its length
and breadth. The inference seems irresistible that this
universal existence of episcopacy is the result of apostolic
direction, and according to the mind of Christ. In the
earliest records of the succeeding age, we find that the
succession of bishops was preserved in all churches of which
we have any account. Ignatius suffered martyrdom about
the tenth year of Trajan, which was only about four years
after the death of St. John, at which time he had been forty
years bishop of Antioch. He is said by Theodoret to have
immediately succeeded Evodius, the first bishop, and to
have been appointed by St. Peter's own hand. The
epistles of Ignatius to the various churches are full of
exhortations to private Christians to be obedient to the
clergy, and to the lower orders of the clergy—viz., presbyters
and deacons—to be obedient to their bishops. In the
beginning of his epistle to the Magnesians he speaks of
Damas their bishop, Bassus and Apollonius their presbyters, and of Zotion their deacon; * the last of them he
praises because he was subject to the bishop and presbytery,
and he exhorts all of them to reverence their bishop,
and to do all things in godly peace and concord, " their
bishop presiding in the place of God, the presbyters as the
council of apostles, and the deacons as the ministers of

* Chap. II.

Christ . . . Neither do ye anything without the bishop
and presbyters." *   In the epistle to the Trallians he names
their bishop, Polybius.†   He says : " Let nothing be done
without the bishop, even as your wont is ; subject yourselves
to the college of presbyters, as to the apostles of Jesus
Christ . . . and let the deacons study to please all men ;
without [the threefold ministry] there is not even the
name of a Church " ‡   Again, having cautioned them to
beware of " strange herbage which is heresy," he adds,
" And so ye will, if ye are not puffed up, and not separated
from God, Jesus Christ, nor from the bishop, nor from the
ordinances of the apostles . . . Whoever doeth anything
without the bishop, the presbytery, and the deacons, his
conscience is defiled." §   To the Ephesians he says :
" Let no man be deceived ; whoever is without the altar is
deprived of the bread of God. . . . Let us have a care of
opposing the bishop, that we may be subject to God." ǁ
In the same epistle he speaks of bishops " settled in the
farthest parts of the earth, who are after the mind of Jesus
Christ, even as Christ is the mind of the Father." ¶   In the
epistle to the Philadelphians : **   " Be not deceived, my
brethren ; if any man follows one who maketh a schism he
shall not inherit the kingdom of God. . . . Endeavour,
therefore, to observe one Eucharist ; for there is but one
flesh of Christ, and one cup in the union of His blood, and
one altar, as there is one bishop with the presbytery and my
fellow-servants the deacons ; that whatever ye do may be
done according to God."   To the Church of Smyrna †† he
writes : " Let all of you follow the bishop, as Jesus Christ
doth the Father ; and the presbytery as the apostles ; and
respect the deacons as the commandment of God.   Let no
man do anything which concerns the Church without the
bishop.   Let that Eucharist be accounted valid which is
ordered by the bishop, or one whom he appoints.   Where
the bishop appears there let the people be, even as where
Christ is there is the Catholic Church.   Apart from the
bishop it is neither lawful to baptize nor to celebrate the

---

* Chaps. VI. and VII.   † Chap. I.   ‡ Chaps. II., III.
§ Chap. VII.   ǁ Chap. V.   ¶ Chap. III.
     ** Chaps. III. IV.   †† Chap. VIII.

feast of charity, but that which he approves is well-pleasing to God."

Irenæus, the disciple of Polycarp the disciple of St. John, was first a presbyter and afterwards Bishop of Lyons, succeeding the venerable martyr Pothinus. He makes the appointment of bishops in all the churches by the apostles and their regular succession an argument against the heretics who had crept into the Church in his days. " We," says he, " can reckon up those whom the apostles ordained to be bishops in the several churches, and who they were that succeeded them down to our own times. He adds, " Because it would be endless to enumerate the successions of bishops in all the churches he would instance that of Rome."

About the same time (A.D. 170) lived Hegesippus, who travelled through a great part of the world to learn the doctrine and traditions left by the apostles in the churches they founded. After this inquiry he uses against the heretics the same argument as Irenæus. He says he had conversed with many bishops, and received the same doctrine from all :—" In every succession " (of bishops), he says, " and in every city, the same doctrine is received which was taught by the Law, the Prophets, and the Lord."

Polycrates, Bishop of Ephesus, writing A.D. 196, says that at that time he had been sixty-five years a Christian. He was therefore born about thirty years after the death of St. John, and was contemporary with Simeon of Jerusalem, Ignatius, Polycarp, and other disciples of the apostles. He, writing about the time of keeping Easter, appeals to the tradition of former bishops and martyrs, and the practice of those of his own time. Among others he mentions Polycarp, Bishop of Smyrna and martyr ; Thraseas, Bishop of Eumenia and martyr ; Sagaris, Bishop of Laodicea and martyr ; seven bishops of his own kindred, and great multitudes of bishops who assembled with him to consult about the Easter question.

Clement of Alexandria (A.D. 192), the greatest scholar of his age, speaks of the gradual promotion of bishops, presbyters, and deacons, which he likens to the orders of angels.

Origen, in the beginning of the third century, speaking of the " debts " in the Lord's Prayer, first insists on the debts or duties common to all Christians, and then adds: " Besides these general debts, there is a debt peculiar to widows who are maintained by the Church, another to deacons, another to presbyters, and another to bishops, which is the greatest of all, and exacted by the Saviour of the whole Church, who will severely punish the non-payment of it." In another place he gives the same rule for maintaining orthodoxy which has already been quoted from Ignatius, Irenæus, and Hegesippus, to adhere to the rule of the celestial Church of Christ according to the succession of the apostles.

Cyprian (248) was Tertullian's scholar, and Bishop of Carthage. His epistles and tracts contain a most full account of the Church officers, and the method of transacting all ecclesiastical affairs which was then observed, both in his own and in other churches. He says, writing to Cornelius, Bishop of Rome : " This is and ought to be our chief care and study, that we maintain the unity which was delivered by our Lord and His apostles to us their successors." In another place he says that " there being only one Church and one Episcopacy all the world over, and orthodox and pious bishops being already regularly ordained through all the provinces of the Roman empire and in every city, he must needs be a schismatic who laboured to set up false bishops in opposition to them."

Firmilian, Bishop of Cæsarea in Cappadocia (A.D. 233), contemporary with Cyprian, also calls the bishops the successors of the apostles, and affirms " that the power of remitting sins, which our Lord conferred on His apostles, was derived from them to the bishops who succeeded in their places."

Eusebius, the historian of the early Church, who lived in the latter part of the third and early part of the fourth centuries, derives the bishops of all churches from the apostles. He gives exact and authentic catalogues of the bishops who presided in all the principal cities of the Roman empire from the apostles down to his own time.

" There is such a multitude of unexceptionable witnesses for this fact," says Archbishop Potter, " as can scarce be produced for any other matter of fact, except the rise and progress of Christianity ; so that whoever shall deny this may with better reason reject all histories whatever." " It is as impossible for an impartial man to doubt whether there was a succession of bishops from the apostles, as it would be to call in question the succession of Roman emperors from Julius Cæsar, or the succession of kings in any other country."

All bishops all the world over were accounted equal as to their spiritual authority. To use St. Jerome's words : " Wherever a bishop is, whether at Rome or Eugubium, at Constantinople or at Rhegium, at Alexandria or at Tani, he is of the same worth and the same priesthood ; neither the power of riches nor the humility of poverty makes a bishop higher or lower ; all are successors of the apostles." * St. Cyprian's way of putting the matter † is that there is but one episcopacy, which is shared by the whole college of bishops. He distinctly affirms that every apostle was invested with the same dignity and power which was given to St. Peter, and every bishop in the world is a successor of Peter as well as of the rest of the apostles, and has the same station and authority within his own diocese which our Lord conferred upon Peter. For the sake of order, how-ever, every bishop limited the exercise of his episcopate to his own Church only. In theory every bishop was without superior, and every Church—i.e. every local community of Christians with its bishop and clergy—was independent ; but in fact, at a very early period, the churches were organised in groups. The Church's growth naturally suggested such an organisation. One Church, usually the Church of the principal city, was historically the mother Church of the whole district, and this would tend to make the daughter churches regard themselves as specially united and all to look up to the mother Church as their natural head. It was natural also that churches connected by ties of race, language, or civil organisation, should acknowledge a special bond of brotherhood ; it was almost inevitable that their bishops should meet occasionally to discuss the com-mon interests of their churches, and make arrangements for the general advantage. These meetings would naturally take place at the principal city of the district, and the bishop of that city would preside. In the early part of the

* Ep. 146 ad Evagrium.   † Ep. IV.

third century we find this provincial organisation already thoroughly established, and spoken of as an ancient recognised system. The "Apostolic Constitutions" * lay down as a custom of the Church " that the bishops of every nation should have a regard to the first among them, and account him their head, and attempt nothing without him besides what concerns their own particular dioceses, and that he should do nothing but by consent of the rest."

This ecclesiastical organisation usually coincided with the civil divisions of the empire. The words Diocese and Parish originally expressed civil divisions of the empire, the parish a territorial division which formed a bishopric, the diocese a still larger district of country which constituted a Patriarchate.

The dignity of the chief bishop of a district was usually assigned to the bishop of the chief city, the metropolis of the district, who thus came to be styled Metropolitan. But this was not always the case, for in Proconsular Africa the chief bishop of the province was elected ; at one time Cyprian of Carthage, at another Augustine of Hippo, was chief bishop.

We have an interesting example of an adaptation of ecclesiastical organisation to the political facts in the case of Judea. Jerusalem was the mother Church of Judea and of all the Churches ; but Cæsarea was the ecclesiastical metropolis of the province, because Cæsarea was the civil capital ; and it was not until the fourth general Council,† when the veneration for the holy places, and the fashion of pilgrimages, had directed the eyes of Christendom to the Holy City, that it was raised to the dignity of a patriarchate *causâ honoris*.

A still more important example is that of Byzantium. The little town on the Bosphorus had been subject to the primate of Heraclea, in Thrace ; but when Constantine made it the seat of empire the Bishop of " new Rome " was speedily raised to patriarchal dignity. From ancient times the bishops of Rome, Alexandria, and Antioch had held a pre-

* The date of this work is the fourth century ; but the first part of it is believed to be a collection of the rules and customs observed during the previous ages of the Church.
† Page 171.

eminent position, because those cities were the capitals of the three great divisions of the empire, and Rome held the first place of honour because of the dignity of the imperial city. The western empire having been destroyed by the barbarians, and Rome depopulated and despoiled, while " new Rome " had grown into the most populous and magnificent city in the world, and the capital of the empire, the patriarchs of Constantinople attempted to take precedence of the popes of Rome. But Rome was still a great name, and the eastern bishops assembled at the general Council of Chalcedon, still allowed it precedence of honour while they placed Constantinople next in order after it.

Each bishop was chief ruler of his own Church. A metropolitan had no right to interfere in the internal affairs of another diocese ; his chief duties were to preside in the synods of his province, and to see that canons there passed were generally observed. He supervised the consecration of all bishops within his province ; he represented his province in communications with other provinces of the Church. The rights of a patriarch were of a similar kind. He presided in the occasional greater synods of his patriarchate, saw that its canons were promulgated and observed, exercised the office of visitor over the metropolitans of his patriarchate without any right of interference in the internal affairs of their provinces, and represented the great branch of the Church of which he was the head.

This ancient organisation into provinces and the customary rights of metropolitans were recognised and sanctioned by the first general Council of Nicæa (A.D. 325). Some individual churches had never been included in any province, nor had their bishops been subject to any metropolitan, and it was then decreed that these *autocephalous* churches should retain their ancient freedom.

The constitution of the empire, ever since the time of Augustus, made the emperor the source of all power and authority, legislative and executive, civil, military, and religious. The emperor held the title of Pontifex Maximus, and Constantine on his accession had been solemnly installed into the office of chief pontiff of the ancient religion of Rome. The imperial exchequer had been accustomed to make grants for the support of temples and the celebration of religious ceremonials ; the laws had allowed immunities and privileges to priests and sacred persons. When the emperor became Christian it was inevitable that he should cease to support heathenism, and as a Christian use his authority and wealth to support and propagate the Gospel. As legislator it was right that he should make the laws of the empire conform to the laws of God and give the Church such immunities and privileges as would tend to the well being of the people. As chief magistrate, it was right that he should restrain his subjects from actions contrary to God's law.

This attitude of protection, support and control, the Church welcomed, without any formal preliminary definition of the proper limitation of the relations between Church and State. These limitations were gradually worked out as occasion arose, and more speedily and easily than might have been expected. Even from the first whatever influence was exercised by the emperors was exercised under legal ecclesiastical forms. Hosius, Bishop of Cordova, Constantine's most trusted adviser in religious matters, wrote thus to him : " Intrude not yourself into ecclesiastical matters, neither give commands unto us concerning them ; but learn them from us. God hath put into your hands the kingdom ; to us He hath entrusted the affairs of His Church ; and as he who should steal the empire from you would resist the ordinance of God, so likewise fear on your part, lest by taking upon yourself the government of the Church you become guilty of a great offence. It is written, ' Render unto Cæsar the things that are Cæsar's, and unto God the things that are God's.' Neither, therefore, is it permitted to us to exercise an earthly rule ; neither have you, sire, any authority to burn incense."

The emperor, as we have seen, tolerated all religions, but he invited all his subjects to embrace Christianity ; and he formally recognised Christianity as the religion of the State. He did not endow the Church throughout the empire, but he repealed the edicts which prohibited it from holding property, and he set the example of building and endowing churches out of his own possessions ; he recognised the validity of ecclesiastical legislation within its own sphere, and used his authority to secure obedience to canonical decisions.

Where the power of the State fails, there the power of the Church begins. Cæsar can only maintain external obedience by the sword ; the Church bids the citizen render a willing obedience, not only for wrath, but also for conscience' sake. The civil power can punish crime, but it fails to repress vice, and it cannot touch sin. The Church especially deals with sin, which is the root of all social and civil disorder. In short, the State can deal only with the material interests and the external life and order of society ; the Church deals with the internal life—the beliefs and hopes and aims of the soul, which are the inner springs and regulators of the external life of man. Only religion can make a man a good citizen. The Roman empire had found out long ago that civil government was inefficient without religion, and we have seen that some of the bitterest persecutions of the Church were a part of the efforts of the best emperors to revive the ancient religion and manners of Rome. The union of Church and State under Constantine was the true fulfilment of these aspirations after the revival of the religious element in civil society.

CHAPTER XIV

THE CHURCH BUILDINGS. THE CATACOMBS

THE first place of Christian assembly for public worship was that upper room in Jerusalem, probably in the house of Mary the mother of Mark, in which the Holy Communion was instituted ; in which the apostles were gathered together when the risen Lord appeared in the midst of them, saying, " Peace be unto you," on the first day of the week after the resurrection, and again on the first day of the week following ; and in which the hundred and twenty disciples were assembled on the day of Pentecost, when the Holy Spirit descended upon them, and the Church of Christ began to be.

There is evidence that in other towns also either the upper room, or the atrium of the house, of some convert, afforded a meeting-place for the brethren. The author of the Dialogue called " Philopater," about the time of Trajan, tells how the Christians carried one Critias into an hyperoon (upper room), the place of their assembly, to make him a proselyte of their religion.

The first church opened for public worship is said to have been in Rome. The Pudens saluted by St. Paul (2 Tim. iv. 21) was perhaps the distinguished senator of that name, in whose house St. Paul is said to have lived ; and the grandson of this Pudens, Pius I., Bishop of Rome from 142 to 157 A.D., is said to have converted a part of the family mansion into a church. The present church of Sta. Pudenziana occupies the same site. Beneath the church, portions of the Roman house have been discovered, and three halls which have been thrown into one may have been this first public church. It was not unusual for wealthy Christians to give to the Church the houses thus hallowed by the church assemblies, to be converted to the permanent use

of the community. The same Bishop Pius, writing to
Justus of Vienne, says that a pious matron, Euprepia, had
given her house to the poor, " where now, dwelling with the
poor, we celebrate the Divine offices." The early Christian
Romance, called the " Recognitions of Clement " (bk. x. 71),
in saying that a certain Theophilus converted his palace at
Antioch into a church, shows what was customary at that
period.

The idea that the Church was in hiding all through the
first three centuries, and that it was only " when the
persecuted Church emerged from the catacombs to bask in
the sunshine of imperial favour " that they ventured to
build churches for public worship, is a popular error. The
Christians were not so continuously harassed by persecution, and were not compelled to keep their religion so
secret as is popularly imagined. Now and then there
was an outbreak of persecution, and Christians, especially the leaders, were compelled to hide ; but intervals
of peace lasted for whole generations, during which
Christians made no secret of their religion ; and probably
they began to build churches almost as soon as the congregations were numerous enough to make it necessary.
There were twenty-five public churches in Rome, and fifteen
suburban basilicas connected with the different catacombs,
before the Diocletian persecution in 303 ; and other
churches had been built all over the empire. Diocletian
too, sent a body of troops to wreck the Church of Nicomedia,
which was a large and conspicuous building on a hill in full
sight from his own palace.

Another popular error is that the two basilicas which
Constantine assigned to the Christians at Rome for their
public worship were the first examples of the use of this plan
for churches. It had been adopted long before the time of
Constantine. Some still remain, little injured, to show
what the plan and arrangement of the early churches were.
One of the earliest is at Djemila (the ancient Cuicul), in
Algeria. It is a rectangular hall, 92 feet long by 52 feet
wide, divided by pillars into a body and two aisles, with a
lofty square enclosure at the upper end on the usual site
of the chancel. Its floor is covered with a fine mosaic
pavement, so purely classical in design as to leave no doubt

of its early date.* Another very early church at Announa
(the ancient Thibilis), also in Algeria, is of the common
basilican plan—a body and two aisles, with a semicircular
apse at the upper end ; this is about 45 feet square. A
basilica at Orleansville, the ancient Castellum Tingitanum,
erected, according to an existing inscription, in the year
A.D. 252 and the most ancient dated church in Africa, is
80 feet long by 52 feet wide, divided by four rows of pillars
into a body and double aisles entirely paved with mosaics,
with an apse at the lower as well as the upper end. Another
very similar example at Ermet, the ancient Hermonthis, in
Egypt, is 150 feet long by 90 feet wide.

The basilicas which Constantine gave at Rome for
churches were, St. Peter's—a very large building, 380 feet
long by 212 feet wide, as large as most medieval cathedrals,
with a very lofty body and double aisles—and St. John
Lateran. He also built an octagonal baptistry, adjoining the
latter church, and a round church outside the Porta Pia as
a mausoleum for his daughter Constantia. At Jerusalem
he adorned the rock-tomb, which was believed to be the
site of the holy sepulchre, with costly marbles, and paved
the surrounding area, and enclosed it with a colonnade. At
the eastern side of this area he erected a basilica in honour
of the resurrection, with an atrium at its east end ; and
ordered that these should be such buildings as not to be
exceeded in magnificence by any in his dominions. He
also built a fine octagonal church at Antioch, at whose
dedication a synod of bishops famous in the history of the
Church was convened. He built, as has been said, two
churches at Constantinople, and others in other cities.
The empress-mother Helena built a fine basilica at Bethlehem, over against the Grotto of the Nativity, which, with
additions by Justinian, still remains.

A considerable number of other churches of early date
remain in many different countries. In Northern Syria are
numerous basilicas of the fourth, fifth, and sixth centuries,
so perfect that they need little more than re-roofing to
be again available for use. Thessalonica has basilicas of

* The basilica described was built by Bishop Cresconias in the fifth
century. An earlier one (fourth century) has since been discovered at
Djemila.—Ed.

the fifth and sixth centuries. The Cathedral of Ravenna, built A.D. 400, has unfortunately been destroyed, but the Church of St. Apollinare Nuovo, built by Theodoric the Goth (A.D. 493—525), remains, 315 feet long ; as does the Church of St. Apollinare in Classe, begun A.D. 538, and dedicated 549, a very fine church, 216 feet long. At Parenzo, in Istria, is a basilica, built A.D. 542, with a very complete plan—a body and two aisles, each terminated with an apse, a western narthex (or porch), an atrium (court), westward of the church, a circular baptistry west of the atrium, and a more modern addition of a circular tower west of the baptistry. Another basilica remains at Hierapolis, on the border of Phrygia.

We have in this long and uninterrupted series abundant evidence as to the early churches. The earliest examples are more than a century earlier than the time of Constantine's conversion. There is no reason to think that earlier lost examples were of a different plan from those which remain. Nor was there any change of plan in the time of Constantine. There were occasional varieties ; especially churches built for baptistries or tombs were circular ; but the normal plan of a church, from the second century certainly, and probably from the first, down to the twelfth, was the basilican. The Basilica of St. Clement, Rome, is the best remaining illustration of the general arrangement and furnishing of a basilica, and is so exact a reproduction of a church of the earliest type that it was always believed to be the original erection of Constantine, until a still earlier church was discovered immediately beneath the present one. On the chord of the apse stood the altar ; the bishop's throne was elevated on steps at the end of the apse, facing down the church, and there were elevated stone benches round the apse for the presbyters. A space was railed off westward of the altar by cancelli for the choir ; on each side of this choir were the raised pulpits (*ambones*), from which the epistle and gospel were read, and some other services sung, and occasionally the sermon delivered. The nave was the place of the faithful ; the catechumens stood in the narthex. In the middle of the atrium was commonly a fountain. The floor had always a mosaic pavement, usually specially designed ; the walls of the apse and the sacrarium

were usually ornamented with mosaics, a colossal figure of
our Lord attended by angels or saints usually occupying the
semi-dome of the apse.

The exterior of the church was nearly always studiously
plain, all the architectural decoration being reserved for the
interior—thus differing from heathen temples, where the
people stood outside to worship at an altar placed in front
of the building, and where the exterior of the building was
adorned with colonnades, and its cornices and pediments
with sculpture.   In the interior of the churches, however,
there was never any abstinence from the use of costly
material and the highest art.   The architect made as finely
proportioned an interior as his skill and circumstances
allowed ; he used marbles and bronze, sculpture, mosaic,
and mural painting, freely, and in the furniture of the
churches there was no affectation of poverty or plainness ;
they had gold and silver vessels for the Communion, silver
lamps, and silken hangings.

Eusebius of Cæsarea gives an account of the new church
built at Tyre, after the death of Maximin, in which he
himself delivered the inaugural discourse on its reconstruction.   It illustrates the power and opulence of the Church
even in a city which had just taken a leading part in the
attempted revival of paganism. The new church was built on
the old site ; for though a more convenient and imposing
place might have been found, the piety of the Christians
clung with reverence to a spot consecrated by holy associations. The whole site was surrounded by a wall ; a lofty
propylæon,* which faced the rising sun, afforded an imposing
glimpse of the magnificence within.   The space between the
propylæon and the church was laid out as a cloister, with
four colonnades, enclosed with a palisade of wood.   The
central square was open to sun and air, and two fountains
sparkled in the midst.   The uninitiated proceeded no
farther than the cloister, but might behold at this modest
distance the mysteries of the sanctuary.   Several other
vestibules, or propylæa, intervened between the cloister and
the main building.   The three gates of the church fronted
the east, of which the central was the loftiest and most
costly, " like a queen between her attendants " ; it was

* Ornamental entrance gate.

adorned with plates of brass and richly sculptured reliefs. Two colonnades, or aisles, ran along the main building, above which were windows ; other buildings for the use of the ministers adjoined. Eusebius does not give the actual dimensions, but speaks in general terms of eulogy of the spaciousness, loftiness and splendour of the interior. The roof was of beams of cedar, the floor inlaid with marble. In the centre rose the altar, already called the place of sacrifice, and guarded from approach by a trellis of most slender and graceful workmanship.

While we contradict the popular idea that the Church was hiding in the catacombs during the first three centuries, we must tell the origin and use of those ancient and interesting excavations. They were not excavated for building material, but expressly for burial-places. The Jewish colony in Rome made catacombs for the interment of their dead, and the Christians adopted this custom of their spiritual ancestors. The ancient Jewish cemeteries (catacombs) at present known in Rome are six in number, discovered at various times between 1842 and 1920. It has been suggested that some of the great Roman families who practised interment instead of the national custom of cremation used catacombs. All but six of the existing catacombs of the first three centuries seem to be Christian. They are forty-two in number, distributed all round the city, and contain 350 * miles of galleries two to four feet wide, with both sides pierced for graves, and seventy-six chambers, the sides of which are also pierced for graves, with occasionally a larger chamber which served for a chapel. Originally some belonged to private families who had embraced the Christian faith ; the entrances were not originally secret, and some were ornamented with architectural façades ; one, that of Calixtus, belonged to the Christian community, and all the Roman bishops of the third century were buried in it. The graves in the sides of the galleries, when occupied, had their openings closed by a stone, on which there is often an inscription. The chambers and chapels were often ornamented with paintings of the same character as those which decorated the Roman tombs and

* This is Northcote's estimate (in 1869), an estimate in 1925 is 544 miles.—Ed.

baths ; and these paintings are the earliest remaining examples of Christian art. Much is merely decorative, in the style used in the secular public buildings at the time, but paintings of Scripture subjects are freely introduced. For example, in the catacomb of Calixtus is a lofty vaulted hall, built in the fine brickwork of early date, whose walls and vaults are adorned with decorative painting of classical character ; winged genii (representing the four seasons) are sporting among gracefully intertwined branches of trees, foliage, and vines ; at the back of an arched recess is a picture of the Good Shepherd.

The figure subjects were chiefly allegorical. Orpheus charming the wild beasts with his lyre was a familiar subject to the pagan ; to the believer it was typical of Christ by His doctrine taming the wild hearts of men. A shepherd carrying a lamb on his shoulders was to the one a pastoral incident, to the other an allegory of the Good Shepherd Who came to seek and save that which was lost. When scriptural subjects were used it was usually with an allegorical meaning. Jonah cast into the sea, swallowed by the sea monster, and issuing forth again from his three days' imprisonment, was a type of our Lord's resurrection. Daniel in the lions' den and the raising of Lazarus appear with the same meaning. Noah in the ark was a type of baptism. A company of persons reclining at a feast, or a representation of the turning of the water into wine, serve for the other sacrament of the Gospel. The Good Shepherd is the oft-recurring and characteristic figure, as the Lord in glory was in the next period of the mosaics of the basilicas.

In times of persecution the clergy and others specially sought after took temporary refuge in the intricacies of these subterranean galleries, and Divine service was conducted in the greater chambers. At all times Divine service was performed in these chapels on the festivals of noted martyrs interred within them or in the neighbouring galleries. Interments continued to take place in the catacombs till the close of the fifth century ; and long afterwards—till the thirteenth century—the martyrs' graves in them were visited by pilgrims to Rome. It is possible that the recollection of these subterranean galleries and chapels gave rise to the construction of crypts under great churches, and to the side chapels of the medieval churches.

The Roman catacombs are those best known to the world, but similar catacombs exist at Naples and other places in Italy, in Malta and Sicily, and also at Kertab in South Russia, at Alexandria in Egypt, and Sousse in Tunisia, which are similarly adorned with early decorative and scriptural paintings.

CHAPTER XV

THE WORSHIP OF THE PRIMITIVE CHURCH

WHAT kind of service was performed in the churches described in the preceding chapter? Justin Martyr, who died about sixty years after St. John (about A.D. 140), gives in his Apology a sketch of the worship of the primitive Church : " Upon the day called Sunday we have an assembly of all who live in the town or in the country, who meet in an appointed place, and the records of the apostles, or the writings of the prophets, are read, according as the time will permit. When the reader has ended, then the president admonishes and exhorts us in a discourse that we should imitate such good examples. After that we all stand up and pray, and, as we said before, when that prayer is ended, bread is offered and wine and water. Then the president also, according to the authority given him, sends up prayers and thanksgivings ; and the people end the prayer with him, saying, Amen. After which distribution is made of the Eucharistic elements, which are also sent by the hands of the deacons to those who are absent."

We are able, to some extent, to fill up the outline which Justin sketches. Many ancient liturgies still in existence can be traced back to four or five originals of very early date known by the names of apostles.* The Liturgy of St. James, or of Jerusalem, was used in Palestine and Mesopotamia. It seems to be the same with a synopsis of a liturgy, called the Liturgy of St. Clement, contained in the "Apostolic Constitutions," a work written probably in the fourth century, but embodying much earlier matter. It agrees with Justin's description above given, and it is

---

* The word " Liturgy " in early times was restricted to the office for the holy Eucharist.

almost certain that the Liturgy of St. James, as still used by the monophysite churches of the East, and that which is used by the orthodox Church of Jerusalem on the Feast of St. James, are versions of the primitive liturgy used by the churches of Judea and surrounding countries in the age immediately following that of the apostles.

The Liturgy of St. Mark, or of Alexandria, is similarly traceable to the second century, to which it is assigned by Bunsen. Palmer says, " There is nothing unreasonable in supposing that the main order and substance of the Alexandrian Liturgy, as used in the fifth century, may have been as old as the apostolic age, and derived originally from the instructions and appointments of the blessed evangelist." The Liturgy of St. Peter, or of Rome, may also " reasonably be assigned to the age succeeding the apostles."

The Liturgy of St. John, or of the Church of Ephesus, is the original of that used in Britain during the earlier ages of Christianity. It was disused in the Ephesian dioceses as early as the fourth century, but meantime had been carried by missionaries from that Church into Gaul, Spain, and Britain, probably about the middle of the second century, and continued in use in France till the time of Charlemagne (eighth century), in Spain till the tenth century, in England till the time of Archbishop Theodore.

But, further, these four ancient liturgies * have so much in common that they must have had a common origin, or have been constructed on the same principles. Probably the apostles used an unwritten liturgical form, always retaining the same elements, but presenting them with a certain amount of freedom, and as liturgies were not committed to writing till the second century, the tradition of the apostolic liturgy would have by that time in different churches assumed different forms which were then perpetuated. These liturgies afterwards received modifications and considerable additions, as one great patriarch or another saw fit to adapt them to the requirements of his time.

In order to complete the scene of a primitive Church and its worship, let us ask next, What were the official vestments of the clergy ? At the beginning of the Christian era, and

* A fifth primitive liturgy is that of Thaddeus from which most Nestorian liturgies derive.—ED.

for some centuries afterwards, all people of a certain social position, in all civilised countries, wore the same costume—viz., a tunic and pallium. The tunic was ordinarily worn by men short and with short sleeves; on occasions of state and ceremony men wore a long tunic down to the ankles. Tunics of people of the senatorial order were distinguished by a broad purple stripe (*clavus latus*) down the front of the tunic; people of the equestrian order had their tunics marked with two narrow purple stripes (*clavus angustus*), reaching from the shoulders straight down the front. The pallium was a large square, or nearly square, woollen robe worn in various ways. One of the commonest was thus: passed over the left shoulder, drawn behind the back under the right arm, leaving it free, and thrown again over the left shoulder, covering the left arm. Great dignitaries had a broad ornamental border to the pallium, and sometimes the whole robe was embroidered. A heathen offering sacrifice or attending a religious ceremony wore an orarium, a square of cloth laid like a veil over the head; this was reduced in the first century to a narrow strip of cloth laid over the shoulders. A Roman, Greek, or Syrian, offering sacrifice at his temple or taking part in any high religious ceremonial would wear a long tunic with sleeves, a pallium, and an orarium over his shoulders, and the colour of all these would be white. Our Lord and His apostles are always, from the earliest representations of them in the second century, represented in tunic and pallium, which, no doubt, they were accustomed to wear. Bishops and saints in the paintings of the sixth century are also represented in tunic and pallium; and probably the clergy of the early Church in their ministrations wore this customary dress of religious ceremonial. The bishop and priest wore the full dress, the deacon the tunic only.

Not till the fourth century do we find any clear mention of the vestments of the clergy. Athanasius was accused by his enemies of laying a tax on the Egyptians to raise a fund for the linen tunics of the clergy. Jerome says: " What harm is it if a bishop, presbyter, or deacon come forth in a white vestment when they administer the sacraments ? " Chrysostom speaks of " the deacons walking about the church in their white tunics." Severanus, Bishop of

Gabala, contemporary with St. Chrysostom, speaks of the deacons ministering at the sacred mysteries " with their veils on their left shoulders "; this veil was doubtless the orarium. The Council of Laodicea (A.D. 370) allows the use of the orarium to bishops, priests, and deacons, and forbids its use by subdeacons, singers, and readers.

Let us now try to picture a church and its services of these first ages. The Church is filling with people, the men taking their places on one side and the women on the other. We see an unusual mixture of classes—the high-born Roman lady, the citizen's wife, and the slave girl side by side; patricians of the city with embroidered pallium thrown over the shoulder, and a soldier of the garrison here and there, with breast-plate and sword, amidst a mixed crowd of burghers and slaves. The double row of singers in white tunics, within the cancelli, are conspicuous above the heads of the people; and beyond all is the bishop in his white robes, seated aloft in his raised stone chair, looking over the whole church; his presbyters in the same costume on their raised bench form a semicircle on either side of their chief; the deacons, in their white tunics, stand beneath, and the deaconesses and Church virgins also have their special place. The service begins, the people stand; there are no seats, and Christians do not kneel at public worship on Sundays except for the blessing. The priest recites the prayers in a sustained and measured tone, the people responding with a loud AMEN, which rolls along the aisles like a peal of thunder; then they take part with the singers in the responsive chanting of the psalms. The bishop delivers his address, still seated in his lofty sedile; then a deacon comes down the church and gives the signal that the service of the catechumens is over. If it be an assembly of the first century, comparatively few will depart; if one of the fourth or later age, many, alas! will leave—as large a proportion, perhaps, as in a modern English congregation. Then the sacred liturgy proceeds, the bishop himself officiating with solemn reverence, standing behind the altar and looking towards the people. The prayers are said, the memorial made, the deacons come down among the people, who are now kneeling, and give them the sacred elements, saying to each as he delivers into his hands bread or cup—τὸ σῶμα τοῦ Κυρίου, τὸ αἷμα τοῦ Κυρίου—" The Body of the Lord ; " " The Blood of the Lord." The Bishop concludes by blessing the kneeling flock. In a few minutes the clergy have defiled in procession into their sacristy, while the crowd of worshippers have crossed the great court and are again among the crowds in the busy sunlit streets of the city.

CHAPTER XVI

EARLY HERESIES AND SCHISMS

OF the faith held by the primitive Church we have no lack of evidence. The disciples had been exhorted to hold fast the faith once for all delivered to the saints of which they had the permanent record in the Gospels and Acts and Epistles. That they did so we have the evidence of the early writers of the Church—1. In their Apologies (or defences) of Christianity ; 2. In their controversial books, in which they maintain the truths of Christianity against Jews, heathen, and heretics ; 3. In their expositions of the Scriptures, in homilies, essays, and letters addressed to the faithful. These evidences enable us to say that, for six centuries at least, the sacred deposit of the faith and discipline of Christ was kept whole and undefiled though not without struggle and controversy, by the churches of Christ all over the world.

From the earliest times, however, there were heresies and schisms. All the heresies (except the last, Pelagianism) sprang up in, and were almost entirely limited to, the churches of the East. They were the results of Oriental mysticism or of Greek speculation. The earlier heresies, as Gnosticism and Manicheism, were not so much erroneous doctrines, springing up in the bosom of the Church, as wild theories of men studying the Church of Christ from without, and endeavouring to combine their previous religions and philosophies, with what they chose to select out of Christianity, into new eclectic religious systems of their own. They were transitional phases of the mind in its passage from Pagan philosophy to the Christian religion. The later heresies—Arianism and the series of heresies which sprang from it—all relate to the mystery of the Being of the undivided Trinity ; they were the erroneous speculations of

Christian theologians who missed their way, one on this side and another on that, in the process, which occupied the mind of the fourth, fifth, and sixth centuries, of casting the truths contained in Revelation into philosophic modes of thought and expression. The last of the early heresies, Pelagianism, sprang up in the West, turned on the relations of grace and free-will, and belongs to the practical sphere of human conduct.

As Gnosticism and Manicheism were the result of the combination of the Oriental religions with Christianity, so Neoplatonism was the result of the attempt to take up into Greek philosophy those elements of Christianity which commended themselves to the Greek mind.

All varieties of Gnosticism agreed in claiming a degree of enlightenment superior to that of the vulgar. As the philosophers professed the old paganism, but claimed to explain the vulgar mythology by their intellectual theories, so the Gnostics professed Christianity, but claimed to soar as much above the vulgar Christianity as the philosophers did above the vulgar paganism. They all busied themselves with the speculation which underlies all Oriental philosophies, the origin of evil. We find as common to all GNOSTIC systems a belief in one Supreme God, dwelling from eternity in the *pleroma*, the fulness of light. From him proceed successive *Æons*, or spiritual beings, the chief of which appear, from their names, to be impersonated attributes of the Deity. Matter is regarded as eternal and essentially evil. Out of matter the world and bodies of men were formed by the *Demiurge*, a being represented by some as a subordinate agent of the Divine will, by others as a hostile and malignant being. The soul of man is imprisoned in his body. Christ was also an emanation from God, and was sent into the world to free man from the tyranny of the Demiurge. Since they believed the body to be evil, they did not believe that Christ had a true body, or that man when delivered would have a body—*i.e.*, they denied the divinity of our Lord and His incarnation, and the resurrection of the dead. In practice, some of the Gnostics sought the victory over their evil nature in an ascetic life, others taught the moral indifference of our actions and wallowed in sensuality.

Simon Magus is regarded as the precursor of Gnosticism.

After the incident mentioned in the Acts of the Apostles, he soon abandoned the apostles' fellowship, and mixing up Christianity with his system continued to teach it ; and Justin Martyr says that, in his day (about A.D. 140), Simon was worshipped as the chief god by almost all the Samaritans, and had adherents in other countries.

Cerinthus is the next great leader of this school. He taught in Ephesus at the time that St. John was living there, and both in his gospel and epistles the apostle refers to the errors of a teaching like to that of Cerinthus.

The system was at its height from about A.D. 120 to A.D. 140. In all the great cities of the East in which Christianity had established its most flourishing communities this rival sprang up beside it. After Cerinthus, Saturninus taught in Ephesus. Basilides and Saturninus taught in Alexandria, and the latter for a time in Rome. Bardesanes was another teacher, whose hymns for a long time were popular even among orthodox Syrian Christians.

The other great system of false Philosophy of this period was introduced towards the close of the third century by Mani, a native of Persia, deeply skilled in the learning of his age. It consisted of an eclectic system of doctrines, having the Zoroastrian religion of his native country for its basis, combined with doctrines gathered out of the Christianity of the Roman empire on one hand, and out of the Buddhism of India on the other. Mani gave himself out to be the promised Paraclete, by which he does not seem to have intended to claim to be the Holy Spirit, but a man invested with a Divine mission, whose office it was to complete the revelation and work commenced but unfulfilled by Christ. He put forth a gospel, in an illuminated volume, which was to supersede the orthodox gospels. His community was organised on the Christian model, and at his death he left twelve apostles, seventy-two bishops, and a priesthood. His doctrines met the eclectic philosophical taste of the times, spread with great rapidity, were embraced with zealous fervour, and lasted for a considerable period. St. Augustine, though brought up in Christian doctrine, for several years of his early manhood embraced the Manichean heresy.

The above were rather false religions than Christian heresies. Other variations from the truth, which are commonly called heresies, as Montanism, Novatianism, and Donatism, were rather schisms based on disciplinary than doctrinal differences, though a certain amount of erroneous doctrine entered into them.

MONTANUS was a native of Phrygia, and had been, it is said, a priest of Cybele. Soon after his conversion to Christianity, which happened about the middle of the second century, he began to fall into fits of ecstasy, and to utter ravings which were dignified with the name of prophecies, and he declared himself to be the Paraclete, meaning, perhaps, no more than that he was the special organ of the Holy Ghost for completing Christianity by a new revelation. This revelation dealt with questions of discipline. The chief characteristic of Montanism was, that it aimed at the introduction of a more rigid system of morals into the Church. It added to the established fasts, proscribed second marriages, denounced profane learning, military service, amusements of every kind ; declared that the Church had no power to remit sin committed after baptism, and cut off such sinners from the communion of the Church on earth, though it admitted that the mercy of God might nevertheless be extended to them. These doctrines appealed to stern, enthusiastic minds, and had many followers. The most distinguished of these was Tertullian, who, though a presbyter of Carthage, and one of the most able and eloquent men of his time, in middle life fell away into Montanism.

About a century later NOVATIAN, a presbyter of Rome started a schism on a point of discipline. After the persecution of Decius some severer spirits denied to those who had lapsed re-admission to the communion of the Church. Novatian,* one of these precisians, and eminent for his learning and eloquence, was irregularly consecrated as an opposition bishop of Rome by three obscure bishops, and so became the head of a schismatical sect. The sentence of exclusion from communion of those who had denied the

* To be carefully distinguished from Novatus of Carthage, who having favoured a treatment of the lapsed more lenient than that of his Bishop, Cyprian, nevertheless on going to Rome procured the consecration of the rigorist Novatian in opposition to Cornelius whom Cyprian supported as bishop although he had differed from him as to the treatment of the lapsed.—ED.

faith was extended to those who had committed deadly sin after baptism. They also adopted the practice (with which many orthodox churches for a time agreed) of refusing to recognise the baptism of those baptized by heretics or schismatics. The sect, though not very powerful, long continued to exist.

The greatest schism of the primitive Church, that of the DONATISTS, arose out of similar questions. The rigid, enthusiastic spirit which existed so largely in African Christianity and had broken out in the Montanist and Novatianist sects, showed itself in the Diocletian persecution. Many thought it wrong to do anything to avoid persecution—either to give up the sacred books, or flee, or evade it in any way ; many courted and provoked martyrdom; in some cases, it is said, impelled by weariness of the hardships of their lot, and in the hope of washing away at once in the blood of martyrdom the sins of a lifetime.

Mensurius, Bishop of Carthage, strongly discountenanced this ill-regulated fanaticism, refused to acknowledge as martyrs those who had voluntarily courted their fate and forbade that they should receive attentions in prison, and the respect from their fellow-Christians, with which those who were really confessors were treated. He himself, on being required to give up the sacred boks, had adopted the common evasion of giving up some heretical writings to be burnt instead. His archdeacon, Cæcilian, had been his chief instrument in this. On the death of Mensurius (A.D. 311) Cæcilian was elected bishop ; but the severer party opposed him, ostensibly because he had been consecrated by Felix, Bishop of Aptunga, who, they said, was a traditor ; * they excommunicated Cæcilian and his adherents, and elected another of the clergy, Majorinus, to the bishopric.

Constantine, after his victory over Maxentius, sent large donations to the African churches ; and hearing of the dispute directed that the gifts should be confined to those who were in communion with Cæcilian. The Donatist party petitioned that their cause might be tried by the bishops of Gaul, who had themselves been exempt from the persecution and its trials. Constantine complied with their request, and

* One who had given up the sacred books.

issued a commission to twenty bishops, who after due inquiry gave their decision in favour of Cæcilian, and suggested, as a way of healing the schism, that both parties should reunite in communion, and that where rival bishops laid claim to a see the bishop first consecrated should be acknowledged. The Donatists appealed against this decision, whereupon Constantine summoned the Council of Arles, consisting of about two hundred bishops, from all parts of the Western empire.*

This council also decided in favour of Cæcilian, and made canons which enacted that a clerical traditor should be deposed ; that the ordination of a cleric by a traditor was valid ; that the baptism of heretics in the name of the Holy Trinity should not be repeated, but the person so baptized should be admitted into the Church by the imposition of hands. The Donatists appealed again from the decision of the council and begged the emperor to take the cause into his own hands. He did so, reheard the case, and decided as the council had done, and issued severe edicts for the deposition and punishment of the schismatics, which, however, were not enforced. The sect held that the true Church existed only in their own communion, and gradually spread in Africa until Donatists became more powerful than Catholics ; the number of their bishops is said at one time to have amounted to four hundred. In nearly every city of Africa were rival bishops and rival churches.

Driven out of their churches by Constantine, and restored by Julian, the Donatists continued to flourish to the time of Augustine, in the beginning of the fifth century. They were guilty of violence against Augustine himself, and others of the Catholic bishops and clergy, and the emperor was petitioned to revive the old edicts against them. In 411, at the request of the Catholics, an imperial commissioner was sent to conduct a conference between the two parties. The bishops of each side assembled in great

* At this council, held Aug. A.D. 314, were present three bishops from Britain—Eborius, Bishop of York ; Restitutus, Bishop of London ; and Adelfius, Bishop of Civitas Colonia Lodinensium, which has been conjectured to be either Camulodunum (Colchester), or Carleon ; with Sacerdos, a priest, and a deacon.

numbers. A debate of several days ensued ; Augustine was the chief advocate on the side of the Catholics. The imperial commissioner gave his judgment against the Donatists ; they appealed to the Emperor Honorius, who confirmed the decision, and enacted penalties against them. Little is known of the latter history of the sect ; it gradually dwindled into insignificance, but is supposed not to have been entirely extinguished till the Saracenic invasion of Africa in the seventh century swept away Catholic and Donatist in a common ruin.

CHAPTER XVII

THE EMPIRE FROM THE DEATH OF CONSTANTINE TO THAT OF THEODOSIUS

CONSTANTINE, on the death of Licinius, reunited the empire (A.D. 324), and ruled it with sole and absolute authority during the remaining thirteen years of his life. He continued in modified form the subdivision of government which Diocletian had introduced, by according his three sons and two nephews the title of Cæsar, and appointing them to nominal governments, surrounding them with ministers and generals whom he trusted, who guided the councils of the youthful princes. Constantine, his eldest son, he appointed to the government of Gaul; Constantius to the East; Constans to Italy and Africa; Dalmatius, to Thrace, Macedonia, and Greece; Hannibalanus to Pontus, Cappadocia, and Lesser Armenia.

On the death of Constantine (A.D. 337) a conspiracy, headed by his ministers and generals and backed by the army, declared against the brothers and nephews of the late emperor. His two brothers, the husband of his sister, seven of his nephews, and Ablavius, his chief favourite and minister, were massacred. Gallus and Julian, two of his nephews, escaped. His three sons—Constantine, Constans, and Constantius—redivided the empire among them, Constantine retaining the new capital, with a certain pre-eminence of rank. After three years, however, Constantine complained that he had not received a just proportion of the empire, and demanded of Constans the cession of several of his provinces. Following up this by an invasion, he was led into an ambuscade and slain (A.D. 340). Constans refused to give his surviving brother any share in his new acquisitions. Ten years afterwards (A.D. 350) Constans fell in a rebellion which raised Magnentius to the purple. War ensued between the surviving son of Constantine and the usurper, which after various fortunes went in favour of the former at the great battle of Mursa (A.D. 353) in which the victors lost more men than the vanquished. Upon a further defeat at Lyons, Magnentius fell on his sword, and left the empire once more united in the hands of Con stantius (A.D. 353). This emperor was of strict morals, but vain and weak, and in the latter part of his reign suspicious and cruel. In religious matters he was under the influence of the Arian party, and his power contributed very largely to the temporary predominence which that heresy attained in the Eastern Church, though his endeavours to force it on the Western Church also, when he succeeded to the sove-reignty of the West, were unsuccessful.

Constantius appointed his cousin Julian to the rank of Cæsar and to a share in the government. Julian developed capacity, and fought three successful campaigns against the Alemanni, who were threatening the frontiers of the empire. This made the Cæsar a favourite with his legions, and consequently an object of jealousy and suspicion to Constantius. To diminish his power the emperor ordered the legions of the West to march to the defence of the Eastern provinces. The soldiers, unwilling to leave their homes and families, and resenting the treatment of their general, proclaimed Julian Augustus, and the death of Constantius left Julian undisputed prossessor of the empire.

JULIAN (A.D. 361), like all the family of Constantine, had been educated as a Christian, and his life is said to have been saved, when so many relatives were massacred, by Mark, Bishop of Arethusa. In his youth he had showed an inclination for the heathen philosophy, and sought the society of leading philosophers, who diligently courted him as the hope of their party. On his accession he at once declared against Christianity, and took steps for the revival of the ancient religion. He withdrew the State support from Christianity ; wrote against it, ridiculed it, harassed it with legal persecutions, which affected the property, and in a few cases the lives, of Christians. He invited the reopening of the deserted temples, and encouraged the

I

re-establishment of the ancient worship. The condition to which heathenism had fallen is illustrated by a story related by Julian himself, that when he was in Antioch, having restored the Temple of Daphne, near the city, he went thither on the day of a great local festival to join in worship ; but instead of the splendid ceremonial and the crowd of worshippers he expected, only one poor old priest was in attendance, with no better sacrifice than a goose which the priest had been obliged to provide at his own cost.

Another enterprise which the emperor undertook was the rebuilding of the Temple of Jerusalem, and the restoration of the Jewish worship and nationality. The destruction of the Temple, the cessation of its worship, and the dispersion of the Jews, were looked upon then, as now, as evidences of the truth of Christianity. The reversal of this would, therefore, have been considered by unbelievers as a heavy blow to Christianity. Julian devoted large sums to the attempt, and invited the co-operation of the Jews. He entrusted the special oversight of the work to his friend Alypius of Antioch, who had been Lieutenant of Britain and was backed by the governor of the province. Workmen were assembled. The Jews naturally embraced the project with religious enthusiasm ; the men wielded tools of gold and silver, as we do at the laying of the foundation stone of a great undertaking, the women carried stones in the laps of their silken robes. But the undertaking was wonderfully frustrated. We have the testimony of Ammianus Marcellinus, a contemporary heathen historian, for this fact, and the admission of Julian himself. The former says that " fearful balls of fire, breaking out from the foundations, continued their attacks till the workmen, after repeated scorchings, would approach no more, and thus the fierce element obstinately repelling them, he gave over the attempt." The Church historians of the next age add other particulars, as that there was a whirlwind which scattered the building materials ; lightning which melted the tools of the workmen and slew some of the workers ; an earthquake which destroyed neighbouring buildings, and disclosed the recesses of the foundations out of which the balls of fire were cast forth.

During an invasion of the Persian kingdom, Julian was

killed in a nocturnal skirmish, after a vigorous reign of one year and eight months.

As he was the last of the family of Constantine, and had not associated any Cæsar with himself, or nominated any successor, the generals met, and avoided the danger of rivalries among themselves by unanimously electing JOVIAN (A.D. 363), a civil official of the household.

Jovian at once repealed all his predecessor's edicts against Christianity, and restored to the Church its property and immunities. The pagan priests and philosophers, who had abused their temporary triumph, sank into neglect, and the Church was more firmly established than ever.

The able VALENTINIAN (A.D. 364), who had commanded in Britain, was unanimously elected as the next emperor. He associated his brother VALENS with himself, assigning him the eastern half of the empire, and taking the western half as his own province. Valentinian was a constant and firm supporter of the Church and of the orthodox party. The pagans fell under the suspicion of magical incantations and immoral rites, and on this ground a terrible persecution was directed against them, especially in Rome itself, which spared neither rank, age, nor sex.

Valens put himself into the hands of the dominant Arian party in Constantinople, and continued to support it, though showing personal respect for Athanasius, Basil, and other great men of the Catholic minority. The election of Damasus Bishop of Rome during Valentinian's reign marks an era in the external history of the Church. The position of Bishop of Rome had become one of such great wealth and influence as to be an object of ambition. On the death of Liberius (A.D. 366) there were two rival candidates for the office, each supported by a numerous and excited following, who filled the city with riot and bloodshed. Damasus was the successful competitor.

Valentinian died a natural death in A.D. 375, and was succeeded by his son GRATIAN, who had long been Augustus and designated as his successor ; with him was associated his infant half-brother, Valentinian II.

Three years afterwards (Aug. 9, A.D. 378) Valens perished with a great part of his army in the fatal battle of Hadrianople against the invading Goths. Gratian conferred the purple and the government of the East upon THEODOSIUS, the son of a general of the same name, whose exploits in the rescue of Britain from an invasion of the Picts and Scots, and subsequently in Africa, had been among the most splendid achievements of the reign of Valentinian. Theodosius, by his conduct and valour, restored the peace and prosperity of the Eastern empire ; his private character adorned the purple ; under his legislation paganism was finally supplanted, the Catholic faith triumphed over Arianism, and the Church was established as the sole religion of the whole empire. At his death commenced a new era of history—the era of the disruption of the empire and the construction out of its fragments of the nations of Western Europe.

CHAPTER XVIII

THE ARIAN CONTROVERSY

THE history of the Church during the reign of Constantine and down to the time of Theodosius is chiefly a history of the Arian controversy. The gradual absorption of the pagan population into the ranks of Christianity and the building up of converts into saints went on; but the energies of Eastern Christianity were chiefly expended upon this critical controversy. The great Churchmen of the time appear as the heroes in this struggle; the interest of this period hangs upon the great peril and ultimate triumph of the truth. The heresy began in Alexandria, that fruitful seat of philosophical speculation. Arius, a presbyter of that Church, taught and maintained a view of the relations in the Godhead of the Son to the Father which was inconsistent with the doctrine of the true Deity of the Son. According to his teaching " there was a time before the commencement of the ages when the parent Deity dwelt alone, in undeveloped, undivided unity. At a time, immeasurably, incalculably, inconceivably remote, the majestic solitude ceased, the Divine unity was broken by an act of the sovereign will; and the only-begotten Son, the image of the Father, the vicegerent of all the Divine power, the intermediate agent in all the long subsequent work of creation, began to be." * He further held, as to the incarnation, that in it the Son assumed a human body, His nature supplying the place of a human soul.† The Church at large held this to be a novel and false doctrine; if the Son was not coeval in existence with the Father, He must have been created, and created out of that which was not pre-existent.

Arius, persisting in his doctrine, was condemned by his

---

* Milman's *Hist. Christ.*, ii. 358.   † Robertson, i. 208.

bishop. The condemnation was ratified by a synod of Egyptian and Libyan bishops; the heresiarch was excommunicated with his adherents, among whom were two bishops, about twelve presbyters, and as many deacons, and a great number of Church virgins. Arius took refuge in Palestine, and industriously propagated his opinions. Eusebius, Bishop of Nicomedia, and a synod of Bithynian bishops, accepted him as orthodox. The controversy attracted attention, and began to disturb the Church far and wide.

Constantine, on becoming master of the East, found the Church thus troubled, and addressed a letter to Alexander and Arius, treating the controversy as unimportant, and urging them to peace and unity; this he sent by Hosius, Bishop of Cordova, the prelate in whom he had special confidence, that he might compose the strife. The emperor, however, soon found that the doctrine at stake was of vital importance, and he took the important step of summoning a general council of bishops of the whole Church to determine it.

There had frequently been councils of portions of the Church, but this was the first general council since the apostolic council at Jerusalem. It met at Nicæa in Bithynia, in June 325, and consisted of about 300 bishops and many priests; even heathen philosophers were attracted to the assembly and held conferences and disputes with the bishops. Hosius, Bishop of Cordova, presided.

In the earlier sessions, Arius was repeatedly heard in explanation and defence of his opinions. His chief opponents were Marcellus, Bishop of Ancyra, and Athanasius,* Archdeacon of Alexandria, who was in attendance on his bishop, Alexander. About a fortnight after the opening of the council Constantine arrived at Nicæa, and future sittings were held in his palace, the emperor himself acting as moderator.

When the assembled clergy heard Arius' plain statement of his teaching they stopped their ears as at the hearing of blasphemy, and the decrees of the council were ultimately signed by all but fifteen or twenty of the whole 300 bishops.

The famous Creed of Nicæa was not then drawn up for the first time. All churches already possessed creeds,

* Page 132.

the same in substance, though more or less full in their summary of the common faith. The ancient creed of the Church of Cæsarea was adopted as a basis, and discussion turned upon the modification of its statements about the Son that they might exclude the Arian heresy, and express clearly the Catholic doctrine of His co-equal Deity. The word homoousion—of one substance or essence—was at length adopted, and inserted in the creed as an expression of that co-equal Deity recognised in the ancient faith of the Church. A protracted strife continued to rage about this word through many years ; it still stands in the Nicene Creed, the monument of the ultimate victory of the true faith.

The decree of the council failed to terminate the strife. Arianism continued to spread. It found favour at court. Constantia, sister of Constantine and widow of Licinius, who had been under the influence of Eusebius, Bishop of Nicomedia, a leader of the Arian party, was persuaded that Arius was unjustly condemned. On her death-bed she appealed to her brother on his behalf. The condemned Arians were recalled, and, by their influence at court, some leading Catholic bishops, assailed by false accusations, were banished from their sees ; Athanasius, who had succeeded Alexander in the see of Alexandria, was exiled to Treves.

When Constantine died the empire was divided into East and West, the Church into Catholic and Arian. Constantius, his empress, and the eunuchs who directed the government, adopted the Arian interest and sustained it with all the power of the State. Valens, his successor after the brief reigns of Julian and Jovian, was also an Arian, so that for forty years from the exile of Athanasius, under Constantine the Great, to the beginning of the reign of Theodosius, Arianism was dominant in the East. In every city of the East and of Africa Arians filled the sees, held the churches, and formed the more numerous party. Catholics were a despised and persecuted minority, and violent measures were adopted to compel them to conform.

In the western portion of the empire Constantine the younger was of the orthodox faith. The Western mind, then as always, was little exercised by the subtle specula-

tions which engaged the Oriental mind ; so that the Western
Church held on its peaceful course, only hearing afar the
noise of the controversy, and aroused occasionally to keener
sympathy when Catholic bishops, expelled as fugitives from
their own sees, sought refuge in Rome.

But when (in A.D. 353) the death of Constantine II. and
defeat of Magnentius had made Constantius sole emperor,
the Arian persecution swept for seven years over the
Western world. A council was convened at Milan, where
the bishops of the West, overawed by Constantius and his
soldiers, consented to join in the condemnation of Athanasius, and to communicate with the Arians. Athanasius
was condemned ostensibly on other grounds than those of
his orthodoxy ; and, in admitting the Arians to communion,
they were not admitting that the doctrine of Arius was right
and that of Athanasius wrong, but only that the Arian
doctrine did not disqualify its holder for recognition as a
member of the Catholic Church. The bishops who refused
to assent were exiled, and others more compliant put in
their places, and a general persecution was carried on
against the orthodox, who complained that the days of Nero
and Decius had returned. The two leading bishops of the
West still held out—Hosius of Cordova, illustrious for his
age and character, and the prominent part he had so long
played in the affairs of the Church ; and Liberius of Rome,
the bishop of the premier see of the West. The conduct of
Liberius was at first not unworthy of his great position.
Eusebius, the powerful chief of the eunuchs, in vain assailed
him with promises and threats, and at Milan he withstood
the flatteries and threats of the emperor himself with equal
firmness, and was condemned to banishment. Hosius also
withstood all endeavours to induce him to yield, and, after
a year under restraint, he too was banished. The emperor
then proceeded to remove Athanasius from Alexandria by
force. So attached were their flocks to the bishops that
Liberius was abstracted from Rome, for fear of a rising of
the people, by stratagem in the night ; and in surprising
Athanasius, also by night, it was thought necessary to
surround the Cathedral Church of Alexandria with five
thousand troops, and even then the people in the church
resisted, a scene of tumult and bloodshed followed, and

Athanasius was carried safely away by his friends in the confusion.

At length Hosius, now 100 years old, gave way and signed a heterodox creed, as a few months afterwards Liberius also did, and Arianism seemed to be triumphant and its triumph sealed by the acceptance of the Creed of Rimini (A.D. 359). A council of the whole Church was convened by the emperor, and, ostensibly for convenience, the Western bishops were to meet at Rimini, the Eastern at Nicæa. Each party was dealt with separately. The Western bishops signed an ambiguous creed in ignorance of the meaning its propounders put upon it ; the Eastern bishops were talked into signing the same formula ; and " the whole world," says St. Jerome, " groaned, and was astonished to find itself Arian." Many bishops, however, as soon as they understood the meaning put upon the words they had accepted, repudiated the new creed.

But the Arian triumph was only temporary. On November 3, 361, Constantius died, having only shortly before been baptized by the Arian Bishop of Antioch. Julian recalled all exiles, and the orthodox bishops returned to their sees under favour of the general amnesty.

One cause of Arian success had been that it was careful to do as little violence as possible to the belief of the people. Until it had gained the victory the difference between itself and the Catholic faith was made to look as small as possible. Arians used language, both in formal creeds and in popular sermons which was ambiguous and would naturally be taken by orthodox minds in an orthodox sense. So numbers of unpolemical pious souls might hear the sermons, recite the creeds, and use the prayers in an Arian church, and grow in faith and holiness—" the ears of the people, uninjured by the subtle heresy, were purer than the lips of the preachers." This being so, was the matter worth all the widespread and long-continued strife ? Is not Gibbon justified when he sneers at all this strife and bloodshed over the difference of a diphthong? (homoousion or homoiousion *). But the question at issue really was, Who was Jesus of Nazareth ? The answer of the Catholics was that He was very and eternal God. The answer of the Arians,

* Of the *same*, or of *like* substance.

however high they might place Him, amounted to this, that
He was a creature. The difference between the two answers
is immeasurably great. If Catholics were right, it was sin
not to worship Him ; if Arians were right, to worship Him
was idolatry. If Jesus must be brought down from the
Catholic altitude of God to the Arian level of a creature,
the whole Christian scheme must undergo a corresponding
degradation. The notion of the sinfulness of sin ; of the
value of the atonement ; of the love of God in giving the
Son to die for us ; of the exaltation of our humanity in
Jesus ; of the power of Jesus to aid us ; must all be brought
down from the height at which the Deity of Jesus places
them, to a level immeasurably lower. Moreover, grosser
doctrines such as those of Aetius came to light as soon as
Arianism appeared triumphant, and the logical conclusion
to which Arianism led was Theism first, perhaps Atheism
in the end. We learn a great lesson from the spectacle of
Athanasius contra mundum—the lesson that the minority
may be right, and that if it is right, though only one against
the world, it will in the end prevail.

CHAPTER XIX

THE TRIUMPH OF THE CHURCH

WHEN Theodosius was elevated to the purple he ruled the eastern half of the empire, but also guided the counsels of his youthful colleagues in the West. In religious matters he at once threw the whole weight of his power and influence on the side of orthodoxy as against Arian and subsequent heresies, and on the side of the Church as against paganism. In the first year of his reign he was baptized * (February, 380), and immediately issued an edict in the names of the three emperors, declaring their will that their subjects should embrace the Catholic faith, branding other parties as heretics and uttering vague threatenings against them. In 381, after a successful campaign against the Goths, he made his entry into Constantinople, and at once gave Damophilus, the bishop, the choice of subscribing the Nicene Creed or resigning. The Arian bishop resigned, and the emperor handed over all the churches to the Catholics, both there and throughout his dominions.

The violence and cruelty of the Arians when in power had alienated men's minds, and people generally were not indisposed to receive the orthodox creed. On the whole, the Catholics were re-established throughout the East with little disturbance.

In 391 the emperor issued an edict forbidding people to offer sacrifices, or even to enter pagan temples. The zeal of Christians, and especially of the monks, moved them in many places to destroy the temples.

* He had previously been only a catechumen. It was very usual for men to make a profession of Christianity, but to abstain from baptism, for fear of the spiritual penalties that might follow any sin after baptism.

Paganism now in its turn began to plead for toleration. Libanius, the most famous philosopher of his time, addressed an elaborate oration to the emperor " For the temples," pleading against their destruction. In some places the people rose in defence of famous local temples, and pagan worship continued in spite of the imperial edicts. The destruction of the temple of Serapis at Alexandria is an example of what took place. Next to the temple of Jupiter in the Capitol it was the proudest monument of pagan religious architecture, and it was one of the wonders of the world. A vast mass of buildings, the apartments of the priests and ascetics devoted to the god, stately halls adorned with statues, a great library, and other subsidiary buildings, surrounded the temple. The temple was ascended by 100 steps ; it stood in the centre of a vast square, surrounded by an enormous portico of beautiful proportions, supported by 400 pillars, the work either of Alexander the Great or of the first of the Ptolemies.* The god was believed to influence the rise and fall of the Nile, on which depended the harvests of Egypt, the granary of the empire. A religious riot in Alexandria, in which the pagans had used the Serapion as a fortress and had immolated Christians as victims on the altar, called forth a rescript from the emperor ordering the destruction of the temple. The Prefect of Egypt, with the Bishop of Alexandria and a military guard, took possession of the temple. They ascended to the sanctuary. They stood in awe amidst the silence of the deserted temple. The huge image of the god, covered with plates of gold and silver and adorned with jewels, filled the sanctuary. The popular belief was that any injury to it would be the signal for the final crash of heaven and earth. The bishop bade a soldier strike ; he struck it in the face, and no catastrophe followed ; another climbed up and struck off the head of the statue, and a colony of rats leaped out and ran in all directions. Shouts of laughter hailed the incident, and the work of destruction proceeded. The pagans threatened that the vengeance of the god would be shown in the cessation of the rise of the Nile ; and, indeed, that was delayed long enough to cause general anxiety ; but at length the river rose above its usual height. The heathen

* Pompey's Pillar is one of them.

then began to hope that the god would avenge himself by an inundation ; but the waters subsided to their proper level, and all fears of the vengeance of the pagan gods ceased. The example was followed, and other great temples were destroyed, both in Egypt and other provinces of the empire. The power and majesty of the ancient gods were, however, still predominant in Rome. The Capitol was still crowned with their temples and statues. No less than 152 temples and 180 smaller shrines were scattered through the city, in which sacrifices and solemnities were still maintained with splendour by ancient endowments. Most ancient aristocratic families still retained the old religion as part of their ancestral dignity.

In 383 the emperor issued an edict which confiscated the property of all the heathen temples, and deprived the priesthood of privileges and immunities. Symmachus, the Prefect of Rome, a man whose character commanded universal respect, assembled the senate, and they presented a petition to the emperor, pleading for toleration of the ancient religion of the empire. Ambrose, Bishop of Milan, replied to the petition, and the emperor did not relax his suppression of idolatry. In 388 the emperor formally proposed for debate in the senate the question whether the worship of Jupiter or that of Christ should be the religion of the Romans, and by a large majority it was resolved to abandon the ancestral religion. Few really believed in it ; many of the ladies of their families were already Christian ; six hundred families inheriting the great names of the Republic are said to have passed over at once to Christianity.

But, though the temples were closed and sacrifices forbidden, the pagans in many places evaded the laws. On solemn festivals they assembled in some convenient place under the shade of trees, under pretence of a convivial meeting ; sheep and oxen were slain and roasted, and the feast was sanctified by incense and by hymns in honour of the god. Then a last edict of Theodosius, A.D. 390, prohibited any sacrifices, the use of luminaries, garlands, incense, or libations of wine, in any place whatever ; the house or estate where such ceremonies were performed was to be confiscated ; or if performed on the estate of another, a heavy fine of twenty-five pounds of gold imposed. There were few or no persecutions under these laws. Pagans, though forbidden to exercise their worship, were not molested, and paganism was left to die out slowly, though many of its superstitions retained their hold in the minds and customs of the people for centuries.

The changes which had taken place between the reign of Constantine and that of Theodosius may be thus described. Constantine, himself a new convert, first placed Christianity on the throne of an empire only half converted from paganism. Constantius and Valens made half the empire Arian. Theodosius, an hereditary Christian, ruled over a Christian and orthodox empire, in which the lingering traces of paganism and heresy were barely tolerated.

CHAPTER XX

THE EXTENSION OF THE CHURCH OUTSIDE THE EMPIRE — ARMENIAN, GOTHIC, ABYSSINIAN, AND IBERIAN CONVERSIONS

THE Roman empire was not the first of the kingdoms of the world to accept the faith of Christ as its national religion ; that honour belongs to the kingdom of ARMENIA. Gregory, surnamed the Illuminator, was the apostle of the first Christian kingdom. The king of Persia had procured the assassination of Kosrov, the powerful king of Armenia, and annexed his kingdom. Kosrov's assassin had been put to death by the enraged soldiery, and only one of his children, the infant Gregory, was saved from their vengeance by a Christian nurse, who fled with him to Cæsarea.

Towards the end of the third century Tiridates, the son of Kosrov, reconquered his hereditary throne, and Gregory reentered his native country in his train. When the king offered a thanksgiving sacrifice, Gregory refused to join in the idolatrous ceremony. It was made known to the king that the recusant was the son of his father's assassin ; and Gregory was tortured and thrown into prison. A pestilence happened, and the king himself was stricken. His sister, who was a Christian, advised the release of Gregory. The king was healed, the plague ceased ; the king, nobles, and people almost simultaneously submitted to Baptism, and Armenia became the first Christian kingdom. Priests were invited from Greece and Syria, 400 bishops were consecrated and Gregory was made archbishop. Churches and religious houses rose in very quarter ; the Christian festivals and days of religious observance were established by law. Dara, however, the sacred province of the kingdom, resisted the introduction of the new religion in arms, and only by the

sword was its resistance overcome and Christianity established in the province. After the Council of Chalcedon the
Armenian Church unhappily embraced the Monophysite
heresy, but it has continued, despite Moslem persecutions,
to the present day.

In the first inroads of the GOTHS into the Eastern empire
in the reign of Gallienus, the invaders carried back numbers
of slaves, among them many Christians. The slaves
succeeded in converting their masters, and the families of
the captives continued to supply a priesthood to the Goths.
A Gothic bishop with a Greek name, Theophilus, was at the
Council of Nicæa (A.D. 325). In A.D. 348, Ulphilas came
with an embassy from the Goths to the Emperor Constantius, and obtained consecration from the Bishop of
Constantinople, probably as the immediate successor of
Theophilus. Ulphilas first reduced the Gothic tongue to a
written language, into which he translated the Bible for the
use of his people. He held Arian tenets and impressed them
upon the Gothic Church; thence they spread to the kindred
nations, the Vandals and Burgundians; so that while
Arianism was dying out in the empire, it was gaining new
force among the barbarians, and was by their subsequent
conquests, planted again in Italy, Spain, and Africa.

The ABYSSINIAN Church was founded at this period. A
scientific expedition in the early part of the fourth century
under Meropius, a philosopher of Tyre, calling, on its homeward voyage, at a place on the coast, in search of fresh
water, was attacked, and all were massacred by the inhabitants except two Christian youths, the relatives and pupils
of Meropius. They were carried as captives to the king,
who made one of them, Ædesius, his cup-bearer, and the
other, Frumentius, his secretary and treasurer. On the
death of the king, his widowed queen begged the two
strangers to act as regents until her son came of age. They
introduced the Gospel among the people; and when at
length they left the country, Frumentius, on arriving at
Alexandria, told his story to Athanasius, and requested
him to send a bishop to follow up the work. Athanasius
thought no one so fit as Frumentius himself, and accordingly
consecrated him and sent him back to Abyssinia. The
Church thus founded continues to this day. It still

acknowledges obedience to the see of Alexandria, and its patriarch is always an Egyptian monk, chosen and consecrated by the Coptic patriarch.

The IBERIANS, or Georgians, about the same period received the Gospel by means of a Christian woman whom they had carried back a captive after an incursion into the empire. First a child of the king, then his queen were healed of sickness by her prayers, and other miracles are said to have been wrought. The king and queen were converted, many of the people followed their example ; and the Iberians, on application to Constantine, were supplied with a bishop and clergy. In the fifth century, when so many Eastern churches adopted the Nestorian and Monophysite heresies, the Georgian Church adhered to the orthodox faith. After continuing under the patriarchate of Constantinople for 1,500 years, it fell by conquest, in 1801, into the power of Russia, and was transferred from the patriarchate of Constantinople to the rule of the Holy Synod of Moscow.

CHAPTER XXI

FATHERS OF THE CHURCH: ATHANASIUS, CHRYSOSTOM, AMBROSE

EVERY now and then the circumstances of an age produce a cluster of great men. The great masters of the Greek tragedy were contemporaries, so were the great Greek philosophers, so were the great Latin poets. So the great Fathers of the Christian Church are nearly all included within a century. The great Alexandrian and African writers, Clement, Origen, and Tertullian, were rather earlier; St. Gregory the Great and the Venerable Bede rather later. Putting them aside, the Fathers, both Greek and Latin, may be said to begin with Athanasius and to end with Leo the Great, and are included between the dates 330 and 461. In the last year of Athanasius' long reign in Alexandria popular acclamation called Ambrose to the see of Milan. Ambrose was ruling the Church of Milan, and influencing the councils of the Western emperors, at the same time that Augustine was occupying the see of Hippo and writing works which have influenced the mind of Western Europe ever since; at the same time Jerome, in his cell at Bethlehem, was studying Hebrew by stealth with his Jewish teacher, and writing the popular version of the Scriptures which had even more influence on Western Christianity than all the writings of all the Fathers. While Jerome was a young man he travelled through Cæsarea, and made himself known to its bishop, Basil; then he travelled to Constantinople, where he heard Gregory of Nazianzus preach; and he witnessed the elevation of John Chrysostom to the throne of Constantinople, and outlived him by thirteen years. In this list of contemporaries is included all the four doctors of the Greek Church and all the four doctors of the Latin Church, except only Gregory the Great.

Thousands of educated English Churchmen are contentedly ignorant almost of the very names of these great writers of the Christian Church. It has been the fashion to underrate them as men who wrote ponderous tomes long since superseded by the results of modern enlightenment. Let us glance at the men and their work. They afford a curious illustration of the cosmopolitanism of their time, and of the very various sources from which clergy were drawn. To limit ourselves to names already mentioned. Augustine was a Numidian, Jerome a Dalmatian, Basil and Gregory Cappadocians, Chrysostom a Greek of Antioch, Ambrose an Italian. Augustine, before his ordination,was a middle-aged professor of rhetoric ; Basil and Gregory young men of family and fortune, who finished their education in Athens ; Jerome, a student, first at Aquileia then at Rome ; Chrysostom began to practise at the bar ; Ambrose was a middle-aged statesman and governor of a province when he was suddenly called to the bishop's chair. Another remarkable fact is that, differing in so many respects, they are alike in this, that they all had some years of ascetic training before they entered upon their work, with the single exception of Ambrose.

What was their work ? The Gospel had not only to give an answer to simple souls asking for a practical rule by which to live here and win heaven hereafter ; if it was to dominate the whole realm of human thought and life, as it claimed to do, it must deal with the whole range of science and philosophy. It must not only refute and reject the false, but must gather into itself all the true results of human thought which the great races—Egyptian, Indian, Greek, and Jewish—had been maturing for centuries ; all true conclusions which human reason had painfully wrung out of the facts of the universe ; all the prophetic guesses of heart and soul stretching out to the unseen and the future.

The Fathers of the Church, by God's grace, accomplished this great and noble task. Holding the faith once for all delivered to the Church by Christ and His apostles with a firm, unfaltering grasp, they, with a wonderful breadth and depth of learning, and a still more wonderful soundness and sobriety of judgment, gathered round the Gospel all that was true and valuable in the heterogeneous mass of ancient thought. Amidst the confusion which resulted from the break-up of the civil, social, and domestic system of the ancient world, and the inroad of the rude customs of barbarous tribes, they laid the foundations of the civil organisation, the social and domestic habits, the philosophy and modes of thought, of the nations of the modern world.

ATHANASIUS was the central figure round which the Arian conflict (Ch. XVIII) raged. As archdeacon of Alexandria he had probably been the first mover in the opposition to the new and dangerous teaching of Arius ; though but archdeacon, and under thirty years of age, he had been the leading speaker on the orthodox side at the Council of Nicæa. Alexander dying immediately after the council, Athanasius was raised to the bishopric of Alexandria, and held this great and powerful see from the age of thirty to the age of seventy-six. " He displays in his writings a manly and direct eloquence ; a remarkable and unusual combination of subtlety with breadth of mind ; extreme acuteness in argument, yet at the same time a superiority to mere contentiousness about words. His unbending steadiness of purpose was combined with a rare skill in dealing with men ; he knew when to give way as well as when to make a show of resistance. . . . Throughout all his troubles he was supported by the attachment of his people and of the hundred bishops who swore allegiance to the see of Alexandria." *

When the emperor Constantine wrote to Athanasius, requiring him to receive Arius and his followers into communion, the undaunted Athanasius replied that he could not acknowledge persons condemned by the whole Church, and the emperor desisted from urging the matter.

The Arians, however, besieged the emperor with all kinds of complaints against Athanasius ; he was summoned to appear before a council at Tyre, and finding that force would be employed if he did not obey the summons, he appeared at the head of 50 out of his 100 Egyptian bishops. When Athanasius was about to take his seat, Eusebius of Cæsarea, who presided, bade Athanasius stand, as became a

* Canon Robertson.

person accused. On this one of the Egyptian bishops,
Potammon, a man of high repute for sanctity, is said to have
addressed Eusebius : " Do you sit while the innocent Athanasius is tried before you ? Remember how you were my
fellow-prisoner in the persecution. I lost an eye for the
truth ; by what compliances was it that you came off
unhurt ? " The ecclesiastical charges against Athanasius were fortified by others of a criminal kind. A
Meletian bishop named Arsenius was persuaded to go
into hiding. Athanasius was accused of having killed
him and cut off his hand to use for magical purposes ; the
accusation of magic being a popular charge at the period.
This was triumphantly answered by the production of
Arsenius before the council safe and whole. Athanasius
embarked for Constantinople, and appealed to have his case
tried by the emperor himself. The council meantime met
again, condemned him in his absence, excommunicated him,
and decreed his deposition. The Arian members of the
Council of Tyre then adjourned to Jerusalem, and there
brought a new accusation against him. They asserted that
he had threatened to stop the sailing of the Egyptian fleet,
on which the capital depended for its supply of corn. The
possibility was enough to alarm the emperor, and Athanasius was banished to Trèves, where, however, he was
honourably entertained at the court of the younger Constantine, and the emperor refused to allow his see to be filled.
On the death of Constantine (A.D. 338) Athanasius returned
to his see after two and a half years' absence, with a recommendatory letter from Constantius, and was joyfully
welcomed by his flock.

At a council held at Antioch two years afterwards, the
enemies of Athanasius procured the passing of a canon, that
if any bishop deposed by a council should appeal to the
temporal power, instead of seeking redress from a higher
council, he should forfeit all hope of restoration. He was
condemned under it, and Gregory of Cappadocia, an Arian,
was consecrated to the see of Alexandria in his stead.
Gregory was escorted to his see by a military force under the
command of the Prefect of Egypt. When the prefect
announced that Athanasius was deposed, and Gregory of
Cappadocia was their bishop, Athanasius tells us what

ensued : " The people were very indignant, and flocked to
the churches when the news was spread about, determined
that no Arian impiety should defile the faith of the Church.
Philagrius the prefect—the man who once before was known
to have insulted the Church and the Church's consecrated
virgins, a renegade from his faith, a fellow-countryman of
Gregory, who owed his place to the court influence of the
Eusebians, and was therefore, as may be supposed, a sorry
friend to the Church—this Philagrius gathered together by
promises—promises only too scrupulously fulfilled—the
heathen mob, Jews, and all the abandoned characters of
the city, worked them up to a pitch of frenzy, and then
hounded them in pell-mell on the people assembled in the
churches. To give an idea of what ensued is out of my
power ; it is beyond language and expression ; the memory
cannot dwell upon it without sorrowful tears. What
ancient tragedy had come up to it ? In what war or dire
persecution did such things happen ? The churches and
the sacred baptistries were set on fire ; at once the whole
city was filled with the outcries, the wailings, and the grief
of the outraged people, protesting against the prefect and
the brute force employed against them. The sacred and
undefiled virgins were horribly insulted, or nearly killed ;
the monks were trodden under foot and left to die ; some
were brained with the discus ; some killed with swords and
bludgeons ; others wounded and beaten. The holy table
was profaned with indescribable impiety and wickedness.
They sacrificed birds and snails to the glory of their idols,
and burnt all the Holy Scriptures they could find, blasphem-
ing our Lord and Saviour Jesus Christ, the Son of the living
God. In the second baptistry (horrible to relate) the
deicide Jews and unbelieving pagans, unrestrained by
decency, committed such obscenities in word and deed that
I am ashamed to relate them. Nay, some of the impious
crew, imitating the bitterest of the persecutors, would seize
the consecrated women and drag them about, forcing them
to blaspheme the Lord, or if they refused, stabbing and
kicking them. Gregory, who had promised pay and booty
to the heathen Jews and other conquerors in this iniquity,
now fulfilled his promise (for he was well pleased with what
had been done), and gave them the church to sack. What

followed was worse than the horrors of war and piracy. They fell to spoil and pillage ; all the large stores of wine they drank or wasted, or carried off; they appropriated the oil of olives ; doors and railings were borne away as trophies ; wall lamps were pulled down, wax candles taken to burn before idols ; in a word, destruction and death filled the church. But they did not stop here. Priests and many people were torn with scourges ; holy virgins stripped of their veils, dragged before the prefect's judgment-seat, and thrust into prison. Some were outlawed, some beaten with the slave's lash, and they attempted to starve out the colleges of ecclesiastics and consecrated women by intercepting their food. This happened in Lent, when the brethren were fasting ; nay, on the very day of Good Friday itself, Gregory induced the prefect to order to be publicly scourged, during one hour, no less than thirty-four virgins, besides married women and men of gentle birth." (St. Athan. Epist. Encyc., 3, 4.)

Athanasius withdrew on the arrival of Gregory, and went to Rome, where a council of fifty bishops pronounced him innocent. Constans, the emperor of the West, requested his restoration to his see, and at length threatened to restore him by force of arms. Constantius, partly disgusted with the revelation of some of the intrigues of the Arian party, partly desiring the support of the West in his meditated campaign against Persia, put a stop to the persecution, himself invited Athanasius to return, and sent him back to Alexandria with a recommendatory letter. Gregory had died a little while before, and Athanasius was again received with universal rejoicing.

When the death of Constans and the defeat of Magnentius left Constantius sole master of the empire, the machinations against Athanasius recommenced. A council at Milan, overawed by the emperor, condemned him. Athanasius, however, declined to resign his see, or to leave the city. It was feared that the Alexandrians would oppose by force any attempt to remove him, and the general in command of the province proceeded to obey the emperor's orders by a mixture of stratagem and force. In the night of February 9 (A.D. 346), while the bishop and a large congregation were keeping the vigil of St. Thomas, the general, with 5,000 soldiers and a mob of Arians, surrounded the church. The bishop, hearing the noise, calmly seated himself on his throne, and gave out the 136th Psalm, the whole congregation joining in the response, " For His mercy endureth for ever." The doors were forced, the soldiers pressed towards the east end of the church to seize the bishop ; many of the congregation were trodden under foot and crushed to death ; some were pierced by the soldiers' javelins ; the consecrated virgins were beaten. The bishop bade all escape, determined himself to be the last. But those about him at length carried him away by a side door, and he escaped from the city. In a few months another Arian bishop, George of Cappadocia, made his appearance, and behaved against the Catholics with still greater violence even than his predecessor ; bishops, clergy, monks, virgins, and laity were plundered, scourged, mutilated, banished, and committed to the hard labour of the mines. Some bishops died through their sufferings. George was driven away by the people, but, reinstated by the civil power, made himself more detested than ever. On hearing of the death of Constantius, the heathen populace of Alexandria murdered the intrusive bishop George. Julian recalled all the banished, and Athanasius returned to Alexandria ; the churches were surrendered to him and the Catholics restored. Julian, however, afterwards declared Athanasius excepted from the general recall, and banished him from Egypt. Athanasius said, " Let us withdraw ; this is a little cloud, which will soon pass over." He sailed up the Nile ; a galley pursued him. At a turn of the stream he doubled back, evaded his pursuers, and returned to Alexandria ; but soon afterwards again left and took refuge among the monks of the desert. Jovian, on his accession, invited Athanasius to court, requesting his instruction and advice, and replaced him in his see. Valens issued a general sentence of banishment against the bishops who had been banished by Constantius and recalled by Julian, and Athanasius took refuge for a time in his family tomb ; but on its being represented to the emperor that he did not fall under the letter of the edict, Valens permitted his return. He spent his remaining years in quiet possession of his see, dying, c. A.D. 373, at the age of seventy-six.

CHRYSOSTOM leads us to the other great sees of the Eastern Church—Antioch and Constantinople. He was born at Antioch about A.D. 347, the son of a military officer of high rank, and early left to the care of his widowed mother. He studied under Libanius, a heathen, the most famous teacher of his day ; and years afterwards Libanius declared that he would have been his own worthiest successor had not the Christians stolen him. He was destined to practise at the bar, but at the age of twenty resolved to devote himself to a religious life. At his mother's entreaties he continued to live with her, but in the practice of an ascetic life, till her death. He then lived four years in a monastery near Antioch, and spent two years as a hermit in a cave, when ill-health, brought on by his austerities, led to his return to Antioch. Here he was ordained deacon, and in 386 Flavian, the Bishop of Antioch, appointed him as the chief preacher in the church of that great see. His eloquence won him the name of Chrysostom—the golden mouth. A very great number of his sermons, taken down as they were preached, still remain, and justify his reputation as the Church's greatest preacher. His style is clear, flowing, and ornate ; he uses abundant and apt illustrations, constantly introduces topics of passing general interest, and is ready and happy in taking advantage of any little thing which may happen while he is speaking. His homilies extend over the greater part of the New Testament, with certain books of the Old ; he adheres to the literal meaning of Scripture, and his exhortations are distinguished by good sense. He is always making practical applications, and appeals to the hearts of his hearers with a deep knowledge of the human heart.*

A remarkable opportunity occurred for the exercise of the influence of this popular eloquence. Taxes imposed by Theodosius excited great discontent at Antioch. The principal inhabitants presented a remonstrance to the prefect, and an excited mob assaulted the prefect's house. Repulsed in this attempt the mob plundered the public baths ; and, lastly, the statues of the emperor and his deceased empress were overthrown, dragged through the streets, and assailed with insults. At this news the emperor

* Canon Robertson.

gave orders for the destruction of the city which had thus out-raged him. The bishop, Flavian, prevailed on the prefect to suspend the execution of the order, while he, old as he was, undertook a mission to the emperor in the hope of appeasing his anger and obtaining a reversal of the terrible sentence. The people of Antioch were panic-stricken. Day by day some of the principal people were arrested and examined before the prefect with tortures ; the rest waited in terrified suspense. This was the great preacher's opportunity. Every day Chrysostom preached in the principal church, which was crowded with hearers, and applied himself to lead the city to a general repentance of its sins, and an earnest preparation for death, should the emperor's sentence be executed, or on the other hand for a new and holier life, should God hear their prayers and turn the emperor's heart. The emperor was touched by the appeal of the aged bishop, and granted the pardon which he asked in the name of Christ.

The Emperor Arcadius nominated Chrysostom to the see of Constantinople, and he was consecrated A.D. 398. At the capital his preaching and virtues made him popular and influential ; but an ascetic mode of life, and the severe discipline he endeavoured to force upon the clergy, made him many enemies among them ; while his severe con-demnation of the vices of the court, and his public strictures on the Empress Eudoxia, made the emperor and the empress his enemies. The latter part of his life was spent under persecution. Theophilus, Bishop of Alexandria, instigated by the empress, headed a party against him. He was summoned before an irregular synod, called " of the oak," to answer certain charges ; and, refusing to acknowledge the jurisdiction of the synod, was condemned in his absence. He was sent across the Bosphorus on his way to exile ; but the people beset the imperial palace with cries for their bishop ; an earthquake added superstitious fears to the natural apprehension of popular disturbances, and Chrysos-tom was recalled. A few months afterwards, when the court had recovered from its terrors, he was banished to Cucusus, a town among the ridges of Mount Taurus, where he spent three years, exercising great influence by means of correspondence with churches in all quarters, and receiving visitors, who came to see and consult him, amply supplied with funds by his friends, and distributing them bountifully in alms. His enemies, provoked by all this, procured that his place of exile should be changed ; and he was ordered to Pityus, a town on the extreme north-eastern frontier of the empire. On his way thither he died of the hardships of the journey. His body was afterwards brought to Constantinople, and Theodosius II., then emperor, met the procession, and asked pardon of the saint for his persecution by his parents.

AMBROSE, Archbishop of Milan, was the greatest Churchman who had yet appeared in the Western Church. On the death of the Arian Archbishop Auxentius, in 374, the Emperor Valentinian invited the people of the city to nominate his successor. They assembled in the principal church ; but party spirit ran high, and there were symptoms of a riot in the church. Then Ambrose, the Prefect of Liguria, who presided, made a speech exhorting the people to peace and unity. When he concluded a voice as of a little child was heard to say, " Ambrose for Bishop," and the cry was caught up by the whole people. Ambrose, the son of a Prætorian prefect of Gaul, had been educated for State employments, and was now thirty-four years old ; but after the bad custom of the time was only a catechumen. He did not desire the office of bishop, and was with difficulty induced to accept it. Milan was at this time the chief residence of the Emperors of the West, and the position of its bishop afforded great opportunities to a great man. Ambrose set himself diligently to theological study and to the administration of the affairs of his see, and his strong practical sense and statesman's experience and lofty character gave him great influence both with court and people.

On the death of Valentinian, Ambrose acquired great influence over the mind of the young Gratian, though in the empress-widow Justina, an Arian, he had a bitter enemy. Nevertheless, when Gratian was murdered at Lyons by the partisans of the rebel Maximus, the empress-mother placed her younger son Valentinian II. in the Archbishop's arms and entreated him to become his protector. Ambrose accepted the charge, proceeded to Trèves, where Maximus had fixed his court, and negotiated a division of the empire, which ceded to Maximus, Britain, Gaul, and Spain, and secured Valentinian in the possession of the remainder.

Ambrose succeeded in extinguishing Arianism in Milan, but the empress-mother, with some courtiers and the Gothic body-guard, still adhered to the heresy. For their use the empress demanded a church without the walls, and subsequently a large church which had just been built and not yet consecrated. Ambrose was twice summoned before the imperial council, who told him he must yield to the imperial will, but he refused; the people surrounded the palace, the troops sympathised with the archbishop, and the demand was withdrawn for the time. A year afterwards it was renewed, and on his refusal the archbishop was ordered to quit the city. He refused to quit his flock unless compelled by force, and for several nights the people filled the church and its adjoining buildings as a guard, and again the archbishop's firmness prevailed. On this occasion Ambrose, it is said, introduced into the Western Church the custom already in use in the East—that the psalms, instead of being left to the choristers, should be sung by the congregation antiphonally.

When Maximus, in violation of the treaty, invaded the territories of Valentinian, Theodosius marched against the invader, defeated him, and for a time fixed his residence in Milan. The archbishop acquired as strong an influence over the mind of the great emperor as he had done over the younger princes. The most remarkable exhibition of the bishop's firmness and of the emperor's respect was on an occasion similar to that already narrated in the sketch of St. Chrysostom. The people of Thessalonica, on the occasion of a chariot race, had raised a popular cry for the release of a favourite charioteer who had been imprisoned for a shameful crime. The military prefect refused, upon which they broke out into a riot, and murdered him with many of his soldiers and others. Ambrose interceded for the Thessalonians, and obtained the emperor's promise of a pardon; but other advisers urged the impolicy of passing over such an outbreak against the imperial authority, and obtained an order for their punishment, which was kept secret from Ambrose. The people of Thessalonica were

invited to a performance in the circus and surrounded and
attacked by troops, who put them all to death, to the
number of 7,000 men, women, and children. The archbishop at once wrote to the emperor, expressing his horror
at this great crime, and refusing to allow his presence at the
Holy Communion until he should have given proof of
repentance. As Theodosius was about to enter the
principal church, the archbishop met him in the porch, and
desired him to withdraw. The emperor spoke of his
contrition ; the archbishop told him that public evidence of
contrition ought to be given for so public a crime. The
emperor submitted, withdrew, and for eight months
remained in seclusion, laying aside his imperial ornaments ;
he consented to pass a law, intended to guard against like
effects of sudden anger on the part of emperors, that an
interval of thirty days should come between a capital
sentence and its execution ; and on Christmas Day he was
formally received back into the communion of the Church.
When Theodosius returned to the East the young emperor
of the West was, until his violent death, entirely under the
guidance of Ambrose. The great statesman-bishop died
on Easter Eve, A.D. 397

CHAPTER XXII

MONASTICISM : ANTHONY. PACHOMIUS. HILARION. BASIL. JEROME. MARTIN OF TOURS

THERE have always been men who have felt keenly the awfulness of life and the vanity of the ordinary ways of men, and have had the courage to break the chains of custom, and live a life apart. The Christian faith gave a new meaning and dignity and sacredness to the common life of man, but it also revealed more certainly and vividly the grandeur of the Unseen and the Eternal, and gave food and encouragement to the contemplative and ascetic class of minds. From time to time this ascetic spirit has exercised a deep influence on the minds of Christian people, due partly, perhaps, to the external circumstances of the time, partly to the example of some illustrious man, or perhaps to one of those waves of feeling which sweep across the sea of human society, such as that which filled the deserts of Egypt and Syria with hermits in the fourth, fifth, and sixth centuries, the forests of Germany with monks in the eighth, revived the monastic spirit throughout Europe in the eleventh, and gave rise in the thirteenth to the mendicant orders.

ANTHONY was not the first who led a solitary life, but he was the first who attained any great reputation ; for his life was written by St. Athanasius, his contemporary, and he is regarded as the father of the Hermits. He was born A.D. 251 in a village in the Thebaid, of wealthy Egyptian parents ; he was brought up by them as a Christian, and was a thoughtful and religious boy. Before the age of twenty he lost both parents and came into possession of considerable property. One day in church hearing the Gospel of the rich young man who was bidden by our Lord, if he would be perfect,

" to go, sell all that he had, and give to the poor, and come and follow Him," he accepted the words as addressed to himself, to be literally obeyed. He gave his land to the inhabitants of his village, turned the rest of his possessions into money and distributed it to the poor, and embraced the ascetic life. At first he lived near his own village, supplying his frugal wants by the labour of his own hands, and giving to the poor what he could spare. He visited all the most famous solitaries and endeavoured to learn from each his special virtue, and to combine them all in his own character. After a time he left his village and afterwards shut himself up in a tomb, where he continued to live a solitary life for ten years. We may picture him sitting in the shaded entrance to his cell—one of the painted tombs with which the hill-sides are honeycombed—with the silence and solitude of the desert around him, and at his feet the green and fertile valley of Egypt, teeming with a busy population and dignified by the grand monuments of the most ancient civilisation of the world. The hum of awakening life rises faintly up towards him ; he can catch the gleam of the Nile, and see the sails of the boats passing on its great highway ; he says his prayers, sings his psalms, and reads his book ; then busies himself in his little garden in the hollow dell through which the spring trickles down towards the Nile ; in the evening he again says his prayers, sings his psalms, and lies down to sleep in peace.

His reputation spread abroad ; people imitated his example, Anthony consenting to receive them as disciples, and the neighbouring desert began to be peopled with their cells. Multitudes of people came to seek his spiritual counsel ; the Emperor Constantine and his sons corresponded with him and sought his advice. Twice he visited Alexandria : once during the persecution of Maximin, when he went to give courage to the sufferers, and to seek, if it should be God's will, the crown of martyrdom ; but the heathen did not venture to molest him. When he returned he sought out a remoter solitude and dwelt in a cave in the side of a lofty mountain, with a spring of water near, a few palm-trees fed by its waters, and a little patch of fertile land which he cultivated, reaping enough corn and vegetables to supply his own wants and furnish refreshment to his visitors. His second visit to the city was during the Arian controversy, in which he and his disciples were steady and influential supporters of the orthodox belief.

A notable feature in the life of Anthony, to be found also in the lives of many other solitaries, is his believing himself to be assailed by temptations in visible shapes— demons disturbing his meditations by noises and antics, or in the form of beautiful women trying to seduce him into lustful desires, or Satan in person tempting him to despair. Jerome describes his own similar experiences in striking language. Luther, in the solitude of the Warzburg, had visions of the same kind. Anthony died in 356, at the age of 105, and charged his disciples to bury him in secret, to avoid honours being paid to his body.

Pachomius modified the ascetic life by gathering a number of religious persons on an island of the Nile called Tabennisi, where they lived together under a rule of life which he laid down for them. Their dress was, after the fashion of the country, a long linen tunic with a woollen girdle, a black frock, and over it a sheepskin cloak. They usually went barefoot. Their food was bread and water, herbs, vege-tables, oil, and a little fruit. Each had his little cell, furnished with a mat of palm leaves for a bed, and a bundle of papyrus reeds served for a pillow by night and seat by day. A group of such cells was called a Laura. Every morning early, and every evening, the sound of a horn sum-moned the brethren to worship. The service consisted chiefly of chanting psalms, twelve at each service ; at the close of each psalm the whole assembly prostrated them-selves in adoration. On certain days lessons from the Scriptures were read.

The institution, both of solitaries and of monks living in community, spread rapidly. The rocky hills which on each side border the long narrow green Nile valley, and divide it from the enclosing deserts, were peopled with hermits. Ammon established a great colony of them in the hilly desert called Nitria. Macarius founded another in the vast solitude of Scetis. In the fifth century the monks were said to be as numerous as all the rest of the population of Egypt. But as asceticism grew into an institution the

character of its professors deteriorated. Men of the lowest
class sought the Laura as an escape from poverty and toil.
Some carried their mortification to fanatical excesses—wore
iron chains, lived half naked, and fed on grass ; some fell into
excesses of spiritual pride, accounted themselves already
saints no longer needing prayer or sacraments. Some even
made the monk's black gown a cloak for religious vaga-
bondage and secret sensuality. They played an important
part in the religious history of Egypt. In the frequent
religious disturbances of Alexandria, some hundreds of
fanatical Nitrian monks would flock into the city, and, un-
armed as they were, their fierce enthusiasm and contempt
of death made them formidable even to the troops who
were called out to restore order.

From Egypt the fashion spread to other lands. HILARION
introduced it into Syria. We have his life written by St.
Jerome. Born of heathen parents at a village near Gaza,
he was sent by his parents for education to Alexandria ;
there he learnt not only rhetoric and philosophy, but Christianity also, and lived a well-conducted life. Hearing of
Anthony, though a mere boy, he left Alexandria and went to
him, and stayed two months, a diligent listener and close
observer. Disliking the concourse of people who visited
Anthony and disturbed the solitude of the place, he returned
with some monks to his own country, being then only fifteen
years old ; he found his parents dead, assumed the linen
tunic, black gown, and coat of skin, and took up his abode
in the desert near Gaza, in a desolate place, between a
marsh and the sea. Here he first made a little cabin, woven
of rush and sedge, for shelter ; after four years he built himself a hut, four feet wide by five feet high, and a little longer
than his own length. Here he learned the Scriptures by
heart ; had visions and temptations like other solitaries ;
was said to work miracles ; gradually became known ; and
people flocked to him from Syria and Egypt. Others
followed his example ; and solitaries and monks multiplied
in Syria. Mar Saba, founded by Sabas, half-way between
Jerusalem and the Dead Sea in the valley of the Kidron,
is the oldest monastery in Palestine. All around for miles
the hills are honeycombed with rocky chambers, the
deserted dwellings of the thousands of monks who peopled

L

this part of the wilderness. Two, three, sometimes four stories of cells pierce the sides of the valleys, overhang the precipices, or bury themselves below the level of the ground. Some monastic buildings still stand—the domed church, the libraries, the hospice—and twenty or thirty monks still inhabit it. The mountain of Quarantania, behind Jericho, believed to be the secne of our Lord's temptation, is also honeycombed from top to bottom with the cells of hermits ; they still contain many frescoes and inscriptions dating back to the fourth and fifth centuries. Another colony peopled the wilderness adjoining the Red Sea, others the mountains of Sinai.

The spirit of Hilarion was grieved by the multitudes who came to consult him ; he had fled from the world, and the world came to him. So he left his cell, and travelled to the desert where Anthony had dwelt ; and two ancient solitaries, who had dwelt near Anthony and had buried him, showed Hilarion his cell, took him to his grave, and told him stories of his life. Hilarion took up his abode with two monks in that neighbourhood. But in a little while the crowds again found out his retreat ; to escape them he embarked on the Nile, sailed down to Alexandria, and thence up to the other oasis. There also his fame followed him, and once more he fled in search of solitude. With one companion he went on board a vessel sailing to Sicily. He offered to pay his passage with his book of the Gospels, his only possession besides his black gown and his sheepskin cloak ; the captain, however, would not receive payment, but gave him his passage for the love of God. In Sicily again he could not be hid ; his ascetic virtues and miracles betrayed him, and he fled to Cyprus, where, in the course of a two-years' stay, he again attracted the notice which he shunned, and, at his companion's suggestion, moved into the solitary interior of the island, where he stayed five years, and died at the age of eighty.

BASIL of Cappadocia introduced the monkish life into Asia Minor. Born about A.D. 329, of noble and Christian parents, he was sent for education, first to Cæsarea, the principal place of his native province, and then to Athens, where his brother Gregory, afterwards Bishop of Nyssa, Gregory, afterwards Bishop of Nazianzus, and the young prince Julian (the Apostate), the nephew of Constantine, were his fellow-students. Basil and his friend Gregory determined to renounce their prospects of secular eminence and embrace a religious life. Basil was baptized after leaving Athens, travelled in Egypt and elsewhere, returned to his country, and was ordained at Cæsarea. Then he withdrew for five years into Pontus, and founded monastic establishments. Charles Kingsley gives a picturesque sketch of him at this period : " On the south side of the Black Sea, at the mouth of the river Iris, beside a roaring waterfall surrounded by deep glens and dark forests, with distant glimpses of a stormy sea, lived as a hermit, on bread and water, a graceful young gentleman, handsome, a scholar, heir to great estates ; the glens and forests around were all his own. On the other side of the torrent his mother and his sister, a maiden of wondrous beauty, also lived as hermits, with their female slaves, and other women who had joined them." But community life was Basil's ideal : " God," he said, " has made us, even like the bodily members, to need one another's help. For what discipline of humility, of pity, and of patience can there be if there be no one towards whom these can be practised ? Whose feet wilt thou wash, whom serve, how canst thou be least of all, if thou art alone ? "

Basil's rule continues to be the rule of the monks of the Eastern Church. Basil returned to Cæsarea, and on the death of Eusebius in 370 was elected to the see ; he enjoyed the confidence of Athanasius and on his death became the leader of the orthodox of the East.

JEROME introduced the ascetic profession into the Western Church. Born at Strido, near Aquileia, and probably of Dalmatian race, he was brought up a Catholic Christian, educated at Aquileia, and sent at seventeen years of age to complete his education in Rome. There, besides going through his courses of rhetoric and dialectics, he tells us that he fell into some of the sins which beset students of all ages. At the age of twenty he was baptized, and soon afterwards returned home. About that time the Syrian Evagrius visited Aquileia. His description of Syrian monasticism fired the imaginations of Jerome and other young men, who set out for the East. Passing through

Cæsarea he visited Basil. At length he adopted the solitary life in the desert of Chalcis, where he spent three years. He writes of the solitary life to his friend Heliodorus thus : " O desert, blooming with the flowers of God ! O wilderness, in which are found the stones of the city of the great King ! O solitude, familiar haunt of God Himself ! Brother, brother, what dost thou among secular men, thou who art greater than all this world ? How long shall the weight of a roof press upon thy head ? How long dost thou hold thyself a prisoner in the smoke of cities ? What dost thou fear ? Poverty ? But Christ calls the poor blessed. Labour ? But no one that striveth is crowned without hard work. Dost thou dread to lay thy fasting body on the bare ground ? But thy Lord lieth beside thee. Does the infinite vastness of the wilderness frighten thee ? Walk in spirit through the land of Paradise, with thy thoughts up in heaven, and thou shalt never heed the desert." He had the usual visions and temptations of the solitary seeker after perfection.

After three years, his health suffering from his austerities, and being plagued by the neighbouring solitaries, he returned to Antioch. Thence he went to Constantinople, where he listened with delight to the preaching of Gregory Nazianzen. Thence he accompanied Epiphanius and Paulinus of Antioch to the synod held there in 381, under Bishop Damasus. Jerome was appointed secretary to the council, and when it was ended the Pope appointed him to the important and confidential position of his own secretary. He was the foremost priest in Rome, and many regarded him as the probable successor to the see. Jerome had retained all his admiration for the ascetic life, and preached it so effectually in Rome that a group of noble Roman ladies embraced it, and put themselves under his direction :— Albina and her daughter, the learned Marcella ; Asella, another patrician dame ; the wealthy widow Paula and her three daughters, Blessilla, Paulina, and Eustochium. The Pope died in 385, and Jerome left Rome and returned to Antioch ; Paula and Eustochium followed him, and together they made a pilgrimage to Jerusalem, thence to Egypt, penetrated Nitria, and witnessed the monastic life there, tarried at Alexandria and listened to Didymus the Bishop, and so back to Jerusalem. Finally they settled at Bethlehem, where Jerome spent the remaining thirty-one or thirty-two years of his life.

Paula built two monasteries at Bethlehem, one for men, the other for women. Jerome sold his little patrimony and contributed it towards the cost. The Church of the Nativity, built by Constantine, protected the grotto in which tradition said our Lord was born. Jerome lived in a little cell in the limestone rock near the grotto, and there carried on a large correspondence, wrote treatises, took part in the theological controversies of his time ; but especially studied Hebrew and accomplished his great work, a new Latin translation of the whole of the Old and New Testaments from the original languages, which, under the name of the Vulgate, continued to be the authorised version of the whole Western Church till the sixteenth century, and is still that of the Roman communion. He was a man of great learning and vigorous mind, irascible, contentious, intemperate in language, but a sincere Christian and a great man.

ST. MARTIN OF TOURS introduced the monastic institution into Gaul *c.* 360 A.D. A man of noble birth, and a soldier, he abandoned the world and lived as a monk in the island of Gallinaria. Thence he was led to undertake the preaching of the Gospel in Gaul, a great part of which province was still heathen. He gained converts, destroyed the temples and statues, erected churches, founded monasteries at Poitiers and Tours, and earned the title of the Apostle of Gaul. When he was consecrated bishop, he fixed his see in his monastery at Tours, and continued to be both abbot and bishop. At his death he was followed to the grave by 2,000 of his monks, and his shrine became the chief place of pilgrimage of the French Church. The Church of Christ was probably first introduced from Gaul into Britain ; and the Gallic Church as our nearest neighbour, through which all foreign influences flowed to us, for many centuries exercised an influence here. The monasteries of Gaul were famous schools of learning, to which students from these islands resorted, and it is probable that from this precedent of the abbot-bishop St. Martin may be derived the fact that most of the sees of the Celtic churches were founded in monasteries, instead of in great towns as was the earlier custom of the Church.

The lives of these leading ascetics show that solitaries and monks were not all poor ignorant half-crazed enthusiasts, but men of birth, wealth, education, and genius. Indeed, asceticism had leavened the Church, so that all the leading men in it of this period had been trained by some years at least of ascetic life.

Women embraced it with equal ardour. Besides deaconesses attached to every great church in the East (in Chrysostom's time the Church of Constantinople had 100) and a number of poor widows, the pensioners of its charity, there were also a number of unmarried women and widows who consecrated themselves to perpetual chastity and ascetic devotion, many continuing still to live in their own homes. Some letters of Cyprian to the Church virgins of Carthage show us their outward observances and their inner spirit. St. Ambrose, the one great man of his time who had not received an ascetic training, yet preached asceticism so persuasively that mothers of Milan forbad their daughters to attend, lest they should be induced to take vows of virginity.

CHAPTER XXIII

THE DISRUPTION OF THE WESTERN EMPIRE AND CONVERSION OF THE BARBARIANS

TAKE a line from the Firth of Forth down to the east coast of England across to the mouth of the Rhine, strike across Europe to the mouth of the Danube, and right across the Black Sea till it touches the Caspian ; then start again from the south-west corner of the Caspian and draw another line to the top of the Gulf of Suez. Everything south-west of these two lines in Europe and Asia was in the Roman Empire. Add, from the continent of Africa, Egypt to the Cataracts of Syene, and the whole fertile strip of country which forms the southern shore of the Mediterranean, and we have before us the whole of the Roman Empire. On the death of Theodosius (A.D. 395) this empire was again divided, according to the Diocletian constitution, between his two youthful sons— ARCADIUS taking the eastern, and HONORIUS the western division. Their accession marks a great era in history, the beginning of the disruption of the empire by the invasion of the barbarians. It was a mighty fabric, which had been gradually consolidated during 400 years. In the space of 100 years more, the western empire had been broken into pieces, ravaged by successive hordes of barbarous tribes, and finally partitioned into independent sovereignties, represented by the modern nations of Europe. In the space of another half-century, the Eastern empire had been stripped of provinces east, west, north, and south, but retained with a diminished territory its imperial city, its constitution, civilisation, and religion, down to the fifteenth century.

The rapidity of this revolution fills us at first with amazement, and it needs a careful consideration of the state

151

of Roman society to perceive its causes. The population of the cities consisted of wealthy proprietors whose estates were scattered over adjoining provinces ; their households were very numerous, and consisted of slaves, with two or three freedmen as upper servants. The manufacturing and trading class was small ; the actual handiwork of all crafts and trades was done by slaves. The rural districts were chiefly divided into great estates, cultivated by slaves under the supervision of the steward of an absent master. The legions for many years past had been recruited chiefly from among the warlike races on the frontiers of the empire. When the barbarians burst upon the empire there was nothing but the legions to oppose them, and when the legions were weakened or crushed in some great defeat, there was neither a sturdy peasantry nor a spirited town popula-tion out of which to recruit them. The country could offer no resistance to an invader. The fortified towns might muster enough soldiers and citizens to man the walls and resist an assault, but they could do little to arrest the progress of the invasion.

In the fourth century some great movement in Eastern Asia impelled the Tartar population, which inhabited the vast central steppes, in a westerly direction. One wave of emigration pushed another before it, until at last the Goths, who touched the eastern border of the Roman empire, unable to resist the pressure behind them, asked leave of the Emperor Valens to cross the boundary of the Danube and take refuge within the empire (A.D. 376). The Roman officers who superintended the immigration computed the Gothic warriors at 200,000 men—the whole people probably numbered a million. Shortly afterwards the Ostrogoths also, in spite of imperial prohibition, crossed the Danube to seek shelter within the empire. The imperial officers plundered and oppressed the refugees, who sought redress by force of arms. They overran Thrace, defeated the army sent against them in the great battle of Hadrianople, and ravaged the country from the walls of Constantinople to the foot of the Julian Alps. The great Theodosius at length defeated them, and reduced them to obedience. They were permitted to settle as subjects of the empire— the Visigoths in Thrace, the Ostrogoths in Asia Minor—and were required to furnish 40,000 troops for the service of the empire.

On the death of Theodosius (A.D. 395) this Gothic contingent revolted. Alaric, a prince of the nation, had been their commander, and on the accession of Arcadius aspired to command the armies of the East. Being disappointed, he raised the standard of revolt. The Goths of the empire and the kindred tribes across the Danube flocked to his camp. He ravaged Greece, invaded Italy, and approached Rome. The Emperor Honorius was compelled to flee from Milan and seek shelter amidst the marshes of Ravenna, which thus for 350 years afterwards came to be the capital of the Western empire. But Stilicho, the able minister of Honorius, had by this time collected the scattered garrisons from all quarters, gave battle at Pollentia, in Liguria, and inflicted a defeat on the invaders.

After three years of peace a vast host of Suevi, Vandals, Burgundians, and Alani, under Rhagasius, burst upon the empire (A.D. 405), and marched unopposed from the northern extremity of Germany almost to the gates of Rome, leaving the emperor shut up in Ravenna, and Stilicho in his camp at Pavia, painfully endeavouring, by enlisting slaves and barbarians, to raise an army to meet them. Florence at length, animated by Ambrose, detained the invaders before its walls till Stilicho was able to act. He did not give battle, but with great strategical skill enclosed the besiegers within intrenchments, and at last reduced them by famine to surrender.

In 408, 409, and 410, Alaric once, twice, and thrice besieged Rome. The first time he accepted a ransom ; the second time the city surrendered, and he placed a puppet emperor on the throne, and marched to Ravenna to demand the confirmation of his power. Being refused, he retraced his steps, forced his way into Rome, and the eternal city, the mistress of the world was given up to sack and plunder by the barbarous Goths.

Alaric had been so far influenced by the religion he professed that he bade that life should be spared, and commanded that the churches of the apostles should be inviolate. An incident related by Orosius will illustrate the force of this Christian feeling. A soldier entered the dwelling of an aged Christian virgin in search of plunder, and demanded the surrender of her treasures. The vessels and ornaments of the principal church had been placed under her care. She calmly showed them to the astonished soldier— vessels of gold of great size and beautiful workmanship. " These," she said, " belong to St. Peter ; I, a defenceless woman, cannot protect them ; my soul is free from sin, if you dare, take them, and answer to God for it." The soldier sent a message to Alaric. He ordered that the virgin and her charge should be safely conducted to the Church of the Apostle. The vessels, and the virgin, with an escort of troops, wound through the streets, while the people broke out into hymns of thanksgiving at the sight.

But the palaces and temples were plundered of their riches, the spoils of ages of conquest ; many of the noblest families were reduced to slavery ; many fled before the conquerors ; and the cities of Africa, Egypt, and even of the East, swarmed with the unfortunate exiles.

Innocent, the bishop, was absent at Ravenna, seeking in vain for aid from the emperor. He returned to find ancient Rome ruined, and the ancient Roman society dispersed. But the churches and houses of the people remained. Pagan Rome was destroyed, but Christian Rome rose out of its ruins. Henceforward the bishop was beyond question the greatest man in Rome, and his power continually increased. The imperial prefect represented the distant and waning authority of the emperor, but the bishop was the elect of the people ; he had large revenues, and the ecclesiastical organisation easily supplied the machinery of a constituted government.

Alaric ravaged all Italy and Sicily, and was embarking for the conquest of Africa when death arrested his career.

Then came the invasion of Spain by the Suevi, Vandals, and Alani, kindred tribes from beyond the Rhine, who, after some alternations of fortune, finally made good their occupation of Spain and Aquitania. About the same time the Burgundians and Franks obtained settlements in the distracted province of Gaul.

But another horde, which had been pressing forward the Goths and Germans, now reached the empire, which lay like a huge monster in his dying throes at the mercy of all the

beasts of prey. The Huns made their appearance in Gaul
in A.D. 451, and next year invaded Italy. They were
Tartars by race, heathens in religion, savages in manners ;
travelling on little active horses, with their families in
waggons ; living in the open air, feeding on flesh only ;
a nomad race, they did not spare towns they did not propose
to occupy, or vineyards and fruit-trees they did not intend to
cultivate ; and calmly slaughtered tens of thousands in cold
blood ; they were led by Attila, the sublime savage, with
genius and consciousness of a Divine mission, calling himself
the " Scourge of God." Rome had to care for her own
safety. The bishop was looked up to by all as their leader,
and Leo was not unequal to the crisis. One of the most
wonderful pictures of this wonderful time is that presented
by the embassy of Leo, the Bishop of Rome, in the vestments of his office, with a procession of his clergy singing
psalms, proceeding to the camp of the Tartar horde pitched
a few miles from the gates of Rome. The " Scourge of
God " listened to the Bishop of Rome, accepted an immense
ransom, and spared the city.

Meantime the Vandals, under their king, Genseric, had
established themselves in the African province, A.D. 439
(St. Augustine died in A.D. 431 in his see of Hippo, while the
city was besieged by the barbarians) ; and on the murder
of Valentinian III. (A.D. 455) they sailed for the Tiber, and
marched on Rome. Again Leo went out to meet the
conqueror, and obtained a promise that the city should
not be fired nor the captives tortured ; but Rome was given
up for fourteen days to pillage. The spoils of the Temple of
Jerusalem, brought by Titus to Rome, were carried off to
Carthage, with all the valuables of the city and a host of
captives.

The nominal emperors were henceforth the puppets of
some successful soldier, who wielded the real power behind
his purpled representative, until Augustulus (475) resigned
his nominal dignity. The senate signified their intention
not to elect another emperor, and sent the imperial ensigns
and sacred ornaments of the throne and palace to Constantinople. The Western empire was entirely extinct,
and the general Odoacer openly ruled Italy. He, after a
vigorous administration of fourteen years, was superseded

by Theodoric, King of the Ostrogoths, with whom the modern history of Italy begins.

In the year 410 Honorius had withdrawn the legions and the civil administration from the distant province of Britain, and left its inhabitants to form a government of their own and provide for their own safety. The helpless state of the abandoned province invited the incursions of the piratical people from the opposite coast of Germany. Saxons, Jutes, and Angles came in different expeditions under different leaders, and gradually forcing the Britons back into the western extremities of the island, Cornwall and Wales, and into the north, established small independent kingdoms.

Thus the empire of the West was divided among the Franks in Northern Gaul; the Burgundians in the country watered by the Saone and the Rhone; the Visigoths in Spain and Gaul south of the Loire; the Suevi in the north-west corner of the peninsula; the Ostrogoths in Italy and Dalmatia up to the Alps and the Upper Danube; the Vandals in Africa; and the Saxons in Britain.

The Goths had long since embraced Christianity, but in its Arian form; the rest of the tribes who permanently settled in the empire had received Christianity from the Goths, and therefore were also Arians; all except the Franks, who embraced Catholic Christianity, as we shall relate, and the Saxons, who continued heathens for the next two hundred years.

The Frankish conversion is an important event for the history of modern Christendom. Clovis, King of the Franks, had married Clotilda, the niece of the Burgundian king. Clotilda, though brought up in an Arian court, had imbibed the Catholic faith, and tried to induce her husband to embrace her own creed. He allowed his children to be baptized, but himself retained his ancestral religion. In the crisis of the great battle of Tolbiac, near Cologne, against the invading Alemanni, he invoked the God of Clotilda, and on his subsequent victory acknowledged the God Who he believed had responded to his call. His subjects were willing to follow the example of their chief; and in the Cathedral of Rheims, together with three thousand of his warlike followers, Clovis was baptized into the Catholic

Church (A.D. 496).* His dominions increased. The Catholic bishops were powerful in the cities of Gaul and well disposed towards the Catholic king ; and Clovis, partly by treaty and partly by force, gradually acquired the whole of Gaul, and established the Catholic religion in it. Burgundy also yielded to the valour of Clovis and his sons.

In 510 the emperor of the East acknowledged the conquests of Clovis by bestowing on him the title of Consul. Clovis accepted the honour, rode to the Church of St. Martin and thence to the Cathedral at Tours, wearing the purple tunic, mantle and diadem, and scattering a royal donative among the people, who hailed him as Cæsar and Augustus. He was at that time the only Catholic sovereign in the West, and the Church added to his honours the title of Eldest Son of the Church, which his successors on the throne of France ever after retained.

When the Goths and their Allies had completed their conquests, and came to settle among the conquered people, they had to deal with the fact that the Catholic clergy and people of the land refused to recognise the religion of their Arian conquerors, or to enter into religious communion with them. Different courses of action were taken in different countries.

In Italy the Ostrogoths retained their own creed, but tolerated the creed and did not molest the clergy of the conquered race. This continued till Arianism was extinguished, together with the Gothic monarchy of Italy, by the conquests of Belisarius (A.D. 537) and Narses.

In Africa a fierce persecution of the orthodox by the Vandal conquerors, Genseric and his successors, Hunneric, Gundamund, Thrasimund, with a short interval of toleration under Hilderic, and a renewal of the persecution by Gelimer, extended over a miserable seventy-seven years, terminated by the overthrow of the Vandal dominion by Belisarius.

In Spain the Suevi, under Theodoric, returned to the Catholic faith in A.D. 569 ; the Visigothic portion of the peninsula under King Reccared, who, succeeding to the

---

* These phenomena of a barbarian king converted through the influence of a Christian wife, and of his people consenting to change their religion with him in a mass, are repeated several times in the history of the conversions of these northern races.

throne in A.D. 586, avowed himself a Catholic. A synod of seventy bishops, at Toledo in A.D. 589, established the true faith among his people. At this synod the Nicene Creed was adopted by the council, with the addition of the " Filioque," which afterwards became the chief point in dispute between the Eastern and Western divisions of the Church of Christ.*

* Who suggested this interpolation, and under what influences this obscure council of a race just emerging from Arianism took upon itself to alter the venerable Nicene symbol, received through all the churches of the world, is not known. The subsequent history of the clause is briefly this : Charlemagne patronised the addition, and got it formally recognised by a council of the bishops of his dominions, held at Friuli, A.D. 796. Then he tried to induce the Bishop of Rome, Leo III., to adopt it ; but the Pope declined to do so, and, on the contrary, had the ancient creed engraved on two plates of silver, and hung up in his Church of St. Peter's, as monuments of the true form of the Catholic Creed. At last, without any formal act of the Church, the alteration was quietly adopted by the Popes. It is said that Pope Benedict VIII., at the suggestion of the Emperor Henry II., first introduced the singing of the Nicene Creed into the service of the mass, and that the form of the creed so introduced contained the " filioque." From Rome it gradually spread over all the Western Church.

CHAPTER XXIV

THE EASTERN EMPIRE FROM THE DEATH OF THEO-DOSIUS TO THAT OF JUSTINIAN

IN the last chapter we saw that on the death of Theodosius the Great (A.D. 395) his son Arcadius took the
Eastern portion of the empire. The reign of this
virtuous but weak emperor is chiefly interesting to us as the
time in which Chrysostom lived. The writings of Claudian,
and of Chrysostom himself, give a vivid picture of the age :
the intrigues of the palace, directed by the young, beautiful,
and faithless Empress Eudocia, the rapacity and cruelty of
the favourite Rufinus, the still more open avarice and vanity
of his successor, the aged eunuch Eutropius, the venality
and corruption of the state, the luxury and frivolity of
society, the worldliness and self-indulgence of the clergy,
with the ascetic and eloquent bishop endeavouring in vain
to stem the tide of ungodliness.

On the death of Arcadius (A.D. 408), at the age of thirty-one,
his eldest daughter, PULCHERIA, received the title of Augusta,
and began to reign as guardian of her brother, THEODOSIUS II.,
who was only two years younger, but who appears to have
inherited the feebler character of his father. Pulcheria
and her two sisters, Arcadia and Marina, publicly took the
profession of Church virgins ; they formed their female
attendants into a religious community, and turned their
palace into a monastery ; the usual religious exercises were
diligently carried on ; the princesses expended large sums in
building and endowing churches, charitable institutions,
and monasteries ; yet this imperial nun firmly, wisely, and
successfully administered the affairs of the Eastern empire
for nearly forty years. The Empress Eudocia, the wife of
Theodosius II., known in her earlier pagan days by the more
famous name of Athenais, in her middle age retired to Jeru-

salem, and spent her last sixteen years in devotion, her alms and pious foundations in the Holy Land exceeding even the munificence of the Empress Helena.

Pulcheria, on the death of her brother (A.D. 450), called to her assistance the military talents of MARCIAN, and gave him the dignity of a nominal marriage with herself and the imperial title. On his death (A.D. 457), following four years after that of his wife, LEO OF THRACE, by favour of the powerful Aspar, the commander of the troops, was elected emperor by the senate, and received his crown from the hands of the Patriarch of Constantinople, the first example of this symbolical representation of the truth that " the powers that be are ordained of God," and that kings are God's ministers.

For our purpose we may pass over the succession of emperors until JUSTINIAN (A.D. 527), whose remarkable reign of thirty-seven years demands notice. The military genius of Belisarius, widely extended his dominions. In a three months' campaign (A.D. 534) that great general defeated the Vandals, and reconquered Africa after it had been nearly 100 years severed from the empire. Next, turning his arms against the Ostrogoths, he conquered Sicily and Italy, and entered Rome, where he was welcomed as a deliverer ; withstood a siege of Rome ; followed the Goths to their stronghold in Ravenna, which surrendered to him (A.D. 539), and all Italy was annexed to the Eastern empire. The civil achievements of the reign were equally remarkable. The genius of Tribonian digested the laws of the empire since the time of Hadrian into three great works—the Code, the Pandects, and the Institutes of Justinian—which were established as the system of civil jurisprudence throughout the empire. Justinian encouraged commerce and manufactures ; in his time the silkworm was introduced from China into Greece. The frontiers of the empire were strengthened by chains of fortifications ; the provinces, subject to inroads of the Scythian horse, were furnished with castles and towers of refuge ; the great cities strengthened ; Constantinople itself made impregnable. The empire was adorned with magnificent public buildings. Almost every city obtained the solid advantages of bridges, hospitals, and aqueducts ; innumerable churches were built with lavish expenditure. In Constantinople alone and the adjacent suburbs the emperor dedicated twenty-five churches in honour of Christ, the Virgin, and the saints. The greatest of all his works, the Church (now the mosque) of Sancta Sophia, still stands, after twelve centuries, a monument of the munificence of the sovereign and the genius of his architects, Anthemius and Isidore. At its dedication the emperor exclaimed, " Glory be to God, who hath thought me worthy to accomplish so great a work ! " and then, with an outburst of vanity, added, " I have vanquished thee, O Solomon ! " The Church of Sta. Sophia is one of the great landmarks in the history of architecture. The style which we know as Byzantine had now grown into its full development and perfection ; and Byzantine art continued to exercise an influence for many centuries.

But Justinian allowed his subjects to be oppressed by a favourite minister ; the administration was incurably corrupt ; the empire, notwithstanding the victories of Belisarius in the West, was feeble and unwarlike and its home provinces were constantly plundered by barbarians, and the subjects of Justinian groaned under the weight of his taxes. For twenty years in the latter part of his reign a feeble but destructive war was waged with Chosroes, King of Persia. Rebellions broke out in Africa, and successive wars almost depopulated that once fertile province. The Goths revolted in Italy under Totila, and many years of war ensued under Belisarius and Narses. Rome was taken and retaken before the Gothic power in Italy was finally broken, and Italy once more annexed as a province to the Eastern empire, under an exarch seated at Ravenna.

M

CHAPTER XXV

THE SECOND, THIRD, FOURTH, FIFTH, AND SIXTH GENERAL COUNCILS

WE have seen that Theodosius the Great (A.D. 378–395) was an earnest orthodox Christian who suppressed the paganism which lingered in the empire and the Arianism which had flourished in the East by the encouragement of his predecessors. He also, at an early period of his reign, took steps to obtain a settlement of other questions of doctrine and discipline which were disturbing the peace of the Eastern Church.

The first of these was the rival claims of Gregory of Nazianzus and Maximus to succeed to the see of Constantinople. Gregory in bygone years had, contrary to his own wishes, been consecrated by his friend, Basil of Cæsarea, Bishop of the city of Sasima ; but a dispute arising, he willingly resigned his pretensions to the see, and retiring to his father, who was Bishop of Nazianzus, and old and infirm, acted as what would now be called his coadjutor. After his father's death, during the earlier part of the vacancy Gregory continued to act as bishop, but then withdrew to Seleucia, and passed some years in retirement.

On the death of Valens, which seemed to offer a new prospect to the orthodox, Gregory was induced by their leaders to go to Constantinople and endeavour to rally the orthodox and to uphold the true faith there. He commenced his work in the house of a friend, where his little church was called the Anastasia, the place of the resurrection of the true faith ; it was afterwards enlarged into a splendid church. At first he encountered much opposition from the dominant Arians and even from his own friends. One Maximus, an Egyptian, who had been in Gregory's confidence, allowed himself to be set up in opposition to Gregory. Some Egyptian bishops, who were at Constantinople acting under the direction of Peter of Alexandria, got access by night to the metropolitan church of Constantinople, and there consecrated and enthroned Maximus as its bishop.

When Theodosius arrived at Constantinople in 380 he summoned the Arian bishop, Demophilus, before him, and on his refusing to subscribe the Nicene Creed he ejected him and all the Arian clergy from the churches, and a few days afterwards formally put Gregory into possession of the principal church of the capital.

The other questions which needed the decisions of a council were the Macedonian and Apollinarian heresies. The Apollinarian heresy had sprung up in the latter part of the life of Athanasius out of the discussion of the nature of Christ. Apollinarius, Bishop of Laodicea, taking the Platonic analysis of man's being into body, animal soul, and rational soul, started the theory that the Son of God, in taking man's nature, took only the body and animal soul, and that the Divine Person supplied the place of the rational soul. Finding his theory not received, he formed a sect, setting up rival bishops at Antioch and elsewhere. The heresy known as the Macedonian was also a remnant of the Arian heresy. Some of that party, who had come to acknowledge the Godhead of the Son, continued to deny the personality and co-equal Godhead of the Holy Spirit.

The Second General Council, summoned by Theodosius at Constantinople to settle these questions, met May 2, 381. It was attended by one hundred and fifty orthodox prelates, entirely from the Eastern Church, among them being Meletius of Antioch, Gregory of Nyssa, and Cyril of Jerusalem ; there were also thirty-six bishops of the Macedonian party.

The earlier sessions were presided over by Meletius, and dealt first with the pretension of Maximus to the see of Constantinople. The council decided in favour of Gregory, and he was solemnly enthroned as Bishop of Constantinople. Meletius died, and Gregory assumed the president's seat. Timothy, Bishop of Alexandria, who had just succeeded his brother Peter, then arrived with a train of Egyptian bishops, and was greatly offended that the council had been begun without him, and dissatisfied with its confirmation of Gregory to the throne of Constantinople. He revived the pretensions of Maximus, and argued against the appointment of Gregory, on the ground that he had been consecrated Bishop of Sasima and acted as Bishop of Nazianzus, and that the Nicene canon forbade translations. Gregory, with his usual spirit of self-denial, resigned the see ; but Maximus was not accepted as his successor. A list of those considered eligible was presented to the emperor ; among them Nectarius, an aged man of senatorial rank and excellent character, who, after the bad custom of the time, was as yet only a catechumen. His, however, was the name selected by the emperor, and Nectarius was at once baptized, and after a few days, being consecrated bishop, took his seat as president of the council, wearing the episcopal robes over his white baptismal dress.

The Apollinarian heresy was condemned ; its founder, however, retained his bishopric till his death, some ten years afterwards, and his peculiar tenets did not long survive him.

In dealing with the Macedonian heresy the council revised the Nicene Creed. First it seems to have added several clauses * to the statement of doctrine about the second person of the Trinity ; and then officially added all the clauses which follow " I believe in the Holy Ghost."

Epiphanius, however, in his " Anchorate," written some time before this council, says that every catechumen repeated at his baptism, from the time of the General Council of Nicæa to the tenth year of Valentinian and Valens (A.D. 373), a creed in the following words—and he recites the Niceno-Constantinopolitan Creed almost exactly as we now have it. " We must infer, then, either that a larger as well as a shorter creed was put forth at Nicæa, such as Epiphanius has recorded ; or that such a longer form had existed of old time, and that the Nicene council only

* " Begotten of the Father before all worlds." " By the Holy Ghost of the Virgin Mary." " Was crucified also for us under Pontius Pilate." " Sitteth on the right hand of the Father." " Whose kingdom shall have no end."

specified those parts which bore particularly on the controversy of the day ; or, lastly, that shortly after the
Council of Nicæa the Nicene fathers, or some of them, or
others who had high authority, enlarged and amplified the
Nicene symbol, and that this enlarged form obtained
extensively in the Church." *

The creed thus enlarged was, after the Council of Constantinople, accepted by the whole Church everywhere, and
formed the great symbol of the Church's unity of doctrine.†
The third canon of this council gives to the Bishop of
Constantinople precedence among bishops next after the
Bishop of Rome, and assigns as the reason, " forasmuch as
it is a new Rome," implying that the Bishop of Rome
obtained his precedency because of the political grandeur
of his see in the ancient capital of the Christian world.

The events which led to the THIRD GENERAL COUNCIL,
held by the Emperor Theodosius at EPHESUS in A.D. 431,
were as follows.

Nestorius, a presbyter of Antioch, was appointed to the
see of Constantinople (A.D. 428). He had been a monk of
blameless life, had some reputation for learning and
eloquence, but is charged with vanity and love of popularity.

He signalised the beginning of his episcopate by severe
measures against the Arian, Novatianist, Macedonian, and
other separatist bodies in the capital.

A presbyter who had accompanied Nestorius from
Antioch, and was much in his confidence, attacked in a
sermon, the use of the title *Theotokos*, as applied to the
Virgin Mary. The word had been used by Athanasius, the
two Gregories, of Nazianzus and of Nyssa, and other great
orthodox Fathers. It did not mean that the Virgin-mother
communicated the Divine nature to the Saviour, but it
expressed the truth that the conjunction of the Godhead
with the humanity took place simultaneously with the
miraculous conception of the humanity. Nestorius, in a
series of sermons, supported the view of his presbyter. He
was understood to teach that a man was born of the Virgin,
and then the Divine Person entered into and united Him-

---

* Bishop Harold Browne, Thirty-nine Articles, i. 296.
† For the subsequent interpolation of the " filioque " clause, see p. 158.

self with this man, which would imply that there were two persons in our Lord. The question roused great excitement throughout the city. The bishop was frequently interrupted in his sermons by expressions of dissent. On the other hand, when a distinguished presbyter preached in Nestorius' presence in defence of the title Theotokos, Nestorius rose and objected to his doctrine as being a confusion of the two natures into one mixed nature. The clergy and the monks were against the bishop, the court supported him, the majority of the people at first were in his favour.

Then Cyril, the Patriarch of Alexandria, took up the question. Cyril had, like so many eminent Churchmen of the period, spent some years of his early life in ascetic discipline among the Nitrian monks. He was strong-willed, eloquent, ambitious. By help of his army of Parabolani,* and his allies the fanatical Nitrian monks, and his wealth and popularity, he exercised such power and authority in the great city of Alexandria as no Churchman before him. On one occasion, the prefect failing to restrain outrages of the Jews against the Christians, he plundered the Jews' quarter and drove them (numerous as they were) out of the city. On another occasion the monks attacked the prefect himself and nearly killed him. The prefect executed a monk who had struck him with a stone ; the bishop rescued his body, gave him sumptuous burial, and canonised him. Cyril had accompanied his uncle and predecessor Theophilus, to Constantinople on the occasion of the Council of the Oak,† when Chrysostom was deposed. His action against Nestorius seems to have arisen partly out of the jealousy which Alexandria entertained of the precedence given to the new see of Constantinople.

Cyril denounced the teaching of Nestorius in a pastoral letter to his church, and entered into angry correspondence with Nestorius himself. Nestorius threatened to bring Cyril before a council for alleged misdemeanours ; Cyril retorted that he should rejoice in the opportunity of bringing Nestorius' heresies before a council. Both parties

---

* District visitors, first organised by Cyprian on the occasion of the plague mentioned, p. 74 ; in the time of Cyril, a numerous organisation of Church servants, paid by the Bishop, and at his service.　　† P. 138.

sought the support of the great Western see. Celestine, Bishop of Rome, held a synod, which condemned the opinions of Nestorius, and threatened him with deposition and excommunication. Cyril also held a synod, which condemned Nestorius, and he drew up twelve " anathemas," in which he stated what he held to be the true faith in opposition to Nestorius' errors, and called upon Nestorius to subscribe to them. The Eastern bishops, headed by the Patriarch of Antioch, and including Theodoret, the greatest theologian of the time, declared on the other hand, that Cyril's anathemas involved the Apollinarian heresy.

The four great patriarchs were, therefore, divided—those of Rome and Alexandria on one side, those of Constantinople and Antioch on the other. Clearly a THIRD GENERAL COUNCIL, to which all appealed, was needed, and the Emperor Theodosius II. summoned the fathers of the Church to EPHESUS, and sent Candidian, one of his chief officials, with a sufficient guard to regulate the proceedings. Nestorius came under the protection of Candidian. Cyril came with fifty bishops and a large train of monks and Alexandrian sailors. Memnon, Bishop of Ephesus, on the side of Cyril, had the support of the local clergy and mob. Celestine of Rome deputed two bishops and a presbyter to represent him and the whole council of the West. John of Antioch and the Syrian bishops, delayed by local disturbances and heavy floods, had not arrived. The 200 bishops assembled waited a fortnight, then they received letters from the Syrian bishops apologising for their delay, and announcing their arrival within a few days. But the council would wait no longer. On the 21st June, 431, it opened its session. Cyril, by right of the dignity of his see, presided. Nestorius refused to appear till the Orientals should arrive. Theodoret and sixty-seven other bishops protested against proceeding without them. Candidian, in the name of the emperor, demanded delay. But on the morrow the council pronounced a sentence of deposition against Nestorius.

On the 27th of June, John of Antioch and the Oriental bishops arrived. On hearing what had been done they constituted themselves, with twenty-nine others who joined them, into a rival council, and proceeded to consider Cyril's conduct and the " anathemas " he had put forth. They found him guilty of turbulence, and of reviving the Apollinarian heresy, and condemned him and all bishops who had adhered to him. The representatives of the Western Church arrived after this, recognised the Cyrilian Council, and at a subsequent session of its members subscribed its decree.

Deputations from both councils appeared before the emperor ; but meantime he had issued an order that Nestorius should resign his see and retire to his monastery. Maximian was consecrated in his place, and the Church was left to choose between the rival councils.

The history of this third council is not edifying, and calls forth little sympathy for either Nestorius or Cyril. The statements of both were, perhaps, one-sided, and each might, with patience and charity, have explained himself to the satisfaction of the other, and so a great and lamentable schism been avoided, which has lasted from that day to this.

The great body of the Church has ultimately accepted the condemnation of the doctrine attributed to Nestorius, and the Council of Ephesus counts as the third of the six general councils. Cyril subsequently gave an explanation of his anathemas, which was accepted as satisfactory, and John of Antioch, Theodoret, and the rest of the Syrian bishops, accepted the decrees of the council, and the bishops who refused were persecuted. But the opinions of Nestorius were zealously propagated and widely adopted in the Further East. The teachers of the famous school of Christian learning which had long existed at Edessa adopted and taught them. The Catholics, the head of the Church of Persia, induced the Persian king to recognise the Nestorian tenets as those of orthodox Christianity, and to expel from his dominions those who refused to adopt them. Nestorianism was thus confirmed in possession of the ecclesiastical establishment of Persia, which it retained ever afterwards. A famous school founded at Nisibis became a great centre of missionary enterprise throughout the East, and spread Christianity and learning from the Euphrates to China, from the north of Tartary to Ceylon. The prosperity of this great Church of the further East culminated in the beginning of the 11th century, when it may be doubted whether Pope Innocent III. possessed more spiritual subjects than the Patriarch of the City of the Caliph. The see was moved successively from Ctesiphon to Baghdad, to Mosul, and to Kochanes. The descendants of this Church still exist in the mountains of Kurdistan, about Mosul, and in the plain of Urumiyeh in Persia.

The FOURTH GENERAL COUNCIL was preceded by a false council, whose painful history must be told.

Twenty years had passed since the Council of Ephesus. Dioscorus had succeeded Cyril in the see of Alexandria, Proclus and then Flavian had succeeded Maximian at Constantinople, when Eutyches, abbot of one of the great monasteries near Constantinople, was accused of teaching a doctrine the opposite to that held by Nestorius, viz., that the Godhead and the manhood were not distinct in the person of Christ, but that the two natures were united in a third mixed nature, neither wholly God nor wholly man. Flavian tried to prevent the new dissension, but was obliged to proceed synodically against Eutyches and to condemn him. Eutyches appealed to a general council, and a council was summoned in the same church at Ephesus in which the third general council had been held. Dioscorus of Alexandria attended with a train of Parabolani and monks, Barsumas, a Syrian abbot, with a thousand monks. Leo of Rome in vain endeavoured to have the council held in Italy, excused himself from personal attendance on the ground that Roman bishops were not accustomed to attend councils beyond the seas (in fact no Pope was present in person at any of the six general councils), and sent three legates as his representatives, and by them a letter (Ep. 28) on the doctrine of the Incarnation, which, under the name of his " Tome," became famous in the history of the controversy and remains as the clearest and most convincing statement of the orthodox view. Dioscorus presided at the council. The proceedings were disorderly from the beginning. The orthodoxy of Eutyches was acknowledged and his opponents condemned amid cries of " Drive out, burn, tear, cut asunder, massacre all who hold two natures." At the demand of Dioscorus the imperial commissioners and their guard were called in, and all present were compelled by threats to sign the decrees, and Flavian suffered personal violence. Theodosius II., under the influence of his minister the eunuch Chrysappius, confirmed the proceedings, and proceeded against the deposed bishops. Leo, however, disavowed the action of his legates, held a synod at Rome, which declared the proceedings at Ephesus invalid, and gave to the council a name which has adhered to it ever since, the *Concilio latrocinium* (the council of robbers).

Theodosius died a few months afterwards ; Chrysappius was put to death ; and the new emperor, Marcian, expressed his willingness to hold another council. Leo again tried to have it held in Italy, but the emperor persisted in summoning it at CHALCEDON (A.D. 451), a suburb of Constantinople, on the Asiatic shore of the Dardanelles. The number of bishops assembled is traditionally said to have been 630, the council itself reckons 520, all from the East, except the two bishops who represented Leo of Rome and the Western Church, and two African bishops. The Roman legates and Anatolius of Constantinople sat as presidents of the clergy, but the real direction of the council was in the hands of the imperial commissioners. The results of the council were : (1) the deposition of Dioscorus, and the restoration of the bishops deposed by the *Concilio latrocinium ;* (2) a definition of the orthodox faith against the errors of Eutyches in these words which were almost those of Leo's Tome, " That Christ is perfect alike in Godhead and in manhood ; very God and very man, of a reasonable soul and human flesh ; co-essential with the Father as to His Godhead, and co-essential with us as to His manhood ; like to us in all things except sin . . . ; one and the same Christ, Son, Lord, only-begotten, to be acknowledged in two natures, without confusion, change, division, or separation ; the difference of natures being in no wise taken away by reason of their union, but rather the properties of each nature being preserved, and concurring into one person and one hypostasis,* not as it were divided or separated into two persons, but one and the same Son and only-begotten, God the Word."

Some decrees were also made as to ecclesiastical prece-

* Substance.

dence and jurisdiction. The wording of one canon is important, since it declares still more explicitly than the second council that the precedence of Rome rested on political grounds. " New Rome," it says, " ought to be magnified in ecclesiastical matters, even like the elder Imperial Rome, as being next to it." The see of Jerusalem had long been subject to the see of Cæsarea, the capital of the province, but Jerusalem, by reason of the vast confluence to it of pilgrims from all countries, had latterly assumed a much higher importance, and the claims of the see of the mother Church to a special reverence were prominent in the minds of all Christians. The council therefore, on the application of Juvenal, Bishop of Jerusalem, raised his see to the dignity of a patriarchate, and gave it jurisdiction over Palestine, leaving to Cæsarea the honorary title of metropolitan.

Leo's representatives had opposed the canon on the see of Constantinople, and Leo challenged its assertion that the precedence of his see arose out of the political importance of his city ; he declared the canon annulled by the authority of St. Peter, and threatened to excommunicate Anatolius. The emperor and the Eastern Church, however, held by the acts of the council ; Anatolius said conciliatory things to Leo, which he accepted as satisfactory, and the matter remained as the council had settled it, and its decrees have been accepted as those of a general council by the whole Church ever since.

The opinions of Eutyches gradually died out of the Greek Church, but the doctrine of one nature in Christ, variously modified, took permanent root and spread in the East and in Africa. The adherents of these sects were known by the general name of Monophysites (believers in One Nature). Just as the Nestorians had a second founder in Barsumas, so the Monophysite heresy seemed on the brink of extinction, when the genius and eloquence and industry of Jacob Baradæus revived and propagated it far and wide beyond the limits of the empire. He died Bishop of Edessa, A.D. 588, leaving his sect in a very flourishing state in Syria, Mesopotamia, Armenia, Egypt, Western Abyssinia, and other countries, in some of which it has continued to be the prevalent form of Christianity. In Egypt the adherents of Dioscorus established a Monophysite Church, which still survives in the Coptic Church, the only present-day representative of the ancient Christianity of Egypt.

THE FIFTH AND SIXTH GENERAL COUNCILS are of less theological importance than their predecessors, but of considerable historical importance in their bearing on the modern pretensions of the Roman see.

Monophysite opinions were not silenced by the Council of Chalcedon, but were still held by many and influential persons within the patriarchate of Constantinople. The Emperor Anastasius (491—518), a zealous Monophysite, appointed Severus a learned monk who held the same opinions, to the patriarchate of Antioch and excited deplorable seditions and tumults in the Church. His successor, Justin I., laboured with equal zeal to restore the Catholic faith. Justinian was also a supporter of the decrees of the council, but his wife Theodora was an avowed Monophysite and protected its professors. She invited Severus, who had been expelled from the see of Antioch, to take up his abode at the capital ; she procured the appointment to the see of Constantinople of Anthimus, a secret enemy of the decrees of Chalcedon. Towards the latter part of their reign Justinian was induced, by the influence of Theodora, to enter into plans for promoting Christian unity by setting aside the decrees of Chalcedon.

Pope Agapetus, who had been sent by Theodahat, the Gothic King of Italy, on a mission to Constantinople, died there. Vigilius, his archdeacon, who had accompanied him, was urged by Theodora to become a candidate for the papacy, and Justinian promised to support him with influence and money, on condition that he would concur in setting aside the decrees of Chalcedon, and hold communion with the Monophysites. Before he reached Rome, however, an election had been made, and Sylverius consecrated as Pope. In the following year Belisarius, who was at that time defending Rome from the besieging Goths, sent for Sylverius, accused him of treasonable correspondence with the enemy, and sent him off by sea into exile. Vigilius was then elected in his room, and paid Belisarius two hundred pounds of gold for his interest. Justinian sent

Sylverius back to Italy for a fresh investigation of his case, but through the contrivance of Vigilius he was seized and carried off to the island of Palinaria, where he died of hunger.

Now commenced the controversy of the Three Chapters. Theodore, Bishop of Cæsarea, persuaded Justinian that the opposition of the Monophysites to the Council of Chalcedon was not due so much to dislike of its definition of doctrines, as to its recognition of persons suspected of Nestorianism, such as Theodore of Mopsuestia, the reputed father of Nestorianism, Theodoret, and Ibas. The emperor published an edict (A.D. 544), in which he ordered the works of the above-named writers, known by the name of the Three Chapters, to be condemned, without prejudice, however, to the authority of the Council of Chalcedon. It was required that this edict should be signed by all bishops. The Eastern bishops in general subscribed, the few who refused were banished ; the African bishops resolutely opposed the edict. Vigilius of Rome was under secret engagements to Theodora to concur in action against the Council, but the Western clergy were opposed to the edict, and Vigilius refused to sign it. The emperor summoned him to Constantinople, where he was detained seven years, vacillating from side to side with pitiable weakness. A synod of seventy Western bishops was summoned to Constantinople, but they refused to concur in the condemnation of the Three Chapters. Vigilius next endeavoured to satisfy both parties by issuing a document, known as his *Judicatum*, in which he condemned the Three Chapters, but professed at the same time to uphold the Council of Chalcedon. An African synod, under Reparatus of Carthage, excommunicated him. The Pope's own deacons returned home to agitate against him. Vigilius appealed to a general council, and meantime withdrew his *Judicatum*. The emperor then issued a declaration of faith, which he required the Pope and other bishops to sign. He refused, and took sanctuary in a church. A guard was sent to seize him. The Pope laid himself under the altar, and when the soldiers tried to drag him away, laid hold of the pillars which supported the altar ; these gave way, and the altar would have fallen upon him if some of the clergy present had not supported it. The loud denunciations of the spectators shamed the officer into putting an end to the scandal. Vigilius was induced by oaths to leave his sanctuary, but effected his escape from his guards to the suburb of Chalcedon, and took refuge in the Church of the Deipara, the same in which the council had been held exactly a century before.

At length the FIFTH GENERAL COUNCIL met at CONSTANTI-NOPLE in May, 553. It was attended by 165 Eastern bishops, including all the Eastern patriarchs, but from the West there were only five African bishops. Reparatus had come but as it was found that he would oppose the imperial designs he was banished on the charge of a crime against the State, and another put in his place whose concurrence had been previously secured. Vigilius refused to attend the council. At last the emperor caused the secret engagements to which Vigilius had subscribed to be laid before the council, and demanded his exclusion from the communion of the Church. The council acted as the emperor desired. It then confirmed the decrees of the four earlier councils, condemned the Three Chapters, and declared that they were not countenanced by the Council of Chalcedon. It condemned Theodore of Mopsuestia as a heretic, but spared the memory of Theodoret and Ibas.

Some months later Vigilius made a humiliating submission to the decrees of the council, in which he ascribed his past difference of opinion to the devil. The emperor then gave him leave to return to his see, but he died on his journey, having greatly damaged the prestige of his see. His archdeacon, Pelagius, was by Justinian's influence appointed in his place, and accepted the decrees of the council; but the Western bishops were very slowly brought to concur. The metropolitan of Aquileia and the Istrian bishops remained in separation for a century and a half.

The Monothelite controversy was the last phase of the discussion, which had continued through so many centuries, as to the mode of the union of the Divine and human natures in our Lord Jesus Christ. Sergius, Patriarch of Constantinople, was the author of it. About A.D. 616 he started the notion that there was only one will and one operation in Christ—viz., the Divine will, which used the humanity as the agent of its operations. The Emperor Heraclius desired to promote the reconciliation of the Nestorians to the Catholic Church. He was led to believe that Sergius' new notion of one will might supply a middle term upon which this might be effected. The doctrine seemed undisputed among Catholics, and some Nestorians seemed willing to admit it. In the year 626 the emperor consulted Cyrus, the Bishop of Phasis, on the subject, who wrote to consult Sergius, and, convinced by his reply, encouraged the emperor's plan. Cyrus was soon elevated to the patriarchate of Alexandria, and succeeded in reconciling the Monophysite sect of the Theodosians by a compromise in which it was admitted that our Lord wrought the acts pertaining both to God and man by one *theandric* (*i.e.*, divinely human) operation.

Sophronius, a learned monk of Palestine, who was then at Alexandria, opposed the doctrine on which this compromise was based, but was induced by the two patriarchs to keep silence. In the following year, however, he became Patriarch of Jerusalem.* Sergius, in anticipation of his re-opening the question, wrote to Honorius of Rome. The Pope replied in a document, which continued for a century one of the main supports of the monothelite opinions. The Church was distracted with this new question. Heraclius thought to settle the controversy after the manner of Justinian, by issuing an imperial edict called the *Ecthesis*, or Exposition of the Faith. He declared that " one will was to be confessed, agreeably to the doctrine of the holy fathers, forasmuch as the Saviour's manhood never produced any motion contrary to the inclination of His Godhead "; but he forbade a discussion of the question as to one or two operations. The Eastern patriarchate received the Ecthesis, but Honorius was dead, and his successor John IV., with a Roman council, refused it; whereupon Heraclius disowned the authorship, and threw the onus on Sergius. In 648 Constans II. put forth a new formulary, called the Type, to supersede the Ecthesis. It simply forbade the discussion of the subject and the use of the obnoxious terms on either side, under severe penalties. A Roman council under Martin, known as the first Lateran Council, refused to be silenced by the imperial decree, and declared that

* It was he who negotiated for the surrender of Jerusalem to the Caliph Omar. See page 185.

there are two natural wills and operations—the Divine and the human—the one Lord Jesus Christ working our salvation both as God and as man, and the council anathematised Theodore, Cyrus, Sergius, Pyrrhus, and Paul, and the most impious Ecthesis and the most impious Type, but spared the name of Honorius.

Three years later the Exarch of Ravenna arrived at Rome, and by imperial orders seized the Pope and sent him a prisoner to Constantinople, where he was treated with great cruelty, imprisoned six months, and at length banished. Other bishops who refused to receive the Type were similarly persecuted. The Emperor Constantine Pogonatus, the successor of Constans II., desirous of restoring peace to Church and empire, summoned the SIXTH GENERAL COUNCIL at Constantinople. It lasted from November, 680, to September, 681. The emperor presided, and the proceedings were conducted with ability, impartiality, and decorum. The Monothelite opinions were condemned as destroying the perfection of our Lord's humanity by denying it a will and operation.* In its anathemas this council included the name of Honorius, declaring that " in all things he had followed the opinions of Sergius, and sanctioned his impious doctrines."

A supplementary council, which claimed to be œcumenical, held in the same place ten years afterwards to make some necessary canons on questions of discipline, was called the Quinisext (or Trullan) Council, as being an appendix to the fifth and sixth. Its decrees contain some canons contrary to Roman customs,† and in two instances expressly call upon

---

* That is to say, in the one person of our Lord are united two whole and perfect natures. That He had two whole and perfect natures implies that He had two wills, and that both these wills were operating and active. There is no question about the existence and operation of the Divine will; the question is, 1. Whether there was a human will also; and 2. Whether, if there was a human will, it was not the mere instrument of the Divine will, so that it never operated or acted of itself. But our Lord's human nature would be imperfect without a human will, and the human will is a free will; therefore our Lord's human will wrought (operated) independently—i.e., He had two wills and two operations.

† E.g. that married men when ordained should not put away their wives; it also condemned the custom which had arisen in Armenia of not mingling water with the wine of the Sacrament; and forbade the celebration of the Agape in churches.—Ed.

the Roman Church to adopt the new canons. They were signed by the two representatives of Rome, and by Basil, Bishop of Gorlyna, in Crete, who professed to sign as representing the " whole synod of the Roman Church," but the Pope (Sergius I.) refused to ratify them. In these canons we have one of the earliest open steps towards the breach between the Greek and Latin churches.

TABLE OF THE FIRST SIX GENERAL COUNCILS

Date.	Place where held.	Emperor under whom held.	Heresiarch condemned.	Heretical tenets condemned.	Remarks.
I. 325	Nicæa	Constantine the Great	Arius (Presbyter of Alexandria)	Denial of the true Deity of Jesus Christ	Hosius (Bishop of Cordova) presided. Athanasius the chief defender of the faith. Homoousion.
II. 381	Constantinople	Theodosius	Macedonius (Bp. of Constantinople)	Denial of the personality and Deity of the Holy Ghost	Meletius of Antioch, Gregory Nazianzen, and Timothy of Alexandria, successively presided.
III. 431	Ephesus	Theodosius II.	Nestorius (Bp. of Constantinople)	That there are two persons in Christ	Cyril of Alexandria presided. Theotokos.
IV. 451	Chalcedon	Marcian	Abbot Eutyches, and Dioscorus, Bp. of Alexandria	That there is only one nature in Christ (Monophysite)	Anatolius (Bishop of Constantinople) and the Envoys of Leo the Great, presided.
V. 553	Constantinople	Justinian	Theodore of Mopsuestia	The "Three Chapters"	The vacillation of Pope Vigilius.
VI. 680-1	Constantinople	Constantine Pogonatus	Sergius of Constantinople, Honorius of Rome	That in Christ there is only one will and one operation	Called the Monothelite heresy.

CHAPTER XXVI

THE EASTERN EMPIRE FROM THE DEATH OF JUSTINIAN TO THE EMPRESS IRENE

THE great Justinian was succeeded (A.D. 565) by his nephew JUSTIN II. In his reign the Lombards and allied nations under Alboin overran the greater part of Italy, and for the next 200 years that country was unequally divided between the Eastern empire and the Lombard kingdom. The empire was represented at Ravenna by an exarch, who exercised a limited sovereignty over the dissevered provinces of Rome and Venice. The Lombard kingdom ruled the rest of Italy, with Pavia for its capital. In this reign also hostilities were recommenced with the Persian monarchy under the great Nushirvan. Justin, incapacitated by disease, resigned the purple, and appointed TIBERIUS (A.D. 574) as his successor. The choice was a happy one. Tiberius, after an administration of eight years, in turn chose for his successor MAURICE (A.D. 582) who justified the choice by a wise and vigorous reign of twenty years. During his reign Gregory the Great was Bishop of Rome. A revolution in Persia drove Chosroes, the grandson of the great Nushirvan, to seek refuge under the power of Rome. Maurice reseated the refugee on his paternal throne ; but the diversion of his forces to the East left the West exposed to the Avars, and these ferocious Tartars ravaged Europe from the Danube to the walls of Constantinople, and from the Euxine to those of Rome. The cessation of the Persian wars left Maurice at liberty to turn his arms against this barbarian foe. After some considerable but transient successes, the emperor's endeavour to restore the discipline of his troops, roused a revolt, which replaced Maurice by an ignorant and brutal centurion, PHOCAS, who massacred the family of his predecessor and their adherents and imitated the vices and cruelties of the earlier empire.

HERACLIUS, exarch of Africa, refused to recognise the usurping tyrant, and was induced, by entreaties from the leading inhabitants of Constantinople, to attempt their deliverance. His son sailed with the Egyptian fleet for the Hellespont ; the tyrant was seized by his own guards and slain, and Heraclius was unanimously solicited to ascend the vacant throne. His reign was signalised by the conquest of Persia. Chosroes, on the murder of his benefactor Maurice, had declared war against his murderer. The incapacity of Phocas and the disaffection of his subjects left the empire helpless before the great king. From the long-disputed boundary of the Euphrates and the Tigris, the Persians extended their conquests over Asia Minor, Syria, Palestine, up to the Thracian Bosphorus, where they established a camp over against Constantinople. South-ward they penetrated into Africa, subdued Egypt and the province of Africa. The conqueror ruled his new subjects with an iron hand, drained their wealth by tributes, despoiled the temples of their treasures, and during a long reign was the most powerful, magnificent, and absolute monarch of the world. In the midst of this power and magnificence he received an epistle from an obscure Arabian named Mohammed, inviting him to abandon the ancestral worship of the Persian monarchy and to acknow-ledge him as the prophet of God. Chosroes tore up the letter with contempt. " Thus," said Mohammed, when the reception of his message was told him, " will God tear the kingdom and reject the supplications of Chosroes."

The Avars, returned from the ravage of Italy, pressed upon the empire from the north and west, while the Persian arms threatened it from the other side of the narrow strait. The empire was reduced to the walls of Constantinople with the remnant of Greece, Italy, and Africa, and some maritime cities from Tyre to Trebizond on the Asiatic coast. The capital was affected by famine and pestilence, resistance appeared hopeless. Heraclius was about to abandon the city and transfer the government to Carthage, when the clergy and people entreated him to remain.

He now adopted a great resolution. Borrowing the

accumulated treasures of the Church, he therewith hired the services of barbarians, mustered the native troops, and equipped a great army. Authorising the patriarch and senate even to surrender the city if it should become necessary, he himself, putting off the purple, and clad as a warrior and penitent, embarked with his troops and sailed round to the Issic Gulf, in the north-east angle of the Mediterranean, and, having there organised and drilled his raw levies, commenced a march which, in the course of three years, carried a victorious army through Cappadocia and the mountains of Armenia into Persia, up to the outskirts of the capital itself. Meanwhile the garrison of Constantinople had repulsed a siege of the Avars, and compelled them to retreat. A domestic conspiracy terminated the life of the Persian king. His son and successor gladly concluded a peace with the Romans, and Heraclius returned to his capital the deliverer of the empire. As he was returning he received at Emesa one of the ambassadors of Mohammed, who invited the princes and nations of the earth to the profession of Islam ; and, while the emperor was celebrating his triumph at Jerusalem, an obscure town on the confines of Syria was pillaged by the Saracens who cut in pieces the troops sent to its relief. The robbers were the apostles of Mohammed, who had just emerged from the desert ; and in the last eight years of his reign Heraclius lost to the Arabs the provinces he had rescued from the Persians.

By these conquests of the Arabs the Greek empire became permanently restricted to the city of Constantinople and the corner of Europe in which it is situated, but continued to exist for another 800 years, until the capture of the city by the Turks, A.D. 1453. The city was the greatest, most magnificent, wealthiest, and most civilised in the whole world. Though its territory was small, it was the emporium of a considerable commerce ; and the empire, though thus reduced, retained something of its ancient dignity, and continued to be the great storehouse of ancient learning and the ancient arts. The Crusaders introduced some of this ancient civilisation of the East into medieval Europe. The flight of the Greeks before the conquering Turk spread the revival of this ancient learning in modern Europe.

The Heraclian dynasty lasted till A.D. 711, and then, after three usurpers had succeeded one another, there followed the Isaurian dynasty, whose founder, LEO THE ISAURIAN (A.D. 726),* is known as the Iconoclast, The hatred of the Mohammedans for images, and their charge of idolatry against the veneration of images in the Christian Church, was perhaps one great cause of the rise of a party in the Church itself which was opposed to this veneration.

In his tenth year, Leo felt himself strong enough to issue a decree retaining the use of images, but removing them from the altar and sanctuary as objects of adoration ; this was followed by another edict proscribing the existence of religious pictures. Forthwith in all churches of the East the statues of Christ and the saints were destroyed, and pictures on the walls obliterated by a coat of plaster.

Under the next emperor, CONSTANTINE COPRONYMUS (A.D. 741), a council of the Eastern Church met, A.D. 754, in the suburbs of Constantinople, attended by 338 bishops assembled from the emperor's dominions only, and unanimously decreed that all visible symbols of Christ, except the Eucharist, were blasphemous or heretical, and ordered their destruction. The people resisted the execution of the decree, and insurrections ensued, which imperilled the emperor's throne. The Eastern monks also resisted, and suffered great indignities and cruelties in consequence. St. John Damascene, the last of the Greek fathers, wrote against it.

LEO IV. (A.D. 775) succeeded Copronymus ; and his widow IRENE, as empress-guardian of her infant son, A.D. 780, repealed the decree against images. Another council, convened at Nicæa (A.D. 787), at which the legates of Pope Hadrian and the Eastern patriarchs were present, decreed that bowing and an adoration of honour should be paid to sacred images, but that this external and inferior worship (*dulia*) should not be confounded with the true and supreme worship (*latria*) which belongs only to God. This council was also recognised by the Latin churches ; but the Franco-German Church in synod at Frankfort under Charlemagne, took a middle line, allowing statues and pictures as historical memorials and adornments, but

* Page 200.

forbidding any adoration of them.   During five succeeding reigns the strife continued, and at length image-worship was restored by a second empress-guardian, THEODORA, the widow of THEOPHILUS, who had himself been the most cruel of the Iconoclasts.

Gregory II. was Pope when the iconoclastic decrees of Leo the Isaurian were issued ; the emperor promised him the royal favour if he complied, and threatened him with degradation and exile if he disobeyed.   Gregory urged the Italians to resist.   Rome, Ravenna, Venice, and the cities of the exarchate, at once threw off their allegiance to the distant emperor, and prepared for self-government and defence.   Rome consummated its final separation from the Eastern empire when Leo III. placed the imperial crown on the head of Charlemagne, and hailed him emperor of the West.   Irene was then the empress of the East.

CHAPTER XXVII

THE MOHAMMEDAN CONQUESTS

ICONOCLASTIC controversy throughout the East had allowed the Mohammedan power to advance almost unchecked.

Mohammed was born at Mecca, in Arabia (A.D. 570), of the chief family of the tribe of Koreish, the most illustrious of Arabian tribes, princes of Mecca and hereditary guardians of the Kaaba, the idol temple and place of pilgrimage of the Arabs. Left an orphan in infancy, with a very small patrimony, at the age of twenty-five he entered the service of a rich widow, Khadijah, whom he shortly married, and lived as a well-to-do merchant till the age of forty. Then he entered upon his religious career, proclaiming the unity of God, and claiming to be the last and greatest of the prophets of God. First he converted his wife Khadijah, his faithful friend Abu- Bekr, his cousin Ali, and his slave Seid. The circle of believers very slowly increased ; three years produced fourteen disciples, seven years about 100. Warned of the resolve of the principal men of the city to kill him, he fled to Medina A.D. 622. This flight (*Hejira*) is the era from which Mohammedan chronology dates. The people of Medina embraced the faith he proposed, and accepted him as their chief. In 629 Mecca yielded to his arms ; the Arabian tribes then flocked to his victorious standard, and by A.D. 632 all Arabia acknowledged him as king and prophet. On his death in A.D. 632, leaving no son, Omar and Ali, his cousins—the latter married to Fatima, the prophet's favourite daughter—seemed to have equal claims to be his heirs. Omar decided the contest by proclaiming Abu- Bekr, the father of Ayesha, the prophet's favourite wife after Khadijah's death. After two years Abu- Bekr died, naming Omar as his successor (A.D. 634). Omar was assassinated, and Othman, who had been Mohammed's secretary, was elected caliph (A.D. 644). After a feeble reign of eleven years, he too fell the victim of a conspiracy, and at length Ali succeeded to the throne (A.D. 660). Moawiya (of the house of Ommiyah, the rival branch of the family of the Koreish, and in his early days the fiercest opponent of Mohammed), who governed as the caliph's lieutenant in Damascus, set up a rival claim to the caliphate. A truce was arranged ; the Syrian pretender gained the provinces of Persia, Yemen, and Egypt ; Ali was assassinated ; Moawiya induced the son of Ali to relinquish his pretensions ; and finally secured the succession to his own descendants.

The religion of conquest began at a period favourable to its success, in the most degenerate and disorderly period of the Persians, the Romans, and the Barbarians of Europe. It boldly attacked at once the Persian monarchy and the Roman empire ; and within a hundred years from the flight from Mecca, the power of the successors of Mohammed extended from India to the Atlantic Ocean, over Persia, Syria, Egypt, Africa, and Spain.

The conquest of Syria began in the year of the false prophet's death, and occupied two years. Damascus alone detained the invaders long before its walls. The imperial troops marched to raise the siege, but were overthrown with great slaughter in the battle of Aiznadin, A.D. 633 ; and Damascus, after a brave resistance, capitulated. Its fate was that of most cities which fell into the power of the Moslem. The majority of the inhabitants accepted the condition of tributary subjects of the caliph ; seven churches were left to them, the rest turned into mosques. Part of the people preferred exile, carrying with them their most precious possessions. After four days allowed for their departure, the fierce Khalid pursued them with a body of horse into the heart of the unconquered territory, massacred them, and returned with their spoils. Aleppo, Antioch, Cæsarea, city after city, submitted in despair.

The invaders marched next against Palestine. Jerusalem made a brave defence, and when it capitulated Sophronius, the patriarch, required that the caliph himself should come to ratify the treaty. Omar consented, and rode from Medina on a camel which carried not only the sovereign of Arabia, Persia, and Syria, but all his baggage also, namely, a bag of corn, another of dates, a wooden dish, and a leathern bottle of water. He pitched his camel-hair tent in the Moslem camp, and received the envoys of Jerusalem seated on the ground. When the capitulation was completed he entered Jerusalem fearlessly, walked about with the patriarch, visited the places of interest, knelt in worship on the steps of Constantine's Church of the Resurrection, and ordered a mosque (the mosque of Omar, still standing) to be built on the site of Solomon's Temple.

Persia was first attacked in the first year after Mohammed's death, and the Arabs marched victoriously to the Euphrates. In a four days' battle at Kadessia the strength of Persia was broken. A last stand was made among the hills south of Ecbatana, where the Arabs gained the decisive victory of Navahend. Ctesiphon, the capital, was taken, sacked, and deserted, and a new capital, Cufa (Baghdad), rose upon the Tigris. Yezdegerd, the grandson of Chosroes, fled beyond the frontier, and died (A.D. 651), the last of the long line of Persian kings.

After the conquest of Palestine, Amr invaded Egypt; after thirty days' siege he took Pelusium. This opened the road to Memphis. A seven months' siege and assault captured the fortifications of the bridge across the Nile, and the city surrendered. The native Christians were Monophysites, who, having been oppressed by the orthodox Greeks, were not averse to submitting to new masters, by which they secured revenge for the past and toleration for the future. Alexandria, twice rescued by the forces of the empire, which found easy access to it from the sea, was as often retaken by the Arabs, and finally remained in their hands, after a siege of fourteen months.

A successful campaign of fifteen months in North Africa, in A.D. 647–8, gave Tripoli and its spoils to the Arabs; but the conquest of North Africa was delayed for twenty years by the internal dissensions of the Saracens, and then proved more difficult than any conquest which had preceded it.

Akbar at length penetrated the country from coast to desert, from Egypt to the Atlantic Ocean, and conquered alike the Roman inhabitants of the cities and the savage heathen tribes of the interior.   The emperor sent the forces of Constantinople to succour the fairest province of the empire, and hired a powerful body of Goths from the King of Spain, and the port of Carthage afforded a gate through which the reinforcements entered.   The contest was protracted for twenty-four years (A.D. 665—689), before the Arabs established themselves permanently over the whole of this once flourishing province.   The Church of Cyprian and Augustine maintained a feeble existence for a time, but at length utterly perished.   North Africa is the only part of the world in which the Church, once planted and flourishing, has, except for a Coptic remnant and modern missionary efforts, ceased to exist.

Spain was the last of the great Mohammedan conquests. Ceuta, the single spot of Africa which had hitherto resisted the Saracen arms, was held by Count Julian on behalf of his sovereign, Roderick, king of the Goths.   The licentious king had dishonoured Count Julian's daughter, and the injured father in revenge not only surrendered Ceuta, but joined the infidels with his forces, and acted as their guide in an invasion of Spain.   The contending races met at Xeres ; the Goths were defeated and dispersed (A.D. 711).   Roderick fled, and was never more seen.   The conquerors pressed forward to Toledo, the capital, which capitulated, and thence marched without serious opposition to the Pyrenees. The mountaineers of the north alone successfully resisted the invaders, and a Gothic and Christian kingdom maintained itself amidst the Asturian mountains throughout the Moorish occupation of the Peninsula.   The numerous Jews, in the Peninsula aided the invaders and were rewarded by the toleration of their religion and the permanent favour of the conquerors, under whom they acquired wealth and dignities.   The Moorish monarchy of Spain developed the resources of the country, cultivated learning and the arts during the period of their greatest depression in the rest of Europe, and flourished for 700 years.

In A.D. 750, the descendants of the house of Abbas, by a successful revolution, replaced the dynasty of the Ommyades upon the throne of Damascus. In the proscription of the Ommyades, a royal youth named Abdalrahman alone escaped destruction and fled from the Euphrates to the Atlas mountains ; thence he was invited to Spain and acknowledged as sovereign ; thus the dynasty of the Ommyades established a separate caliphate in Spain in opposition to the Abbasides reigning at Baghdad. Similarly the descendants of Ali, in Africa and Egypt, established a separate caliphate, having Cairo for its capital, and the vast dominions of the followers of the prophet were thus permanently divided into three rival caliphates, which afterwards suffered further subdivisions.

In A.D. 721 the last wave of Mohammedan invasion dashed itself to pieces against the power of the Franks. Abdalrahman, Caliph of Cordova, conceived the idea of carrying the Mohammedan arms eastward, through France and Italy to Constantinople, and subduing all Europe to the faith of the false prophet. His first attempt, upon the part of southern France long subject to the Gothic monarchy, was successful. A second effort carried him as far as the banks of the Loire. There he was met by Charles Martel and the Franks, routed, and driven back again behind the permanent barrier of the Pyrenees.

The religion of Mohammed was styled *Islam*, a word which implies submission to the will of God. In its first conception it regarded Judaism and Christianity as true but imperfect religions, the Old and New Testaments as true but corrupted, and Mohammed as the last of the prophets, sent to complete the revelation of God's will. His revelations, collected and preserved in the Koran, were dictated by the prophet from time to time, as occasion required ; they contain many striking coincidences with the Old and New Testaments, but also many passages derived from Talmudical legends and Apocryphal Gospels. The tenets of Islam were few and simple : belief in the unity of God and the prophetic character of Mohammed, a belief in the providence of God and His predestination which amounted to fatalism and faith in the resurrection of men and a future state of rewards and punishments. Its positive duties were also few—prayer, almsgiving, fasting, and the pilgrimage to Mecca once in the life-time. Moral duties and brotherly love were strongly urged. Its principal doctrinal defect is the denial of the divinity and atonement of our Lord, and of the personality and eternity of the Holy Spirit. Its principal moral defect is the permission of polygamy and concubinage, and the facility of divorce. It retained the ancient Arabian rite of circumcision, administered at twelve years of age.

CHAPTER XXVIII

THE GROWTH OF THE PAPACY

THERE is no positive evidence whatever of the time when, or the persons by whom, the Church was founded in Rome. But the tradition that it was founded by the joint action, in some undefined way, of the two apostles St. Peter and St. Paul was so early and so widely current that the best historians accept it as a probable truth. The first names on the roll of Roman bishops—Linus, Anacletus, Clement—are not always given in the same order; and they and the succeeding names down to the end of the second century are little more than names,* whose authentic history is a blank.

The Church, we have seen, adopted in its organisation the political divisions of the empire; this gave a certain pre-eminence to the churches of Rome, Alexandria, and Antioch, the capitals respectively of the European, African, and Asiatic divisions of the empire, and among these the primacy of honour was given to Rome, the Church of the imperial city. But this " primacy " was entirely titular and honorary. It did not entitle the Bishop of Rome to interfere in any other patriarchate than his own. It only entitled him to exercise within his own patriarchate such authority as each of the other patriarchs might exercise in his. The metropolitan jurisdiction of Rome extended over the suburbicarian churches, *i.e.*, the churches in the civil diocese of Rome (viz., the seven provinces of middle and lower Italy, with the islands of Corsica, Sardinia, and Sicily). Milan was another metropolitan see in Italy whose political prestige, while Gratian, Theodosius, and

---

* Linus, Anacletus, Clement, Evaristus, Alexander I., Sixtus I., Telesphorus, Hyginus, Pius I., Anicetus, Soter, Eleutherius, Victor I.

Valentinian held their court there, and Ambrose was archbishop, overshadowed that of Rome. Aquileia was another
metropolitan see of Italy. Ravenna afterwards became a
fourth centre of ecclesiastical government. In the early
history we see each of these provincial churches entirely
independent of Rome, and acknowledging nothing but a
primacy of honour in the Roman see.

The idea of basing the primacy of Rome upon the alleged
primacy of St. Peter among the apostles was an after-
thought. It assumes—(1) That Christ gave to Peter the
supremacy over the other apostles. (2) That Peter's see
was at Rome. (3) That the supremacy which Christ gave
Peter was to descend to his successors in that see.

We reply—(1) That there is no evidence in Holy Scripture
or primitive antiquity that Peter possessed any such supremacy ; on the contrary, at the Council of Jerusalem James
presided, not Peter, and Paul claims to be not a whit behind
the chiefest apostles. The three texts which Romanists
adduce as Scripture evidence do not bear any such meaning.
" Thou art Peter, and on this rock I will build My Church "
(Matt. xvi. 18) ; the rock does not mean Peter, but Peter's
confession of the divinity of Jesus, and if it did the text
would not prove that Peter was to be universal bishop and
supreme ruler of the Church. Of all the fathers who have
commented on this text, Origen, Chrysostom, Hilary,
Augustine, Cyril, Theodoret, and those whose interpreta-
tions are collected in catenas, not one understands the rock
to mean Peter, or founds the primacy of the Roman see on
the text. " When thou art converted strengthen thy
brethren " (Luke xxii. 32), does not indicate that Peter was
the authoritative teacher of the whole Church. No single
writer until Pope Pelagius II. near the end of the sixth
century dreamt of such an interpretation ; * all explain it
simply as a prayer of Christ that Peter might not wholly
succumb and lose his faith entirely in his approaching trial.
Our Lord said to Peter, " I will give thee the keys of the
kingdom of heaven " (Matt. xvi. 19), but so He said also to
all the apostles ; so whatever in that phrase Christ gave to

* " Of twenty patristic citations made by Bellarmine in its favour,
all are from Popes, and eighteen of the twenty are from the False
Decretals " (Littledale).

St. Peter, He gave it to him in common with the rest. The ancient fathers always speak of the keys of the Church, not the keys of St. Peter.

We reply to (2) That there is no evidence that Peter ever acted as Bishop of Rome; on the contrary, Clement, the second on the list of Roman bishops, is said to have been appointed by St. Paul, and Linus and Anacletus, by St. Peter; but it does not appear that either St. Peter or St. Paul did more than thus exercise their apostolic authority in the appointment of others to the office of bishop there. The other great patriarchates, Alexandria and Antioch, similarly claimed to be sees of St. Peter; and Gregory the Great, on his accession to the see of Rome, assumes that all three share the representation of the see of St. Peter. He writes to the Bishop of Alexandria: " Your Holiness has said much to me in your letters concerning the chair of St. Peter, chief of the apostles, declaring that he continues to sit in it himself in the person of his successors . . . I have willingly received all that was said, because he who speaks to me concerning Peter's chair is the person who occupies it. . . . " Then quoting the charge given to St. Peter, " Feed My sheep," he goes on: " And thus though the apostles may be many, yet the see of the chief of the apostles (which belongs to me, though it is in three places), prevailed in authority solely by virtue of his [Peter's] chiefship. For it is he which exalted the see on which he condescended to take his rest and finish the present life [i.e., Rome]. It is he who adorned the see to which he sent the evangelist his disciple [i.e., Alexandria]. It is he who established the see in which he sat for seven years, though he was to leave it [i.e., Antioch]. Insomuch, then, as the see over which, by Divine authority three bishops now preside, is one man's [viz., Peter's] and one, whatever good I hear of you I lay to my own account, and if you hear any good of me lay this to the account of your own dessert," etc. The compliment is rather an elaborate one, but the meaning is plain. Gregory assumed the truth of the theory, current before his time, that these three great sees attained their dignity not because they were the three great capitals of the empire, but because they were three sees of St. Peter; and he assumes the other great patriarchs

to be his equals in order and dignity ; though no doubt he
would have been ready to assert on proper occasion that the
see of Rome was first in honour of the three.

(3) That a supremacy over the whole Church was to
descend from Peter to his successors in the see of Rome, is
pure assumption, without a tittle of evidence in its favour
from Scripture or primitive antiquity.   In very early times
the churches founded by the apostles themselves were
looked up to with considerable and natural respect, as
models of apostolic faith and discipline.   Rome being the
only apostolic see in the Western Church, the reverence
paid in the East to Alexandria, Antioch, Ephesus, and other
churches, was in the West monopolised by Rome.   Appeals
on disputed points came naturally to be referred to these
churches for solution ; thus appeals from all the West were
made to Rome.   As Rome stretched her pretensions she
asserted herself to be *the* apostolic see, and claimed to be a
court of final appeal for the whole Church.   Fathers had
made reference to this respect for apostolic sees, and
councils had recognised appeals to them.   Rome, in later
days, endeavoured to fortify her pretensions by the falsifica-
tion of these evidences, making them speak of the apostolic
see instead of the apostolic sees.   Indeed the whole edifice
of the Papal supremacy is, in the language of one of her own
children [Père Gratry], " honeycombed and gangrened with
falsehood."   False   documents   were   forged,   genuine
evidences falsified, so that in reading Roman books nothing
can be accepted without verification.

That the great patriarchates were originally independent
of one another we have the evidence of a canon of the Council
of Nicæa.   Referring to a question of ecclesiastical sub-
ordination which the Meletian controversy had raised in
Egypt, it says : " Let the ancient custom, which has
prevailed in Egypt, Libya, and Pentapolis—that the Bishop
of Alexandria should have authority over all these places—
be still maintained, since this is the custom also with the
Roman bishop.   In like manner at Antioch and in the other
provinces the churches shall retain their ancient prerogatives "—*i.e.*, Rome, Alexandria, Antioch, and the other
patriarchs had each the same authority over their respective
provinces.   The origin of the precedence of Rome is

distinctly stated on the highest possible authority, viz., that
of two general councils, Constantinople and Chalcedon, to
have been political and not religious ; it was because Rome
was the capital of the empire, not because Rome was the see
of Peter. When the little town of Byzantium was made by
Constantine the new capital of the empire, the Church of
this " new Rome," which had been subordinate to Heraclia,
the capital of Thrace, was raised by the second general
council to the honorary dignity of the patriarchate, and
precedence was assigned it above Alexandria and Antioch
and next after Rome, " forasmuch as it is new Rome." The
fourth General Council of Chalcedon said that " the fathers
rightly conceded that rank to the episcopate of ancient
Rome because Rome was the mistress city." Pope Leo the
Great, indeed, was very angry with this assertion, and
refused to recognise the canon ; but the canon remained
unaltered as one of the decrees of a general council universally received by the Church.

Not unnaturally, when the Western empire was destroyed,
Rome plundered and ruined by Alaric and Attila, and
Constantinople had become the sole seat of the Roman
empire, some patriarchs of Constantinople seem to have
contemplated the assertion of the consequent transfer of
the primacy to the see of new Rome. The assumption by
the Patriarch John (585–595) of the title of œcumenical
bishop seems to have been suspected of being a step in this
direction ; a supposition which will explain the energy and
temper with which Gregory the Great protested against it.
His arguments against the ambitious designs which he
attributed to John supply an insuperable argument against
the usurpations of his successors in the see of Rome. He
wrote to the patriarch himself against it, to the other
Eastern patriarchs of Alexandria and Antioch, and to the
Emperor Maurice. To the patriarchs he said that to allow
the title to the Patriarch of Constantinople would derogate
from their own rights and be an injury to the whole order.
" Œcumenical bishop," he argued, must mean sole bishop ;
if, therefore, the œcumenical bishop should err, the whole
Church would fail ; and for a patriarch of Constantinople to
assume the proud and superstitious name, which was an
invention of the first apostate, was alarming, since among

the occupants of that see there had been not only heretics, but heresiarchs. The Bishop of Alexandria replied that he had ceased to use the title in addressing John, as Gregory had commanded (*sicut jussistis*), and in his reply addressed Gregory himself as " universal Pope " ; whereupon Gregory wrote, " I beg that you would not speak of ' commanding ' since I know who I am and who you are. In dignity you are my brother, in character my father. . . . I pray your most sweet Holiness to address me no more with the proud appellation of ' universal Pope,' since that which is given to another beyond what reason requires is subtracted from yourself. If you style me universal Pope, you deny that you are at all that which you own me to be universally. Away with words which puff up vanity and wound charity." To John he writes : " What will you say to Christ (Who is, you know, the Head of the universal Church) in the examination of the last judgment ? You who endeavour to subject to yourself, under the name ' universal,' all its members ? . . . Surely Peter, the first of the apostles, is a member of the holy universal Church. Paul, Andrew, John, what else are they but the heads of particular communities ? Yet all are members under one Head ; and to comprehend all in one brief expression, the saints before the law, the saints under the law, the saints under grace—all these, making up the body of the Lord, are dispersed among the members of the Church, and no one ever yet wished to be called ' universal.' Let then your Holiness acknowledge how great is your pride who seek to be called by that name by which no one has presumed to be called who was really holy."

The superior position of the Roman see grew out of natural causes. In the first two centuries we hear no claim to superiority over other churches. The first evidence of any application from a foreign Church to Rome for the settlement of any question is the synodical letter of Siricius in answer to Hunerius, Bishop of Tarragona, A.D. 385. The first attempts of the popes to exercise authority over foreign churches had been in the case of the Easter controversy, the questions of heretical baptism, and of the treatment of the lapsed. Pope Victor's attempt, at the end of the second century, to enforce the Roman time of celebrating Easter in the churches of Asia Minor was an entire failure. He excommunicated those churches, but the other branches of the Church refused to concur with his sentence; the Asiatic churches disregarded it, Irenæus and other leading men reproved Victor sharply, and, lastly, his excommunication was withdrawn, and the Asiatic churches retained their local custom till the Council of Nicæa (325 A.D.) decreed a uniformity of usage.

The question of heretical baptism arose in the middle of the third century in the African Church, which in a synod denied the validity of baptism by heretics, on the ground that since they themselves were outside the pale of the Church their baptism could not admit any into it. This decision was adopted by an Asiatic synod. Stephen of Rome held the validity of baptism by men who, though heretical, were Christian, and pronounced excommunication against his opponents. He only drew down sharp censures on himself. St. Cyprian, Bishop of Carthage, and St. Firmilian, Bishop of Cæsarea, denied that he had any right to dictate to other bishops and churches, declaring " that in respect of the internal government and particular custom of each diocese (=province) there was no one in the Church of God who could be bishop of bishops, or who could compel them by threats to forsake what they had found established by their predecessors." Again St. Cyprian says : " In which matter we do violence and give the law to no one, inasmuch as every bishop has the free choice of his own will in the administration of the Church, as he will give an account of his acts to the Lord." * The other Eastern churches quietly retained their practice of rebaptizing, unmoved by the opinions or fulminations of the Roman bishop.

In the Arian disputes which disturbed the Church for above half a century, and were discussed in more than fifty synods, the Roman see took no steps to settle the dispute by its own authority; and when at length Julius and Liberius (337–366) did take part in the controversy, they both fell into error. Julius declared, with his synod, the orthodoxy of Marcellus of Ancyra, who was an avowed Sabellian. Liberius purchased his return from exile by condemning Athanasius and signing an Arian creed. This

* St. Cyprian, Ep. lxxiii.

acknowledged apostacy of Liberius sufficed through all the Middle Ages for a proof that popes could fall into heresy like other people.

In the four general councils, we do not see Rome playing any leading part. In the first and most venerable, of Nicæa, Rome was represented by two presbyters on account of the great age of the bishop, but they took no prominent part in the proceedings. In the second council, of Constantinople, the Roman see was not represented at all. The decrees of the council were communicated to Rome, in common with all other churches, and were received by her as by them. In the third council, of Ephesus, the council did not wait for the arrival of the Pope's representatives, who were behind their time, but deliberated and made their decree, and the papal envoys subscribed it at a subsequent sitting. In the fourth council the Pope's envoys took part in the previous " Council of Robbers," and the Pope had to disavow their assent to its proceedings. At the Council of Chalcedon Leo the Great, one of the early assertors of the claims of the see, was Pope ; and for the first time a Pope took such steps unsuccessfully, as we should have expected him to have taken with success at the previous councils had the papal claims then been acknowledged. First he tried to get the council held in Italy, but the emperor declined ; then he claimed that his envoys should preside in his name, and by way of compromise they were allowed to sit with Anatolius, the Bishop of Constantinople, as joint presidents, the emperor's commissioners being the real regulators of the proceedings.

The history of the fifth council is a still less happy one for the see. Pope Vigilius thrice contradicted himself on the subject under discussion (" The Three Chapters "), excommunicating first one side and then the other, and a long schism in the West was the consequence. The heresy of Pope Honorius was one of the causes which necessitated the calling of the sixth general council (A.D. 649). He had pronounced in favour of the Monothelite heresy and written two letters to the patriarchs of the Eastern Church in its defence, which for half a century were the strongest support of the erroneous opinions. The council, presided over by papal legates, pronounced the Monothelite doctrines heretical, and solemnly anathematised Honorius by name as a heretic. In the acts of the council are the following passages : " We have caused to be read the letter of Honorius to Sergius, and have found it altogether alien from the apostolic teaching, the definitions of councils, the doctrine of the eminent holy fathers, and that contrariwise it follows the false teachings of the heretics. We altogether reject them, and abhor them as soul-destroying. . . . And those profane and soul-destroying writings we have caused to be burnt before us for their complete annihilation." The succeeding councils (the seventh and eighth), presided over by popes, and two Roman synods, repeated this condemnation and anathema of Honorius, and the Roman breviary down to its " reformation " in the sixteenth century, on the saint day of Leo II., recited in his honour that he had presided at the sixth council which had anathematised Honorius, while in the oath taken by the popes on their accession, which may be seen in the old " Liber Diurnus," every pope declared Honorius a heretic and anathema.

A century later Pope Adrian approved the second Nicene Council in favour of the adoration of images, but the great council of Frankish and German bishops refused to receive it ; and in 824 the bishops assembled in synod at Paris spoke without ceremony of the " absurdities " of Pope Adrian, who, they said, had commanded an heretical worship of images.

Political circumstances favoured the growth of the influence and power of the bishops of Rome. The absence of the emperors and court from Rome during the time that Christianity was becoming the religion of the mass of the people, and the adherence of the nobles of Rome to the ancient heathenism, left the bishop a conspicuous and influential person ; the ruin of the great ancient families by Alaric and Attila left him beyond question the greatest personage in Rome, and one of the greatest in Italy.

But moral circumstances still more efficiently commended the claims of Rome to general reverence and influence. While other parts were distracted for centuries by successive heresies, the Western Church, saved by its unspeculative temper, had, on the whole, consistently held to the ancient faith, receiving the new definitions as they were definitively arrived at, without suffering from the contests by which the victories of the faith were won. This gave the Western Church, and the Roman bishop as its representative and mouthpiece to the rest of Christendom, a character for orthodoxy. Again, while other parts of the Church were distracted by disputes for precedence—Constantinople seeking to establish a primacy in the Eastern empire, and Alexandria opposing it—Rome had no rival in the Western Church, and grew continually more pre-eminent. These causes rightly gave Rome great prestige in the eyes of the whole Church; her advice was sought, her arbitration requested, her opinion on controverted questions solicited by both disputants. She welcomed all such references to her authority, and gave to her replies the tone of a judge giving sentence or a sovereign issuing decrees.

Early in the sixth century a Roman abbot, Dionysius Exiguus, published a work, in which he had collected the canons of the general and of the more important provincial councils, and to these he added a collection from the decisions (decretals) of the Roman bishops in reply to questions. This work soon obtained authority as a text-book of ecclesiastical law and the fact that he had given so prominent a place to the papal decrees had an important influence in shaping the papal monarchy.

Between the conquest of Italy by the Goths and the defeat of the Lombards by Pepin, the progress of papal power was arrested and the bishops of Rome had a troublous time. Theodoric, while paying every respect to the Catholic clergy, exercised a control over the election and administration of the bishops of Rome, to which under the later emperors they had not been accustomed. That king sent Pope John and five other bishops and four senators on an embassy to Constantinople (A.D. 525) to demand the same toleration for Arians which he allowed to Catholics. John was received with unbounded reverence at Constantinople, but on his return to Italy the king cast him into prison, where he soon died. Again, in A.D. 536, King Theodahat sent Pope Agapetus to the eastern capital to try to avert a threatened attack of Justinian. We have already related * how Agapetus died at Constantinople, and Justinian agreed

* Page 172.

with his archdeacon, Vigilius, who had accompanied him, to support his candidacy for the papacy on Vigilius undertaking, when Pope, to condemn the Council of Chalcedon.

After many variations of fortune, the Italian kingdom of the Goths was at length annihilated by the arms of Belisarius and Narses, and disappears from the page of history.

In 537 A.D. under Belisarius, then master of Rome, Vigilius at length became Pope,* but, hesitating to fulfil his secret engagements with the emperor, was summoned to Constantinople. There he was detained upwards of seven years, trying in vain to steer a safe course through the religious dissensions which agitated the Eastern Church. He suffered from both sides—imprisonment from the emperor, and excommunication from the Catholics—came out of the matter with a ruined reputation, and died on his way back to Rome, having by his conduct greatly lowered the dignity and reputation of his see. These were further weakened by the subsequent schism of Aquileia and the other Italian provinces, which lasted nearly a century and a half. Justinian also established the right of the crown to a confirmation of the papal election, and greatly controlled the action of the popes. He even meditated the elevation of Constantinople to the primacy over the whole Church.

In the reign of Justin II. the non-Lombard parts of Italy were governed by the exarch, deputed by the Greek emperor, and seated at Ravenna.† Rome was nominally subject to this exarch, but appears in reality to have governed itself. An imperial prefect administered criminal justice ; the people took an oath of allegiance to the emperor, and upon any irregular election of the bishop, a circumstance by no means unusual, the emperors held themselves entitled to interfere. The popes seem to have possessed some measure of temporal authority in the city. But the spirit and institutions of the Romans were republican, and the city appears to have possessed a municipal government which conducted its internal affairs.

On Emperor Leo the Isaurian issuing his decrees against images, the Italians refused to concur, and threw off allegiance to the emperor. The Lombards took advantage of this and seized the exarchate of Ravenna. Rome was

* Page 172.　　　　　† Page 179.

next assailed, and the Lombard kingdom might have been completed by its conquest and permanently established in Italy, but the Pope appealed to France for aid. He had a weighty claim on the gratitude of the King of France. The race of Clovis had gradually sunk into mere puppet kings, while the power of the state was wielded by an officer called the Mayor of the Palace. This office became elective, and at last hereditary. Pepin of Heristal transmitted his authority to his son, Charles Martel, the hero who met the Saracens, and won the great victory (A.D. 732) which saved Europe from subjugation to the followers of Mohammed. Pepin succeeded his father Charles Martel; and in A.D. 752, in the name and with the consent of the nation of the Franks, a solemn reference was made to the Pope, Zacharias, as to whether the royal name and dignity ought not to pass from the degenerate Merovingian race to that race which actually for three generations had ruled the nation by its wisdom and defended it by its valour. Zacharias judged that he who possessed the power should also bear the title of king. The unfortunate Merovingian prince was dismissed into a convent and Pepin raised to the throne, the founder of a new and more illustrious dynasty.

The Pope appealed to Pepin for aid against the Lombards. Stephen II., who had succeeded Zacharias, went beyond the Alps, and threw himself at the king's feet, humbly imploring his help. Pepin received him with extraordinary respect and returned with the Pope to Italy, at the head of an army of Franks, who drove the Lombards out of their recent acquisitions and bestowed them upon the Bishop of Rome. Some Byzantine envoys present at the conclusion of the treaty urged Pepin to restore the exarchate to the emperor, but Pepin replied that he had fought for St. Peter and not for the emperor and could not take away from the apostle what he had given him. This " donation " was the beginning of the temporal power of the popes, though for many years to come this temporal dominion was held as a fief of the Frankish crown.

CHAPTER XXIX

THE EMPIRE OF CHARLEMAGNE

THE genius of Charlemagne, son of Pepin, united under one head the various nations of central Europe which had risen out of the ruins of the Western empire; brought for the first time under the influence of civilisation and religion the barbarous tribes of Saxony, Bohemia, and Hungary; and during a vigorous and enlightened reign of nearly half a century fostered the growth of civilisation and religion over this vast extent of territory. His empire broke in pieces again after his death; but it left to modern days the political system of the European family of nations, and their civil and social institutions.

Inheriting half the kingdom of Pepin, he seized the other half on the death of his brother Carloman (A.D. 772), and speedily subdued the kingdom of the Lombards. Next he wrested from the Saracens Spain from the Pyrenees to the Ebro. He prevented fresh irruptions of barbarous tribes upon the settled parts of Europe by thirty years of war against the Saxons. His successes against the Sclavonians of Bohemia and the Huns of Pannonia were equally important, and cost far less. Thus his conquests embraced all Europe between the Elbe and the Ebro, the English Channel and the Mediterranean Sea. Two-thirds of the ancient Western Roman empire were subject to him, and his conquests in the East made the new Western Empire territorially not less extensive than the old.

He exercised a real sovereignty over the papal states, and visited Rome on several occasions. At the Christmas festival, A.D. 800, while Charlemagne was kneeling before the altar of the Lateran Church, the Pope, Leo III., placed a crown upon his head, and the people saluted him with the grand old title of Augustus ; while the Pope set the example of doing homage to him as the new Emperor of the West.

But his fame does not rest merely on conquest. His love of learning was, perhaps, his strongest characteristic. In mature age he learned to read and write, to speak Latin with ease and accuracy, and to read Greek. He drew learned men to his court from Italy and England, the only two countries of Europe which could then supply them. The greatest of these was our countryman Alcuin, who had been educated in the cathedral school of York, under Archbishop Egbert, the brother of the Northumbrian king. Charlemagne established two great schools of learning— one at Metz ; the other, called the Palatine school, of which Alcuin was master, accompanied the movements of the court ; in it were educated the members of the royal family and the noble youths of the household ; the emperor himself was one of its scholars. He urged his nobles to cultivate letters, required it of his clergy, and ordered that the clergy should open schools everywhere for all classes of people. He took measures for the organisation of the Church throughout his dominions, gave liberal endowments to the clergy, and took a deep interest in religious questions. Among the conquered Saxons he founded eight bishoprics, whose sees were the first schools, and grew into the first cities of that savage land. Under his direction the ancient Roman law and the legal customs of the Franks were digested into a system of law, known as the Capitularies of Charlemagne. He gave liberal encouragement to commerce, agriculture, architecture, and the arts.

Two facts synchronise the histories of three great powers at this period. The Emperor Charlemagne carried on a friendly correspondence with Irene, Empress of the East, and there seems to have been some idea of a reconstruction of the ancient empire by a marriage between them. He also exchanged compliments and presents with the famous Caliph Haroun al Raschid.

In his reign the second council of Nicæa (A.D. 787), established a reconciliation between Rome and Constantinople on the question of images. Charlemagne sent a copy of the acts of the council to Alcuin, then in England, and it is said the English bishops joined in requesting

Alcuin to write against the council. He wrote a letter to Charlemagne, and out of this probably grew a treatise, in four books, put forth in the emperor's own name, and known as the Caroline Books. In them the Frankish Church puts forth its objections to that reverence to images which the council had enjoined. It declares their only proper use to be for ornament or historial memorial, and that the rule of the Catholic Church was that images be allowed, but not worshipped.

A council of Frank bishops held at Frankfort considered the question of " Adoptionism," * which had been raised in Spain. This we note as an illustration of the fact, that the Church under the new Emperor of the West held councils, important from the large area of the Church represented at them, and from the learning of some of their members, to deal with the doctrinal questions of the day.

Charlemagne died in 814, and the European world relapsed into confusion and barbarism for seventy years. His son, Louis the Pious, or the Debonair, subdivided the empire into four, intending to reproduce something like the constitution of Diocletian. But the divisions made the empire a prey to its foreign enemies. The Norman pirates ravaged the northern coasts of Europe throughout the ninth century, until in A.D. 912, the French king, Charles the Simple, ceded the province of Neustria to Rollo, the founder of the dukedom of Normandy. The Saracens made themselves masters of Sicily and Sardinia, and in the latter part of the ninth century harassed the southern coasts of Europe ; at the end of the ninth century the Hungarians, pouring from the east upon Germany, Italy, and southern France, recalled the memory of Attila by their devastations.

Charles the Fat was deposed by a diet (A.D. 888), and the governors, bishops, and nobles usurped as sovereigns the fragments of the empire which they held as fiefs. The term of seventy-four years from the abdication of Charles the Fat may be considered a vacancy of the empire till the establishment (A.D. 962) of Otho I. He recovered Germany, part of France, and Italy, and extended civilisation

---

* The theory that " Jesus Christ as to His human nature was the Son of God only by adoption or by name."—D. C. B.

and Christianity by his conquests among the Scandinavian tribes between the Elbe and the Oder, and in the peninsula of Sleswick and Denmark.   In Italy, in 961, he was solemnly crowned emperor, after the title and its prerogatives had been suspended for nearly forty years.   From that time the imperial dignity was associated with Germany ;   the prince elected in the German Diet acquired with the imperial title the subject kingdoms of Italy and Rome ;   but he might not legally assume the titles of emperor and Augustus till he had received the crown from the hands of the Roman pontiff.   He was assumed to succeed to all the rights of the Carlovingian empire.

During the whole period from the disruption of the Roman empire the Church was gaining power.   The national councils of the new nations gave a constitutional position to the bishops as great landowners, while the superior civilisation of the bishops gave them a legitimate leading influence in those councils and in the private counsels of the king.   Religious veneration for the hierarchy greatly increased the influence the clergy derived from their learning and their wealth.   Thus the power of the clergy in the nations of Europe during the ninth and tenth centuries was very great.

The power of the papacy also increased greatly.   Rome was still to the rude nations of the north and west the shadow of a great name, and the Bishop of Rome was beyond question the head of the Western Church.   The disputes of sovereigns, in which the Popes were sometimes invited to arbitrate, and in which they sometimes interfered on the invitation of one side only, gradually gave the opportunity of putting forth the pretension to crown and uncrown kings, which afterwards found its greatest exponents in Gregory VII. and Innocent III.

Dionysius * had done a good deal through three centuries to favour the pretensions of the Roman see by having published the doctrinal letters of Roman bishops, together with the canons of councils, as authorities on ecclesiastical law.   But about the middle of the ninth century a new collection of canons and decretals was issued (by an anonymous writer) under the venerated name of St. Isidore of

* Page 199.

Seville, which, besides genuine canons of councils and letters of popes, contained new canons of hitherto unknown councils, above a hundred new letters of popes from the time of the apostles downwards, and a number of other documents. These documents greatly magnify the prerogatives of bishops, but especially exalt the authority of the Pope. They represent him as having from the earliest times acted as supreme head, lawgiver, and judge of the Church. Many of these forgeries are clumsy enough, but in an uncritical age they passed without detection, and were accepted as defining the principles of primitive ecclesiastical law and usage. When the forged decretals came to general knowledge, Nicholas I. was pope (858–867) and exceeded all his predecessors in the audacity of his designs, in which he was favoured by the confusion which ensued on the break-up of the empire of Charlemagne. Grasping at the new weapon, he assured the Frankish bishops that all these documents had long been preserved in the Roman archives, and he proceeded to act upon the principles thus laid down. For above two hundred years the Roman see was not in a condition to enforce new and extended claims, and nearly three centuries passed before the seeds thus sown produced their full harvest.

CHAPTER XXX

THE DARK AGES OF THE PAPACY

URING the ninth and tenth centuries, with the growth of population, extension of cultivation, and progress of wealth, the revenues of the great European sees had become very great, and, combined with their feudal rights, had made their occupants more or less independent princes. These great positions were often conferred by sovereigns upon their own relations, or bestowed as rewards of service or gifts of favour, or obtained by intrigues and bribes. The lesser benefices were similarly bestowed, and simony was rife throughout the Church. The tendency of the feudal system was to make all offices and tenures hereditary, and this affected the temporalities of ecclesiastical benefices. A few examples will illustrate these statements. In 990 a count of Toulouse sold the see of Cahors. About the same time a viscount of Beziers bequeathed the bishopric of that city and the bishopric of Agde as portions to his daughters. In 925 Herbert, Count of Vermandois, on the death of the archbishop of Rheims not without suspicion of poison, compelled the clergy and people to elect his own son Hugh, a child not yet five years old, and seized upon the temporalities. The election was confirmed by King Rodolph and Pope John X., and the boy prelate was committed to Guy, Bishop of Auxerre, for education, while a coadjutor-bishop administered the see. Seven years later (A.D. 932) Rheims fell into the power of another political party, by whom the claims of Hugh were disregarded, a monk named Artald was nominated archbishop, and invested with the pall by Pope John XI. The contest for the see continued for thirty years. It was discussed at provincial councils; and whereas Hugh had been acknowledged by one pope, and Artald by his successor, the rescript of a third pope, Agapetus II., was exhibited at one of these councils, peremptorily ordering the restoration of Hugh, while Artald exhibited a letter of the same pope of exactly opposite tenor. The corrupt disposal of ecclesiastical benefices, the consequent intrusion of unfit men into the higher offices of the Church, and the scandal of their worldly lives are exhibited also in the history of the popes during this period, and unpleasant as are the revelations they are necessary for a true history of the papacy.

The see of Rome, as the greatest ecclesiastical prize, was throughout the whole period contested by rival factions of Italian nobles.

Formosus, raised to the papacy in 891, held it for five years, and was a man of learning and probity. Boniface VI., who in youth had been of so scandalous life that he had been degraded from the priesthood, next attained the papal dignity by violence, and held it fifteen days, when he was in turn driven out by Stephen VI., a man of equally worthless character. Stephen having suffered in early youth some offence from Formosus, now avenged himself by having the dead pope taken out of his tomb, arrayed in his pontifical robes, and formally tried for the offence of having been uncanonically translated from the see of Pontus to that of Rome. He was, of course, found guilty and degraded; the robes stripped off, the three fingers of his right hand, which had been used in giving benediction, cut off, and the body cast into the Tiber. On the death of Stephen (A.D. 897) the next pope, John IX., reversed the sentence, and restored Formosus to his papal dignity. A rapid succession of popes then took place. The marquises of Tuscany and counts of Tusculum were the most powerful senators, and heads of rival factions, and promoted their creatures to the see as one or other gained the upper hand. Elections, followed within a few months, weeks, or days by deaths, excited suspicion as to their cause; in some cases violence or poison appeared without disguise. At length Adalbert, Marquis of Tuscany, in league with a noble and wealthy Roman widow named Theodora, obtained a preponderance of power. Theodora had two daughters—Theodora and Marozia—both, like herself, beautiful, and all three seem to have assumed the licence of the noblemen of their time

in the unrestrained indulgence of their vices. For upwards
of half a century these three women filled the Roman see
with their lovers, their illegitimate children and grand-
children. Sergius III., pope from 904 to 911, is described as
a monster of rapacity, cruelty, and lust. He lived in open
concubinage with Marozia. The next pope, Anastasius III.,
died in A.D. 913, and was succeeded by John X. Luitprand,
the contemporary historian, tells the story of his elevation :
" In those days Peter, Archbishop of Ravenna, used frequently to send to Rome a deacon of his church named
John, to pay his obeisance to his Holiness. As the deacon
was a very comely and personable man, Theodora, falling
passionately in love with him, engaged him in a criminal
intrigue. While they lived thus together the Bishop of
Bologna died, and John had interest enough to get himself
elected in his room ; but the Archbishop of Ravenna dying
before he was consecrated, Theodora persuaded him to
exchange the see of Bologna for that of Ravenna, and he
was accordingly, at her request, ordained archbishop by
Pope Lando. Lando himself died soon afterwards, and
Theodora exerted all her interest, as she could not live at a
distance of 200 miles from her lover, and got him preferred
to the pontifical chair. John proved himself a vigorous
pope, and probably not subservient to the party which had
elevated him. Accordingly some adherents of Guy, Duke
of Tuscany, the second husband of Marozia, surprised the
pope in the castle of St. Angelo, murdered his brother before
his eyes, and put the pope himself to death either by starving
or by suffocation."

The illegitimate son of Pope Sergius and Marozia was
then elevated to the papal seat under the title of John XI.,
but was restricted to the performance of his ecclesiastical
functions. The government was administered by Marozia
and Hugh the Great, King of Arles, Marozia's third
husband, and afterwards by her son Alberic, who ruled
tyrannically in Rome for two-and-twenty years, while the
papal chair was filled with a succession of his creatures,
whom he held in entire subjection. On the death of
Agapetus II., in 955, Octavian, the son of Alberic, a youth
of eighteen, who two years before had succeeded to his
father's secular power, was advised to strengthen his position

P

by assuming the papacy also. He regarded his episcopal functions as a mere adjunct to his character of prince and soldier, and continued to wear his former dress and live his former life ; and no young prince can have led a more dissolute life than Pope John XII. The Emperor Otho, a religious man, scandalised, with all Europe, at the life of the pope, came to Rome ; but the pope withdrew from the city. The emperor wrote a letter, stating the charges against him—sacrilege, perjury, incest, murder—and calling upon him to answer them. The young prince thereupon assumed the character of pope in the following reply : " John, servant of the servants of God, to all bishops. We hear that you want to make another pope. If that is your design, I excommunicate you all in the name of the Almighty, that you may not have it in your power to ordain any other, or even to celebrate mass." A council decreed his deposition, and Leo, chief secretary of the see, a man of good character, was elected in his room by the clergy and people, and the Romans bound themselves by an oath never to choose a pope without the emperor's consent. After the emperor's departure, however, John regained possession of the city, another council deposed Leo, and the Tuscan party revenged themselves by the mutilation of their enemies. Shortly afterwards John was killed in the act of adultery. The people, notwithstanding their oath, and notwithstanding the previous consecration of Leo VIII., proceeded to the election of a new pope in Benedict. But the emperor reappeared before the city and starved it into surrender. At a council Benedict formally surrendered his dignity to Leo and went into exile.

We may pass over the subsequent struggle between the Romans and the emperors, and the history of the succeeding popes, most of whom were respectable, and some of them men of learning and ability, till we come to the year 1033. In that year the Tuscan party, on the death of Pope John XIX., appointed to the popedom a boy of ten or twelve years of age, cousin of the preceding pope, under the title of Benedict IX. This youth soon appeared resolved to emulate the worst of his predecessors. In 1044 the Romans (for the second time) drove the debauched and tyrannical pope out of Rome, and elected John, Bishop of Sabina, in his place, under the name of Sylvester III. Within three months, however, John succeeded in regaining his position in Rome, and then, to rid himself of the restraints and troubles of the papacy, sold his interest to a priest called John Gratian, who had a great and deserved reputation for austerity of life. But after a short time Benedict resumed his claim to the see ; so that there were three popes at once, each holding possession of one of the three principal churches of Rome : Benedict, supported by the Tuscan party, Sylvester by a rival faction of nobles, Gratian, who had taken the name of Gregory VI., by the people. Peter, the Archdeacon of Rome, went to Germany to request the interposition of the emperor, Henry III. At Piacenza Gregory met the emperor, and presided at a council. Benedict, having retired to a monastery, was not mentioned in the proceedings of the council ; Sylvester was declared to be an intruder and deposed and condemned to be shut up in a monastery. Then Gregory was invited to state the circumstances of his own elevation. He explained that he had expended funds entrusted to him for pious purposes in what he considered the pious purpose of rescuing the Roman see from its calamities and disgrace. He was made to see that in the eyes of the council the transaction was simoniacal, and he resigned, or, according to other accounts, was deposed by the council. The emperor proceeded to fill the vacant papacy with a pope of his own selection in Clement II. (A.D. 1046).

CHAPTER XXXI

THE CONVERSION OF THE NORTHERN NATIONS

WE now relate the history of the conversion, in the sixth and following centuries, of the nations outside the area of the empire.

When Honorius withdrew the Roman legions and imperial administration from the province of Britain, and left it disorganised and defenceless, the barbarous piratical tribes from the opposite coasts of the North Sea—Jutes, Angles, Saxons—fell upon the land like wolves on a sick deer. The conquest extended over 100 years. By the end of that time the whole of England, except its western corners, Cornwall and Wales, had been conquered by the heathen barbarians. The civilisation and the Church of the Roman province had been almost extinguished except in those strongholds, and Saxon England added to that vast extent of Northern Europe—the forests of Germany, the Scandinavian peninsula, and the plains of Russia—in which the Gospel was unknown.

In A.D. 431 the attention of Pope Celestine was directed to Ireland, and he dispatched thither Palladius, whom he had previously consecrated as a bishop; but whether to found a church or to preside over churches already existing is not certain. He landed with twelve companions, baptized a few converts, and erected three wooden churches; but his work did not prosper, and he retired to Scotland, intending to return to Rome, but was arrested by the hand of death.

Within a year he was followed by the missionary whose successful labours have given him the title of the Apostle of Ireland. The original name of St. Patrick was Succath. He was born of Christian parents, his father, Calpurnius, and his grandfather, Potitus, being in holy orders. One

authority says that his mother was a sister of St. Martin of
Tours. The place of his birth is disputed. He himself
calls it *Bonaven Taberniæ ;* Lanigan, Döllinger, and others,
identify this with Boulogne, but it was certainly in Britain
and Dr. Newport White favours the neighbourhood of
Dumbarton, while Bury (*Life of St. Patrick*, 1905) says
his father was a Briton, and suggests that his birthplace
was " in S.W. Britain, perhaps in the regions of the Lower
Severn." Both, alike, reject Daventry as impossible.
The date of his birth was, probably, A.D. 389. He was
trained in the monasteries of Southern Gaul. Amidst the
conflicting legends it seems certain that he spent some time
in the monastery of St. Martin at Tours, under the strict
discipline of that famous seminary ; afterwards studied
with St. Germanus at Auxerre, and thence visited " one of
the islands of the Tuscan Sea," probably Lerins, then a
famous school of learning, in which St. Hilary of Arles and
St. Lupus of Troyes had been educated. It had long been
his desire to preach in Ireland, whither in youth he had
been carried off in a piratical incursion, and had spent some
years as a slave. On the abandonment of his mission by
Palladius, Patrick was consecrated—there is reason to
believe in Gaul—and sailed from Gaul with some fellow-
labourers, A.D. 432.

After seven years his converts had so largely increased
that he sent two of his original companions either to Gaul
or Britain to receive consecration. One special feature in
his work was the founding of monasteries, to which the
native youth flocked for education ; from which the clergy
went forth preaching. These grew into great religious
colonies and centres of civilisation and learning, as well as
of evangelisation. Most of the ancient sees of Ireland
appear to have sprung out of these monasteries, each of
which was presided over by a bishop, a fashion different
from the custom of the Church in the civilised countries
of the ancient empire, but which St. Patrick had probably
learned in Gaul from the institutions of St. Martin, the
Abbot-Bishop of Tours.

The fame of the Irish Church attracted, and was increased
by, an influx of foreign Christians. The invasion of the
empire by the barbarians drove thousands from their homes

to seek refuge out of reach of the fierce hordes, and crowds of these foreigners flocked to Ireland as a secure Christian, if uncivilised, place of refuge. But it soon ceased to be uncivilised. Learning and religion were so diligently cultivated that Ireland became one of the most famous schools of learning and the arts in Europe ; and from this " Island of the Saints " went forth a host of missionaries whose labours in England, Gaul, and Germany we have briefly to record.

In the year 563, ninety-eight years after the death of St. Patrick, Columba, a native Celt, trained in one of the great Irish monasteries, left Ireland with twelve companions and founded a religious house on the little island of Iona, on the west coast of Scotland, near the Mull of Ross. Thence in frequent missionary journeys he converted the neighbouring Picts, and even extended his labours to the distant islands of Orkney and the Hebrides. The house of Iona is specially interesting to us as one of the chief centres from which our Saxon forefathers received their Christianity.

The native British Church had done nothing for the conversion of its heathen conquerors. So long as the war between the two races was still in progress—and it lasted for a century—the conquered race was organising armed resistance to the fierce heathen rather than missions for their conversion, and long before the strife of the races was over in the west and north, the settled tribes of the southeast had already received the Gospel at other hands.

What English youth does not know the charming story of the incident which first interested Pope Gregory the Great in this distant land ? Long before he was bishop, while abbot of the monastery which he had founded on the Cœlian Hill, he was one day crossing the Forum when his attention was attracted to a group of youths of both sexes who were standing there exposed, like other wares, for sale. They had fair complexions, light hair, and blue eyes, a striking contrast to the dark Italians about them. The abbot, asking who these children were, was told that they were *Angles*, from the kingdom of *Deira*, and that their king was named *Ælla ;* and, in fanciful play upon the words, he declared that they looked like *angels*, and ought to be saved *de ira* (from the wrath of God), and taught to sing *Alleluias*. The incident produced a deep impression on Gregory's mind ; he resolved to undertake a mission to England, and, with the Pope's sanction, had actually gone three days' journey, when the people of Rome, who were warmly attached to him, refused to let him leave them, and he abandoned his project. But long years of high employments, as ambassador to Constantinople and Archdeacon of Rome, did not banish his recollection of the fair English slaves, and when at length he succeeded to the papal chair, he carried out his intention of sending a mission for their conversion. For this enterprise he selected forty monks from his own monastery on the Cœlian Hill, with Augustine, the prior, at their head. He furnished them with books and everything necessary for their work, gave them letters of commendation to the Frankish kings and the Gallican bishops, and sent them forth to cross the Alps, the breadth of Gaul, and the stormy channel, to their distant mission field.

A door of entrance had been opened. Ethelbert, King of Kent, had married a Christian princess, Bertha, daughter of Charibert, King of Paris, with the condition that she should retain the free exercise of her religion. A bishop and clergymen had accompanied her as her chaplains, and the king had fitted up one of the ancient British churches at Canterbury for their worship. No doubt the influence of his wife, and the conversation of her learned chaplains, led the Kentish king to receive favourably the religious embassy which the great Bishop of Rome had sent. After some cautious delay the king laid the subject before an assembly of the people, and it was agreed to abandon the faith of their barbarous ancestors, and embrace the religion which now for 200 years had been that of the civilised world ; and we are told that the Italian missionaries baptized the king and his nobles, and 10,000 Kentish men, in the neighbouring river, in one day. Ethelbert obtained leave for the missionaries to preach in the neighbouring kingdom of the East Saxons, where they obtained some temporary success. In the kingdom of East Anglia they were tolerated, but made few converts. Edwin, the king of Northumbria, the leading kingdom in the north, sought the hand of a daughter of Ethelbert and Bertha, for whom, like her mother, it was stipulated that she should retain her religion and have the ministrations of a staff of chaplains. Paulinus was entrusted with this new charge. History repeats itself. After long delay and hesitation Edwin was persuaded in his own mind, and submitted the question of a change of religion to the assembly of the people. Bede, the historian of the Saxon Church, tells how the proposal was received by the thoughtful old thane, glad to hear a religious teacher who offered a solution of the great problems of life—whence do we come, whither do we go? and by the worldly high priest. Again the king, the thanes, and the people accepted the new religion, and Paulinus is likewise said to have baptized his 10,000 Northumbrians in a day. We are not surprised to find that these wholesale conversions were sometimes followed by wholesale apostasies.

Cœdwalla, a British prince, made an alliance with Penda, King of Mercia, defeated and slew the Northumbrian king, and regained the sovereignty over Bernicia and Deira, which he ruled cruelly for two years. Paulinus fled with the widowed queen and her child to Kent, leaving James, a deacon, behind, to keep together the Christians who still clung to their faith. Oswald, a prince of the family which had been dethroned by Edwin, set up the standard of revolt against Cœdwalla, and in the great battle of Heavenfield the power of the British prince was entirely broken, and Oswald established his family upon the Northumbrian throne. During his years of exile among the fathers of Iona, he had become an earnest Christian. Instead, therefore, of recalling Paulinus, the partisan of the rival house and teacher of the rival Church, he sent to Iona, and begged the Celtic monks to undertake the evangelisation of the north. Aidan was sent ; he built a monastery, a second Iona, on the little island of Lindisfarne, off the coast of Northumbria, which became a missionary centre, from which the greater part of England was evangelised. The work accomplished by the two missions may be thus briefly described. The Italian missionaries Christianised Kent and Wessex ; the Celtic missionaries, Mercia ; and a Northumbrian, with a Roman education (Wilfrid of York), introduced Christianity into Sussex. The work was begun by the Italians, and, after having lapsed, taken up and finished by the Celts, in Northumbria and Essex.   The East Anglian Church was founded by Felix, a Burgundian, who was assisted in his work by Fursey, an Irish-Scot.   The part of the Gallican Church in sending Bishop Liudhard with Queen Bertha must not be overlooked.   The two schools held the same doctrine, but some different customs.   They had a different succession of bishops, kept Easter at different times, had a different liturgy, different customs in the consecration of the clergy, and other differences of lesser consequence.   These served to divide the converts of the two sets of missionaries into two religious parties, whom it was obviously desirable to unite more completely than had been accomplished at a synod of Whitby in March, 664.   Accordingly on the death of the Kentish Archbishop, Deusdedit, in July of the same or following year, the two kings who were the special protectors of the two missions—Egbert king of Kent, and Oswy king of Northumbria—with the consent of the churches, agreed to select a man acceptable to both parties, and to send him to Rome to receive consecration from the chief bishop of the Christian Church, that he might return and regulate the English churches.   Wighard, the man selected, died at Rome, and the pope, Vitalian, selected in his place Theodore, a Greek monk, and consecrated him Archbishop of Canterbury.   Theodore, on his return, held a general council of the English churches at Hertford, A.D. 673, and there all the churches agreed in common customs, and were organised into a united Church of England, 150 years before the separate kingdoms were united into one kingdom of England under the sceptre of Egbert of Wessex (827).

Theodore, and Hadrian, who had accompanied him to his English work, were both eminent scholars, and gave a great impulse to the cultivation of learning in England, so that the monasteries of Deira became famous throughout Europe for their learning.   Bede, a monk of Jarrow, ranks amongst the great writers of the Church ; his ecclesiastical history is an inestimable monument of the early Saxon history of our own country.   In the next generation Archbishop Egbert, a man of princely birth, founded a noble library at York, and taught in the schools there, to which students flocked from all Europe. These schools produced Alcuin, named already as one of the greatest scholars of the age of Charlemagne. This brightest period of Saxon learning coincided with the darkest period of literature among the Franks.

The Franks had been zealous converts, but the Frankish Church seems by this time to have lost much of its early zeal, and many of the people were still heathen. Beyond the Rhine, their eastern frontier, stretched the vast forests in which the German tribes still maintained the barbarism and paganism of their ancestors.

A great love of an ascetic life, and a great desire for missionary labours, possessed the religious mind of Ireland and England at that time ; large numbers of monks and priests went out from both countries, like so many spiritual knights-errant, to war against ignorance, idolatry, and sin. Throughout the Continent, almost, the traces of these Irish missionaries are to be met, in the names of saints to whom churches are dedicated and special local honour paid. Some of these British missionaries were men of superior powers, and accomplished results of great and permanent importance.

In 559 Columbanus, trained at the Irish Bangor, with twelve companions, journeyed to the south-east of France, refused the invitation of Guntram, the grandson of Clovis, to settle in Burgundy, and crossed into the wild district of the Vosges. This hilly country, once colonised and culti-vated by Roman legionaries, was now overgrown again with forest and abandoned to the bear and wolf and to tribes of pagan Suevi. Here Columbanus founded three monasteries, at Anegray, Luxeuil, and Fontaines. On their first settlement the monks had to endure great hard-ships, and were sometimes reduced to live on herbs and bark of trees. They cleared the forest and cultivated the land ; people began to settle round them, to whom they taught the arts of life as well as the Christian faith. The Celtic monks maintained the customs of their own Church as to the time of the Easter festival and other peculiarities. This brought Columbanus remonstrances from the popes and from a synod of the local clergy ; but the abbot begged the synod to leave him in peace, and suggested to the pope to reconsider the question of the paschal cycle, since it was his own calculation which was wrong ; and he and his monks persisted in their own ways. The king, Thierry, held him in honour and used to visit him ; but Columbanus rebuked his vices, and Brunehaut, the queen-mother, set herself against him ; and at last the monks were marched by force to the coast and bidden leave the kingdom. Columbanus then made his way by the Rhine into Switzerland, and laboured first near Lake Zurich, afterwards at Brienz, on Lake Constance, then crossed the Alps into Lombardy, where he was received by Agilulf and Theodelinda, the sovereigns of Lombardy, and founded a monastery at Bobbio, where he died, A.D. 615. This monastery afterwards became famous throughout Europe. It existed till 1803, and its library possessed an Irish antiphonarium and missal, MSS. of the date of its foundation, and a very extensive and valuable collection of ancient books.

Gall, one of the companions of Columbanus, was pre vented by sickness from going into Italy. With twelve companions he founded a monastery in the depths of the forest and presided over it for twelve years. During that time he revived the faith in the ancient diocese of Constance and reclaimed from barbarism the district bordering on the Black Forest. After his death his cell became a great place of pilgrimage. His monastery was replaced by a more sumptuous edifice, under the auspices of the mayor of the palace, Philip of Heristal ; during the ninth and tenth centuries it was an asylum of learning and one of the most famous schools of Europe. Its library is still a storehouse of valuable ancient MSS.

Fridolin founded a monastery at Leckingen ; Magnoald another at Füssen, in Swabia ; Kilian, a monk of Iona, laboured successfully at Würzburg ; Emmeran, a native of Poictiers and Bishop of Aquitania, resigned his see and preached in Bavaria ; Rupert, Bishop of Worms, founded Salzburg.

The monastic establishments of those ages were outposts of civilisation ; the industrious monks taught the roaming hunters by their example the methods of agriculture and the arts of life, and gradually Christianised and educated them into orderly, industrious communities. The kings and nobles gladly gave any little company of monks a wide tract of unreclaimed land. This was the origin of the ecclesiastical greatness of the Middle Ages. The towns which sprang up about the monasteries became the great medieval cities; the little oratory grew into the cathedral; the district of forest land, cultivated and inhabited, became a principality; and the privileges of local government, originally given to the abbot to enable him to rule his rude dependants, made the medieval bishop a sovereign prince.

The Franks maintained a border war for many years with their neighbours, the barbarous and fierce Frieslanders, who occupied not only the small district in Holland which still retains their name, but a considerable portion also of the Netherlands and adjacent districts. The kings of the Franks encouraged the introduction of Christianity among all the fierce barbarians on their borders as one means of civilising them, and even in many cases forced Christianity on a conquered people as one of the conditions of peace.

Hazardous and even fatal as the adventure often was, the zeal and courage of the missionaries led them to risk their lives in the foundation of these religious settlements among hostile heathen. Thus, when the conquests of King Dagobert opened the way, Amandus of Aquitaine settled as a temporary bishop among the Frisians about the Scheldt, and ultimately succeeded to the see of Maestricht.

Eligius of Limoges, goldsmith at the court of Clothaire II. and Dagobert, lived a holy life in the midst of a dissolute society, erected churches and monasteries, redeemed slaves, gave large alms to the poor, and at length, in 641, was elected Bishop of Noyon. His diocese was mainly inhabited by barbarous heathen tribes, among whom he laboured diligently and successfully, building churches and planting monasteries. Fragments of his sermons have been preserved by his biographer, St. Ouen, Bishop of Rouen, and are interesting as examples of these missionary teachings. In one sermon, after protesting against the idea that men can win the favour of the Almighty by the mere performance of external ceremonies, he proceeds : " It sufficeth not, my brethren, that ye be called Christians if ye do not the works of a Christian. That man alone is benefited by the name of a Christian who with his whole heart keeps the precepts

and laws of Christ, who abstains from theft, from bearing
false witness, from lying, from perjury, from adultery, from
hatred of his fellow-man, from strife and discord. . . . He
adds stronger commands than these, for He says, ' Love
your enemies, bless them that curse you, do good to them
that hate you, pray for them that despitefully use you and
persecute you.'   Behold, this is a hard and difficult command, and seems impossible to men, but it has a great
reward ; for hear what He declares it is, ' That ye may be
the children of your Father which is in heaven.'   Oh, what
grace is here !   Of ourselves we are not worthy to be His
servants, and yet by loving our enemies we become the sons
of God.   He, then, who wishes to be a Christian indeed must
keep these commandments.   He who keepeth them not
deceiveth himself.   He is a good Christian who putteth
his trust not in amulets or devices of demons, but in Christ
alone. . . . Neither heaven nor earth, nor stars, nor any
other creature is deserving of worship.   God alone is to
be adored, for He created and ordained all things.   Heaven,
indeed, is high, and the earth wide, and the stars passing
fair ; but grander and fairer must He be who made all
these things.   For if the things that we see are so incompre-
hensible and past understanding, even the various fruits of
the earth and the beauty of the flowers, and the diverse kinds
of animals in earth, air, and water, the instinct of the provi-
dent bee, the wind blowing where it listeth, the crash of the
thunder, the changes of the seasons, the alternations of day
and night ; if these things that we see with our eyes cannot
be comprehended by the mind of man, how shall we comprehend the things we do not see ? or what kind of Being
must He be by whom all these things are created and
sustained ?   Fear Him, my brethren, before all things,
adore and love Him, cleave fast to His long-suffering, and
never despair of His tender mercy."

In another sermon he pictures the day of judgment :
" Let us reflect what terror ours will be when from heaven
the Lord shall come to judge the world, before whom
the elements shall melt in a fervent heat, heaven and earth
shall tremble, and the powers of the heavens be shaken.
Then, while the trumpets of the angels sound, all men,
good and evil, shall in a moment of time rise with the

bodies they wore on earth, and be led before the tribunal of Christ. Then shall all tribes of the earth mourn while He points out to them the marks of the nails wherewith He was pierced for our iniquities, and shall say unto them, ' I found thee, O man, of the dust of the earth ; with My own hands I fashioned thee, and placed thee, all undeserving, in the delights of Paradise ; but thou didst despise Me and My words, and didst prefer to follow the deceiver, for which thou wast justly condemned. Yet I did pity thee. I took upon Me thy flesh ; lived on earth among sinners ; endured reproach and stripes for thy sake ; that I might rescue thee from judgment, I endured blows and to be spitted on ; that I might restore to thee the bliss of Paradise, I drank vinegar mingled with gall. For thy sake was I crowned with thorns, crucified, pierced with the spear. For thy sake did I die, was laid in the grave, and descended into Hades, that I might bring thee back to Paradise. Behold, and see what I endured for thy sake ! Behold the mark of the nails wherewith I was fixed to the cross ! I took upon Me thy sorrows that I might heal thee ; I took upon Me thy punishment that I might crown thee with glory ; I endured to die that thou mightest live for ever. Though I was invisible, yet for thy sake I became incarnate. Though I knew no suffering, yet for thy sake I deigned to suffer. Though I was rich, yet for thy sake I became poor. But thou didst despise My lowliness and My precepts ; thou didst obey a deceiver rather than Me. My justice, therefore, cannot pronounce any other sentence than such as thine own works deserve. Thou didst choose thine own ways ; receive, then, thine own wages. Thou didst despise light ; let darkness, then, be thy reward. Thou didst love death ; depart, then, to perdition. Thou didst obey the evil one ; go, then, with him into eternal punishment.' " We quote finally the last words of this saintly seventh-century bishop : " Now lettest Thou Thy servant depart according to Thy word. Remember, O Lord, I am but dust, and enter not into judgment with Thy servant. Remember me, Thou that alone art free from sin—Christ, the Saviour of the world. Lead me forth from the body of this death, and give me an entrance into Thy heavenly kingdom. Thou who hast ever been my protector, into

Thy hands I commit my spirit. I know that I deserve not to behold Thy face ; but Thou knowest how my hope was always in Thy mercy and my trust in Thy faithfulness. Receive me, then, according to Thy loving-kindness, and let me not be disappointed of my hope."

Our able, zealous, turbulent Wilfrid of York was among the missionaries to Frisia. While on his journey to Rome to appeal against Archbishop Theodore, his ship was cast by a storm on that coast in the year 678. He was hospitably received by the king, Aldgis, and the natives ; and finding them still unbelievers, stayed some time among them, and converted the king, several chiefs and some thousands of the people. But Wilfrid soon left them, and Radbod, Aldgis' successor, was a heathen, and the pagan customs were restored. In 690, Wigbert, a Northumbrian monk, spent two years in a vain endeavour to influence Radbod and his people. At this time the successes of Pepin of Heristal in Frisia, appeared to afford a new opening to missionary enterprise, and Willebrord, a Northumbrian educated in Wilfrid's monastery of Ripon, took eleven Irish companions, sailed to France, and offered his services to Pepin. These monks established themselves at Wilteburg, and evangelised a considerable portion of Frankish Frisia. Willebrord was consecrated, by Pope Sergius, Archbishop of the Frisians. Many Anglo-Saxons came to work under him, or attempted independent enterprises in neighbouring countries. Willebrord made a voyage into Denmark in a fruitless endeavour to find an opening for the Gospel there. On his return a storm drove him to take refuge in Heligoland, an island sacred to one of the Frisian deities. It was forbidden to kill any animal on the island, or to drink of the holy well except in solemn silence. The archbishop, detained some time by the weather, killed cattle for food for his crew and for thirty Danish boys whom he had bought and brought back to educate ; and he baptized three of his company in the sacred well. King Radbod sent for Willebrord, and decreed that one of the three proselytes must die to atone for the desecration of the island. Some years afterwards, Wulfram, Bishop of Lens, with a company of monks also came on a missionary campaign into Frisia, baptized a son of Radbod and preached with considerable success. Wulfram once found himself present at a great pagan festival at which human sacrifices were offered. A boy was about to be hung on a gallows. Wulfram expostulated with Radbod, and prayed him to spare the boy's life. The chiefs standing round tauntingly said, " If your Christ can save the boy from death he shall be His servant and yours for ever." Wulfram fell on his knees as the boy was thrown off from the beam ; the cord broke, and Wulfram, finding him still alive, claimed him. The incident was accepted as a miracle, and the fame of Wulfram increased. Another time two boys were to be sacrificed by drowning. They were fastened to a stake erected on the shore, and left to be overwhelmed by the rising tide. As the tide crept nearer, the elder took his brother upon his shoulders. The bishop begged Radbod to spare them, but was met with the old taunt, " If your God Christ will deliver them, you may have them." Wulfram prayed, and the story says the waves suddenly receded, and the bishop rushed forward and released the children, and brought them back by the hand. The Gospel gradually made its way among the people. Radbod's son had been baptized, and the fierce old warrior himself at length consented to be baptized. But at the last moment he asked whether, if baptized, he should meet the kings his ancestors in heaven ; and on being told that they, being unbaptized, would not enter there, he drew back, declaring that he would rather share the company of kings and warriors than sit down in heaven with a handful of beggars, and ultimately the old pagan died as he had lived. On his death Charles Martel reduced the part of Frisia hitherto independent ; and Willebrord was soon joined by the fellow-labourer whose success soon eclipsed his own and won for him the title of " the Apostle of Germany."

Winfrid (afterwards named Boniface), a noble Saxon of Devonshire, of considerable reputation, had the prospect of a useful career at home, but his heart was set on missionary work among the heathen of the German forests. He made a pilgrimage to Rome, and Pope Gregory II. gave him letters authorising him to preach the Gospel in Germany wherever he should find opportunity. At first he preached in Thuringia ; but, hearing of Radbod's death and the new

opening in Frisia, he repaired thither and offered his services to Willebrord, and laboured with him for three years.
Willebrord, feeling the advance of age, desired that the able
and energetic Winfrid should be his successor in the see of
Utrecht.   Winfrid declined, and set out on an independent
mission in Hessia.   He met with speedy success among the
Hessians ; and Gregory sent for him to Rome, and consecrated him missionary bishop, taking from him an oath of
obedience to the Roman see—a step which seems without
precedent, except in the case of the bishops of the proper
patriarchate of Rome.   Winfrid consolidated the work of
the earlier Irish and Anglo-Saxon missionaries ; undertook,
with the consent of Charles Martel, the reformation of
the disorders of the Frankish Church, revived its councils,
and gave new energy to its life.   He covered Central and
Western Germany with the first elements of civilisation and
Christianity.   Monastic seminaries—Amonëburg, Ohrdruf,
Fritzlar, and Fulda—were founded amid the Teutonic
forests.   The sees of Salzburg, Freisingen, Regensburg,
and Passau testified his care of the Church of Bavaria ; the
see of Erfurt told of his labours in Thuringia ; that of
Buraburg in Hesse ; that of Wurzburg in Franconia ;
while his metropolitan see at Mayence, having jurisdiction
over Worms, Spires, Tongres, Cologne, and Utrecht, was
evidence that, even before his death, the German Church
had passed beyond its first missionary stage.   As age
approached, instead of retiring, as he had once contemplated, to end his days among the brethren of Fulda, he
set out on a last missionary journey into one of the earliest
scenes of his labours, into Frisia.   A great number of
converts were to meet him on Whitsun-eve, 755, to receive
the rite of confirmation on the morrow ; but, instead of the
white-robed neophytes, he found himself surrounded by a
band of armed pagans.   He forbad those with him to make
any resistance, and they were massacred on the spot.   The
copy of St. Ambrose on " The Advantage of Death," which
the archbishop had brought, together with his shroud, to
the shore of the Zuyder Zee, was long shown at Fulda as
a precious blood-stained relic of the great archbishop.

Part of the policy of Charlemagne was to win the Saxons
from their ancestral barbarism and ferocity by means of

Q

Christianity ; and in spite of the remonstrances of men like
Alcuin, who protested against the propagation of the
Gospel, as Mohammed spread his false religion, at the point
of the sword, Charlemagne persisted in that policy. Whenever he reduced the Saxons to sue for peace, he required
them to submit to baptism, and left monks and priests
to carry on the work of their conversion. Sturmi, abbot of
Fulda, Willehad, a Northumbrian, Liudger, a Frisian
educated partly in the school of Alcuin at York, are among
the most prominent agents of this Saxon conversion. As
soon as the emperor was engaged in some distant part of
his wide dominions the Saxons would revolt, burn churches
and monasteries, and resume their ancient customs. Then
the emperor would hasten back, and gather his forces for
another Saxon campaign. In the end he gained his object.
Slowly but steadily the wave of conquest passed on to the
Weser, the Elbe, the sea. He established bishoprics richly
endowed, and founded great monasteries as spiritual
fortresses in the newly annexed heathen country. His
eight bishoprics of Osnaburg, Bremen, Münster, Minden,
Halberstadt, Paderborn, Verden, and Hildesheim, grew into
the great cities of medieval Saxony.

The evangelisation of Denmark and Sweden is to be
attributed in great measure to the labours of Anskar,
a monk of Corbie, who won the title of the Apostle of the
North. Hamburg was the centre of his work ; there he
built a church, monastery, and school. After many
vicissitudes, after seeing Hamburg plundered and burnt by
an incursion of the Northmen, he succeeded in obtaining
the permission of King Eric of Denmark for his missionaries
to preach throughout the land, and many of the people
embraced the faith. Thence Anskar proceeded to Sweden,
and obtained leave to preach there from King Biorn and the
popular assemblies ; and there also, with some temporary
checks, the Gospel slowly but surely made its way.

Until the ninth century Norway was still governed by
numerous petty independent chiefs. The people were
rough and fierce. The younger sons of the chiefs muste ed
crews of hardy adventurers, sailed out of their fiords, and
devastated the sea and river coasts of Europe. About
860 arose the king (Harold Haarfager or the Fair-haired)

who united all these principalities into one kingdom of Norway. But the chiefs and bonders (*i.e.*, peasants), indignant at the new yoke, emigrated in great numbers, colonised the Orkneys and Hebrides, the Faroes and Iceland, invaded Russia and Normandy, and harried the coasts of England, Ireland, and Spain.

In 933 Harold Haarfager resigned the crown to his son, Eric " of the Bloody Axe," from whom a deliverer came in the person of Haco, his youngest brother. Haco had been at the court of our Anglo-Saxon king, Athelstan, where he had been baptized, and educated in the faith and in manly exercises. Athelstan furnished him with men and ships, in which they sailed to Drontheim. The people welcomed him who promised to secure to the bonders their rights, and to restore the old customs. Eric was deserted by the people, and Haco accepted by the whole country as king. He sent to England for bishops and priests, and in the district about the capital several churches were built ; and the king, at the great assembly of the people at the Froste-Thing,* proposed that the whole people should transfer their faith from Odin to Christ. The proposal encountered a successful opposition. Harold Ericson, who succeeded to the throne, had also, with his brothers, been baptized during their exile in England ; and they proceeded to pull down the heathen temples, and forbid the sacrifices. The King of Denmark took advantage of the commotions which ensued, and conquered Norway, placing Yarl † Hacon over it as his viceroy. The King of Denmark was a Christian, and had given priests and learned men to the Yarl, bidding him make all the people in Norway be baptized. But Yarl Hacon allied himself with the heathen party, and made himself independent of Denmark ; before the great battle with the Jomsburg pirates, he offered one of his own sons to Thor for victory. But in spite of his compliances, his rule was unpopular, and the people welcomed Olaf, the son of Tryggve, as a deliverer.

Olaf's reign was the turning-point in the conversion of the country. In his youth, as a viking,‡ he had travelled in England, Germany, Russia, Greece, and as far as Con-

* Winter assembly of the people.
† Earl.   ‡ Sea-rover.

stantinople. In the Scilly Islands he had been converted
and baptized with all his crew. Sailing to England, he was
confirmed by Alphege, Bishop of Winchester, in the presence
of King Ethelred; thence he went to Ireland, where he
married the sister of one of the Irish kings, and lived at the
court of his brother-in-law. Here one of the northern
vikings told him how all Norway was groaning under the
cruelty of Hacon the Bad and would welcome a grandson
of Harold Haarfager. Olaf sailed for Drontheim, and there
was chosen by the Thing as king, and drove Yarl Hacon
out of the land. As soon as he was seated on the throne
he destroyed temples and idols, won over his relations and
intimate associates, and then proclaimed his resolve that
Christianity should be the national faith. All the inhabitants of the district more immediately subject to him were
baptized. He went from place to place, holding assemblies
of the people, and proposing to them to accept baptism or
to fight, and in many places the people unwillingly submitted. In the North the people of eight districts were
bidden accept baptism; but they had come armed, out-
numbered Olaf's men, and demanded of him to join in the
customary sacrifices to the gods. The king temporised and
agreed to meet them at the midsummer festival at Mære.
Meantime he assembled some of the chiefs, and told them
if he was to sacrifice at Mære it should be a sacrifice of the
most solemn kind—a sacrifice of men, and that not of
criminals and slaves, but of the greatest men, and he commanded fifteen of the principal chiefs present to be seized
and kept for the sacrifice. They rescued themselves by
submitting to baptism. When the people assembled at
Mære, Olaf and his men entered the temple, and while the
sacrifice proceeded he suddenly struck down the image of
Thor with his battle-axe; his men overthrew the other
idols; and the king proposed his usual condition, that the
people should be baptized or fight. They, disheartened by
the powerlessness of their deities, surrendered, gave hostages
that they would be true to Christianity, and "took baptism."
A young pagan named Endred agreed to decide the question
of his faith by wager of battle against a champion named by
the king. Olaf himself appeared as the champion of Christ.
The contest lasted three days. Olaf beat him in swimming,

diving, archery, and sword play, and having conquered him, instructed him in the faith, and had him baptized. Olaf's zeal for Christianity at length cost him kingdom and life. Sigrid, the beautiful widow of a Swedish king, visited the court of Norway in the hope of marrying Olaf— " the strongest, bravest, most beautiful of men." Olaf was inclined to the match, but on her refusing to embrace Christianity, treated her with contemptuous indignity. She married Sweyn of Denmark, and stirred him up, with the son of her first marriage and some disaffected Norwegians, to invade Norway. Olaf was beaten, and with the last survivors of his crew leaped overboard that he might not fall into the hands of his enemies. The country was governed by the conquerors for fifteen years, until Olaf Haraldson, a descendant of Harold Haarfager, won the throne. He sent to England for a bishop and priests. Bishop Grimkil, " the horned man," as the people called him from the shape of his mitre, compiled a system of ecclesiastical law for the Norsemen. Olaf found that many had relapsed into their old heathen customs, and he went about reclaiming them to the Gospel by high-handed proceedings similar to those of his namesake. After his death he was canonised. When Canute had united the three crowns of Denmark, Norway, and England, he promoted the civilisation and evangelisation of his Scandinavian dominions; schools and monasteries were founded, bishoprics established, churches built; the old faith in Thor and Odin gradually disappeared, and the Northmen became the children of " the White Christ."

CHAPTER XXXII

THE CONVERSION OF THE SLAVONIC NATIONS

THE vast Slavonic population of rude, warlike, pastoral tribes inhabited the rebarbarised provinces on each side of the Danube—Bulgarians, Moravians, Bohemians, Poles—and extended onwards into the heart of the modern Russia. In the early part of the ninth century, when Theodora was Empress of Constantinople, the sister of the BULGARIAN Prince Bogoris fell into the hands of the Greeks, and while in captivity embraced the religion of the empire. After a while a Greek monk was taken by Bogoris, and exchanged for his sister. Bogoris, like Clovis, long listened unmoved to his sister's endeavours to convert him ; but on the occurrence of a famine, prayers to his own deities having produced no effect, while prayers to the God of the Christians were followed by speedy relief, he received baptism at the hands of the patriarch, the emperor himself standing sponsor by proxy.

The divisions among Christians had the same evil results then as now. Missionaries from the Roman and Armenian churches visited the new convert, and sought to win his adherence. Political reasons made him for a time connect himself with the Western empire, and the interference of the Pope led to warm remonstrances from the Greek patriarch. Pope Nicholas claimed the Bulgarian Church, because it was within the limits of the ancient Western empire, the Patriarch Photius because the Eastern Church had introduced Christianity into the country. The controversy called forth works on the theological questions in dispute between the two churches from some of the greatest Western theologians, such as Hincmar of Rheims, Odo of Beauvais, Æneas of Paris, and Ratramn of Corbie. In the end the Bulgarians chose the Byzantine connection, and received a Greek archbishop and bishops.

The conversion of the Bulgarians led to the introduction of Christianity into neighbouring kindred tribes among the Chazars of the Crimea, the Slavic tribes in the interior of Hellas, the Serbians, who extended from the Danube to the Adriatic, and others. The kingdom of MORAVIA had acknowledged the supremacy of Charlemagne, and had received a regionary * bishop and some priests, who had not been very successful. When the empire of Charlemagne was breaking to pieces, Ratislav, the King of Moravia, seeking to recover his independence, and to withdraw his people from Western influence, wrote to the Greek Emperor Michael for religious teachers : " Our land is baptized," he wrote, " but we have no teachers to instruct us and translate for us the sacred books." The emperor sent Methodius and Cyril, who gave them an alphabet, and translated into their tongue the Gospels and Acts, the Psalter and other sacred books, and the Liturgy. The pope, Adrian, summoned the Greek missionaries to Rome, and after some hesitation, approved their use of the Liturgy in the vernacular, appointed Methodius metropolitan of Moravia and Pannonia, and on their return, though hindered by the jealousy of the German clergy, the Greek clergy were very successful among the people.

BOHEMIA received its Christianity through Moravia. Its heathen duke, Borziwoi, about 801, visited the court of the Moravian prince, and with his attendants received Christianity at the hands of Methodius, and on his return to his own country took with him a Moravian priest, who baptized the prince's wife and sons ; and after various fluctuations, Boleslav the Pious, the great-grandson of Borziwoi, assisted by the influence of the Emperor Otho, established a Saxon bishop, Dietmar, at Prague, and the Church slowly won the people from their heathen customs.

The seeds of Christianity are said to have been wafted into POLAND from Moravia as early as the ninth century, and Christian refugees from the invasions of the Hungarians appear to have extended its progress during the tenth. In 965 the Polish Duke Mieceslav I. married the daughter of the Christian King of Bohemia, and embraced the faith, and a bishopric was erected at Posen. A fourth wife, Oda,

* A missionary bishop without a definite see.

the daughter of a German count, erected numerous monasteries and churches, and introduced French, German, and Italian ecclesiastics. Otho III. bestowed the title of king on Mieceslav II., and made Gnesen a metropolitan see, with authority over the sees of Breslau, Cracow, and Colberg. On the death of this king the heathen party, regaining a temporary ascendancy, burnt the churches, and killed or drove away the clergy. At last the Poles agreed to restore the line of their ancient princes. Casimir, the son of the late king, was found in a Benedictine monastery, where he had taken the vows and received ordination. Pope Benedict IX. released him from his vows, and the new king abolished the remains of the Slavonic Liturgy, and brought his Church into closer union with the Roman see.

The conversion of RUSSIA was the greatest missionary achievement of the Byzantine Church. In 955 the Russian Princess Olga, with a numerous retinue, visited Constantinople, and there embraced Christianity, having the Emperor Constantine Porphyrogenitus for her sponsor. On her return she endeavoured to convert her son Swiatoslav and her grandson Vladimir. Some ambassadors whom Vladimir sent to Constantinople returned deeply impressed by what they had seen. The grandeur of the Divine service in the Church of Sta. Sophia; the impressiveness of the building—then, perhaps, the noblest in the world—the splendour of the service, the clergy, the processions, the music, the prostrate people, overpowered their imaginations. " When we stood in the temple," said the ambassadors, " we did not know where we were, for there is nothing else like it on earth; there in truth God has His dwelling with men, and we can never forget the beauty we saw there. No one who has once tasted sweets will afterwards taste that which is bitter. We can no longer abide in heathenism." Thereupon the Boyars said to Vladimir, " If the religion of the Greeks had not been good, your grandmother Olga, the wisest of women, would not have embraced it." Soon afterwards the prince demanded the hand of Anne, the sister of the Emperor Basil. His request was granted on condition of his embracing Christianity. Vladimir having become a Christian, gave orders for the immediate baptism of his people. " Whoever on the morrow," ran the proclamation, " shall not repair to the river, whether rich or poor, I shall hold him for my enemy." Accordingly the people of Kieff flocked in crowds to the river and were baptized. The national idol was dragged to the river and thrown in ; where the temple had stood the prince erected the Church of St. Basil. Michael, the first metropolitan, with his bishops and priests, travelled from place to place, baptizing and instructing the people. Churches were built and schools founded ; the Slavonic Scriptures and Liturgy of Cyril and Methodius, were introduced ; sees were erected at Novgorod, Rostoff, Chernigoff, Vladimir, and Belgorod ; but in the remoter parts of the country long labour and much persecution had to be endured before the Cross triumphed over the ancient superstitions.

The ancient Slavonic religion still maintained a firm ascendancy over a large tract of country ; its hierarchy was powerful, and it was not till the end of the first quarter of the twelfth century that the chief towns of POMERANIA received the Gospel, through the influence of the Suzerain Boteslav, Duke of Poland, and chiefly by the apostolic labours of Otho, Bishop of Bamberg.

At the close of the twelfth century a new agency was employed in the conversion of these Slavonic races. Western Christendom was full of the crusading spirit. At first its idea was to win back by the sword the lands which the Mohammedans had wrested out of Christian hands. Then it proceeded to propagate the faith in heathen lands at the sword's point. Innocent III. directed the crusading spirit against the heretics of the south of France,* and the heathen of the north-east of Europe.

LIVONIA, on the east coast of the Baltic, was the first scene of these northern crusades. Meinhard and Berthold in the end of the twelfth century had successively (1186–1198) laboured in vain for the conversion of the stubborn heathen people. In 1198 Berthold re-entered the country at the head of an army of crusaders. The people submitted to force, but, on the removal of the force, rose against the clergy and their converts. Berthold's successor, Albert of Bremen, came at the head of another crusading army and

* See page 260.

laid the foundations of the town of Riga ; and when the crusading army broke up, he, with the pope's sanction, established a new military order, the Brethren of the Sword, as a permanent military force for the propagation of the Gospel. The new order, as its reward, was to possess the lands they won, receiving baptized natives as subjects, and those who refused baptism as slaves. From Riga the military evangelists spread into the neighbouring country, erecting castles to defend their conquests, under the protection of whose walls German colonists settled. The Bishoprics of Revel, Dorpat, and Pernau were at first so many ecclesiastical fortresses, founded by the Brethren of the Sword to consolidate their conquests, as well as centres for the propagation of Christianity.

The opening of the thirteenth century saw the PRUSSIANS still strongly adhering to their ancient heathenism, the missionaries who had from time to time penetrated into their country having paid for their courage with their lives. In 1210, Christian, a Pomeranian monk, with several brethren, accredited by Pope Innocent III., laboured for four years and met with some success ; then the heathen party rose against them, destroyed their churches, and put many of the converts to the sword. A military order, after the model of the Order of the Sword, was then founded for the conquest and conversion of Prussia, but did not prove successful. Then the Order of Teutonic Knights, quitting the Holy Land, were incorporated, with the papal sanction, with the Order of the Sword, and undertook to expel the last remains of heathenism from the face of Europe. For fifty years the knights waged war against the Prussians, slowly making way and securing their conquests by castles, around which arose the towns of Culm, Thorn, Marienwerder, and Eburg, which they peopled with German colonists. In 1260 the knights were defeated by the Lithuanians ; the Prussians rose in revolt, burnt churches and monasteries, slew the clergy, and wasted the country far and wide. Twenty-two years of sanguinary war ensued, in which successive armies of crusaders came to help the knights, before the struggle between the rival faiths ended.

The neighbouring province of LITHUANIA did not abandon its heathenism and embrace Christianity till

A.D. 1386, and not till well into the fifteenth century did the SAMAITES (of whom the Samoyedes, now living within the polar circle, are probably the surviving representatives) receive Christianity from a Lithuanian priest called Withold, who fixed his see at the town of Wornie or Miedniki. Among the LAPPS Christianity did not become the popular religion till the sixteenth and seventeenth centuries.

CHAPTER XXXIII

THE HILDEBRANDINE PERIOD

THE religious abuses narrated in chapter XXX at length gave rise to a strong and widespread desire for a reformation of the Church. Among the clergy themselves there was a rising party intent on remedying the prevalent evils, and Gregory VI.* had been the representative of their hopes. The emperor, Henry III., was himself resolved to fulfil the duty, which his office was understood to impose upon him, of reforming abuses. Among the people generally the state of the Church excited great discontent, and not a little disaffection, and any measures of reform were sure of their sympathy.

Pope Clement II. summoned a council for the correction of abuses ; but his death and that of his successor delayed any action for some months. The emperor again chose as Pope a German, his own cousin Bruno, Bishop of Toul, a man of great reputation for piety, learning, and eloquence, and not without experience in public affairs. At a great assembly at Worms he was invested with the symbols of the papacy, and set out for Italy in all the state and splendour of pontiff-elect. At one of the halting-places of his cavalcade he was met by Hugh, the famous Abbot of Cluny, accompanied by one of his monks, an Italian named Hildebrand, a meeting which produced memorable results.

This Hildebrand was born of humble parents, but his uncle was Abbot of St. Mary's on the Aventine, and under him the youth was trained for the ecclesiastical profession. Embracing the severe ascetic notions which were spreading in the Church, and discontented with the laxity of his monastery, he crossed the Alps and entered the society of Cluny, which had lately become famous for its revival of primitive monastic discipline.

* Page 211.

At the meeting of the pope-elect and the Abbot of Cluny, Hildebrand put forth the views of the reforming school among the clergy. The genius of Hildebrand at once obtained an ascendancy over the mind of Bruno. He adopted his views, took him into his suite, and, pope-elect and cousin of the emperor though he was, laid aside the pontifical symbols, adopted the dress of a pilgrim, entered Rome barefooted and in a coarse frock, and addressing the people assembled in St. Peter's told them that he had been chosen by the emperor as pope, but had come to submit himself to their decision. He was rewarded by loud and universal acclamations, which hailed him pope under the name of Leo IX.

Leo ordained Hildebrand sub-deacon, and conferred on him the treasurership of the Church and other preferments, and Hildebrand became the soul of the reforming party among the Roman clergy, and the trusted adviser of the pope. Leo undertook in earnest the work of reformation, and set out on a council of visitation. He crossed the Alps and passed through Germany, reforming abuses, redressing wrongs, reconciling foes, consecrating churches, conferring privileges on monasteries. Next he journeyed to Rheims, where he announced his intention to hold there a council for the reformation of disorders in the Church and the general correction of morals, to which he invited the King of France, and summoned the French bishops. This was a novel assumption on the part of the pope, and an invasion of the rights of the French king and Church. The king absented himself on the plea of a military expedition ; but no one ventured to oppose the pope, and the synod was held. The bishops and abbots were required to swear that they had not been guilty of simony either in obtaining or administering their offices. The Bishop of Nantes, who confessed that he had purchased the succession to his father in the bishopric, was degraded to the order of presbyter ; the bishops of Nevers and Coutances confessed that their preferment had been bought for them by relations but without their own knowledge, and on making their submission they were allowed to retain their sees. The Bishop of Langres, accused of many vices, absconded, and was deposed. Twelve canons were passed : one enacted that no one should be appointed to a bishopric without the choice of his clergy and people ; another excommunicated the Bishop of Compostella, who had taken the title of " apostolic," and claimed an independent primacy over the Spanish Church ; another summoned to Rome the Breton bishops, who had long been separated from Rome, and had not obeyed the summons to the present council.

From Rheims the pope proceeded to Mayence (1049), and held another council there. He returned to Italy in triumph, having given a great impulse to the work of reform and greatly increased the prestige of the papal see. The system of visitation thus commenced was continued throughout his pontificate, and established the authority of the pope as the acknowledged chief ruler of the Western branch of the Church, the powerful corrector of abuses in the hierarchy, and censor of the morals of the whole body of the faithful. During this pontificate, and in the year A.D. 1054, occurred the formal breach between the Eastern and Western branches of the Church, which will be related later.*

Leo IX. died 1054, solemnly committing the Church to the care of Hildebrand ; and the clergy and people were desirous of electing him as Leo's successor. Hildebrand, however, induced the people to entrust him with a commission to the emperor, requesting him to nominate a pope acceptable to the Romans, and he suggested Gebhard, Bishop of Eichstadt, one of the emperor's most trusted counsellors. On his arrival at Rome, Gebhard, like his predecessor, was formally elected by the clergy and people, and assumed the name of Victor II. By him the system of reforming synods was kept up, but they were presided over by his legates. In A.D. 1056 the emperor died, bequeathing to Victor the guardianship of his only son, Henry IV., a child of six years of age. The virtual government of the empire was thus vested in the same hands as the papacy, but the pope died in the following year (A.D. 1057).

The Romans took advantage of the minority of the young emperor to choose a pope for themselves. During his short reign, under the name of Stephen IX., synods were held which passed fresh canons against the marriage of the clergy.

* Page 278.

Hildebrand's influence continued unabated. Probably at this time he was ordained deacon and appointed Archdeacon of Rome; and when dying, the pope exacted an oath that his successor should not be appointed without Hildebrand's advice.

On Stephen's death, in Hildebrand's absence, the nobles of the Campagna gained access to St. Peter's by night, and set up as pope a member of their faction under the name of Benedict X. Another party at Rome sent envoys to the empress-mother, requesting her to nominate a pope. Hildebrand returned to Rome, met these envoys, and suggested the name of Gerard, Bishop of Florence, who accordingly was nominated by the empress, while Hildebrand secured his simultaneous election by the cardinals, who had fled to Sienna. Gerard took the name of Nicholas II., and was escorted to Rome by Godfrey of Tuscany, of whose capital of Florence he had been bishop, and who was the brother of the late pope. Benedict submitted to him, and passed the rest of his life in a monastery. In the papacy of Nicholas II. occurred a revolution in the religious affairs of Milan. The Church of St. Ambrose had long held a lofty position. Its archbishop was a great secular prince, and, in the absence of the emperor, the most important personage in the north of Italy; its clergy bore a high character for learning and morality, for the discharge of their pastoral duties and the education of the young. The church had a liturgy of its own, which it venerated as that of St. Ambrose, and its clergy was a married clergy— a privilege which they enjoyed under the sanction of that great father. The same custom was generally observed throughout the churches of Lombardy and Turin also had a married clergy, with the sanction of its bishop, Cunibert. An agitation was got up against the marriage of the clergy and the passions of the mob inflamed against them. A council held at Rome (A.D. 1059) enacted that no married priest should celebrate mass, or the laity attend such a mass. It also passed other important canons. One, that no clerk should take preferment from a layman, either for money or gratuitously, was aimed at the whole system of lay patronage; another, that no layman should judge a clerk, claimed exemption for all the clergy from all civil courts;

another established a new procedure for papal elections, depriving the emperor of his recently acquired right of nomination, and the clergy and people of their primitive right of election, and vesting the appointment substantially in the cardinals.

On the death of Nicholas II., in 1061, a contest ensued. The young emperor treated the recent canon as a nullity, and nominated Cadolaus, Bishop of Parma, as pope, under the name of Honorius II. The Hildebrandine party chose Anselm of Lucca, and after a bloody conflict enthroned him by night in St. Peter's as Pope Alexander II. A political revolution decided the question in favour of the latter. The empress-mother was forced to acknowledge Alexander, and became a nun in the Roman convent of St. Petronilla. Honorius, after much fighting, was compelled to shut himself up in the Castle of St. Angelo, where he held out for two years, and then retired to his see of Parma, which he retained till his death, not formally resigning his pretensions to the papacy, but making no active attempt to enforce them. The Norman conquest of England occurred during this pontificate.

Alexander died in 1073, and at his funeral a loud outcry arose from the clergy and people demanding Hildebrand as his successor. The cardinals elected him. He took the name of Gregory VII., thus at once testifying his gratitude to his first patron, Gregory VI. whose pupil and chaplain he had been, and proclaiming his acknowledgment of him as a legitimate pope.* Hildebrand, with a caution we should hardly have expected, declined consecration until the consent of the emperor had been obtained.

Gregory VII. soon began to develop the dazzling idea of a universal spiritual monarchy which his great genius had conceived. His theory was that the pope is chief governor of the Church ; that bishops can only be appointed with his consent, and may be deprived at his will; that his authority supersedes their diocesan authority ; that he alone is entitled to make new laws for the Church ; and that no council may be accepted as a general council without his decision to that effect. From this he deduced a control over sovereigns. Christ is the King of Christendom, and

* See page 211.

the pope is Christ's vicegerent, and has a right to watch over the conduct of kings as of other men, to correct their morals, to depose them if their government is un-righteous, and to absolve their subjects from their vows of allegiance. He claimed as direct fiefs of the holy see Spain, Saxony, Bohemia, Hungary, Denmark, Poland, Provence, Corsica, Sardinia, England, and Ireland. In cases of conquest and disputed or doubtful successions he assumed power to confer a legitimate title on sovereigns, requiring them to accept their kingdoms as fiefs of St. Peter.

These claims were made possible by the state of the Church and the world. The general dissatisfaction of men with the tyranny of kings and nobles, and with corruptions in the Church, induced them to hail as a heaven-sent deliverer this representative of Christ, who promised to cleanse the Church and control the princes.

The question of Church patronage was the key of the position. The kings, nobles, and lay patrons generally had abused their trust ; Gregory sought to deprive them of it, and to vest it in the hands of the prelates, with a supreme control in the pope over all ecclesiastical benefices of the whole Church. A canon against lay investitures had been made in the last pontificate ; Gregory now renewed it with the resolve to enforce it. But the quarrel of the investi-tures was postponed to other questions more pressing. Germany was in a miserable state of misrule and confusion. Henry IV. was dissolute and tyrannical. Saxony was in rebellion, many of the nobles disaffected. The pope summoned the emperor to appear at Rome to vindicate himself from the charges brought against him by his subjects. This assumption of authority naturally enraged the emperor, who replied by an exercise of the ancient imperial authority over the bishops of Rome ; he sum-moned a council at Worms (A.D. 1076), at which he enter-tained accusations against Gregory, and the council decreed his deposition. The pope replied by excommunicating the king, declaring his subjects released from their allegiance, and depriving him of his dominions. He also excom-municated those who had taken part in the proceedings at Worms. The partisans of the emperor fell away from him, and the emperor found himself almost alone. The prince

R

and prelates of Germany met at Tribur (A.D. 1076), and came
to a resolution that if Henry could obtain the papal absolution within a year from the time of his excommunication
they would accompany him to Rome, and would aid him
in driving out the Normans, who had seized part of his
Italian dominions ; but if unabsolved by the end of the
year he should forfeit his kingdom. Meantime he was to
dismiss his excommunicated advisers and live as a private
man.

The year of grace was drawing towards its close when
Henry left Germany, accompanied by his wife Bertha and
their infant child, crossed the Alps in a winter of extraordinary severity, and found himself honourably received
by his Lombard subjects, who were opposed to the Hildebrandine party, and hoped that the emperor would overcome and depose the pope. The pope was advancing north-
ward to attend a council to which he had summoned Henry
at Augsburg. On hearing of the approach of the emperor
with a large train, he turned aside to Canossa, a strong
Alpine fortress where occurred that dramatic scene which
has ever since been regarded by some as the supreme
display of the power of the Church, by others as the supreme
exhibition of priestly arrogance.

The emperor followed the pope to Canossa and sought
his absolution in order to avert the forfeiture of his kingdom,
offering to submit to any terms. At length the pope proposed that Henry should give proof of his penitence by
surrendering to him the ensigns of royalty and acknowledging that he had rendered himself unworthy of the
kingdom. Henry, driven to extremities, consented. He
was admitted, alone and unattended, clad in the coarse
robe of a penitent and barefooted, within the second of the
three walls which surrounded the castle, and there in the
courtyard he remained three winter days fasting and
neglected. On the fourth day he sought an interview with
the Countess Matilda of Tuscany and Hugh, Abbot of
Cluny, who were present in the castle, induced them to
become sureties for his fulfilment of any conditions imposed
on him, and was then admitted to the presence of the pope.
The king, a man of tall and remarkably noble person, in his
coarse robe and with bare feet, prostrated himself before

the pope, whose small and slight person was withered with austerities and bent with age. The pope was moved, and received him with tears ; and on his promising to submit his conduct to an inquiry at a diet of German princes, at which the pope should preside, and to abide by its sentence, Henry received absolution. The pope celebrated mass, at which the emperor was present, and then the pope received him at his table with friendly conversation.

The German princes, however, set up a rival emperor— Rudolph, Duke of Swabia—and three years of war ensued. Gregory kept himself neutral until Rudolph was victorious, and then declared for the victor. Henry replied by summoning a council at Mayence and appointing a rival pope, Guibert of Ravenna, as Clement III. Loyalty was rekindled by Henry's misfortunes ; in another battle Rudolph was slain ; Henry marched into Italy and besieged the pope in Rome. The siege lasted three years, when Henry took the city ; Gregory took refuge in the Castle of St. Angelo ; the antipope was enthroned in St. Peter's, and Henry and Bertha received their imperial coronation at his hand on Easter-day, 1084. In May the pope's Norman allies, returned from an expedition in the East, for three days plundered and ravaged Rome, and eventually set fire to the city ; this conflagration destroyed a large portion of ancient Rome. Gregory left the capital in disgust and retired to Salerno, and died in the following year (May 25, 1085).

He left a powerful party resolved on carrying out his policy. On his death-bed he nominated Desiderius, Abbot of the great monastery of Monte Cassino, as his successor, or if he should refuse, then either Otho of Ostia, Hugh of Lyons, or Anselm of Lucca. Desiderius (after long reluctant delay) was the next pope, as Victor III., and Otho succeeded him as Urban II.

The quarrel between the emperor and the holy see continued with varying fortune. Henry, taught by his misfortunes, exhibited vigour and firmness, recovered the allegiance of his nobles and the affections of his people. The popes did not withdraw the excommunication, but the German Church disregarded it, and its bishops received investiture from the emperor, in spite of the canons to the contrary. His rebellious son Henry lavishly professed obedience to the Roman see, but as soon as by its help he secured the throne (A.D. 1106) proved a more determined and more successful opponent of papal pretensions than his father. In 1110, having pacified Germany, he crossed the Alps, occupied Rome with a great army, and demanded of the pope his coronation as emperor and recognition of his right of investiture. The pope hesitating, Henry carried him off with the cardinals, and for sixty days kept them prisoners in neighbouring castles, while his troops ravaged the country. The pope yielded, acknowledged the right of investiture, crowned Henry V. as emperor, withdrew the excommunication on Henry IV., and the emperor returned in triumph to Germany. But the emperor being gone, the pope withdrew his concessions and the quarrel of investitures continued through the pontificates of Urban, Paschal, and Callixtus II. At length both parties, wearied by the contest of half a century, came to a compromise at the Diet of Worms (A.D. 1123). The right of free election and consecration to bishoprics and abbacies was secured to the clergy and monks ; on the other hand election was to take place in the presence of the emperor or his deputy, and the new prelate was to receive investiture of the temporalities by the sceptre, without any payment and perform the feudal duties of his estates.

During the next eighty years, down to the election of Innocent III., the pretensions of the papacy were acted on from time to time according to the more or less vigorous character of the pope, and as opportunities occurred. Innocent III. (A.D. 1178) carried the papal authority, during a reign of eighteen years, to a still greater height than Gregory VII. He assumed a supreme authority over the kings of Christendom. His interference in their mutual quarrels, and in their administrations, was often effectual, and his interposition often sought by them. Philip of France appealed to him against Richard of England. When Richard was imprisoned by the emperor, his mother, Queen Eleanor, appealed to the pope to procure his release. " Has not God," she asks, " given you the power to rule nations and kings ? " Innocent enjoined the King of Aragon to restore his debased coin, excommunicated Sweyn for usurping the crown of Norway, compelled the

King of Leon to repudiate his wife, as being within the forbidden degree of relationship, and compelled Philip of France to take back the lawful wife whom he had divorced. Peter II., King of Aragon, voluntarily surrendered his kingdom to the pope, and received it back as a fief of the holy see, thus securing the powerful protection of the papacy against ambitious neighbours. Innocent compelled John of England to lay his crown at Pandulph's feet, and to receive back his kingdom as a fief of the holy see.

The papal prerogative continued at this height throughout the thirteenth century, towards the end of which Boniface VIII. put forth still more extravagant pretensions. He claimed Scotland as a fief, and forbade Edward I. to war against it ; but Edward summoned a parliament, which concurred with the king in a firm repudiation of the papal claim. The pope forbade the clergy to contribute to the revenue of their governments ; but Edward retorted by withdrawing from his clergy the protection of the law, and Benedict gave them permission to pay what the king demanded. Germany made a similar stand, the Diet of Frankfort declaring (A.D. 1338) that he whom the electors chose was king and emperor without needing the approbation of the pope. Philip the Fair of France, also firmly withstood his pretensions. The pope was about to issue a bull deposing the king, when his minister, William of Nogaret, seized the pope's person, who was then staying at Anagni, a town in the Campagna ; and although the pope was rescued, he died after a few days, of fever, brought on by excitement.

The authority of the popes had not depended on the numbers they could bring into the field against emperor or king, but upon the moral influence they exercised over the minds of the subjects of king or emperor. The oppressions of kings and nobles, and their abuses of ecclesiastical patronage had made clergy and people welcome the interference of the popes of the eleventh and twelfth centuries as heaven-sent deliverers. But as the popes of the twelfth and thirteenth centuries developed their extravagant pretensions to a universal temporal monarchy, their ambition shocked the common sense of nations, their aggressions on the rights of national churches offended the clergy, the rapacity and venality of the Roman Curia alienated the whole Christian world, and from that time a steady reaction set in against the papal pretensions. This was assisted by the revival of the study of ancient Roman civil law. The jurists showed from the Pandects of Justinian what had been the relations of emperor and pope in the ancient empire ; and it was generally assumed that through Charlemagne the German emperors were the heirs of that ancient empire of the West. The other great European monarchies also yielded nothing of their own sovereign authority. A Peter of Aragon, or a John of England, might submit from interest or fear, but princes like Henry V., Edward I., and Philip the Fair, were bold enough to defy the superstitions which fenced the papacy ; and, when public opinion had once turned against the popes, were strong enough gradually to force back and limit the once irresistible power. The reaction steadily increased, till it produced the Reformation of the sixteenth century.

CHAPTER XXXIV

THE CRUSADES

AMONG the most remarkable religious movements of the Middle Ages were the expeditions for the recovery of the Holy Land from the power of the Mohammedans, which were called Crusades.

In 637 A.D. Jerusalem had capitulated to the Caliph Omar (p. 185). It was a holy city alike to the Jew, Christian, and Mohammedan. Under the mild rule of the earlier caliphs the Jews retained their synagogues, the Christians some of their churches and monasteries, while the Mohammedans appropriated some churches to their own worship, or built mosques beside them. Pilgrims from all Christendom visited Palestine, and made the round of the sacred places without let or hindrance ; and narratives * which returned pilgrims wrote are still extant and full of curious interest.

In A.D. 969 the Fatimites severed Egypt and Syria from the caliphate of Baghdad, and set up an independent sovereignty, with Cairo as capital. In 1055 the Abbasside Caliph of Baghdad called in Togrul, son of Seljûk, chief of a Turkish tribe which had embraced Islam, who made himself temporal sovereign with the title of sultan, leaving to the caliph the dignity of representative of the prophet and religious head of his followers. Under Togrul's third successor, Tûtûsh, the warlike Turks wrested Syria from the Fatimite sovereignty, and restored it to the caliphate of Baghdad. The government of Jerusalem was given to a fiery zealot called Orthok.

* Those of the Bordeaux Pilgrim, c. 333, Eusebius, A.D. 360 ; Jerome and Paula, A.D. 382 ; Etheria (Sylvia), 385 ; Eucherius, 440 ; Theodorus, 530 ; Antonius Martyr, 570 ; Arculf, A.D. 670 ; Willebald, A.D. 754 ; Bernard the Wise, A.D. 870 ; Sæwulf, A.D. 1103 ; Abbot Daniel, 1106 ; Sigurd, A.D. 1111 ; Benjamin of Tudela, A.D. 1173, and others, down to the " Stacions of Rome " of the 14th and 15th centuries. Most of these are readily obtainable in the publications of the Palestine Pilgrims' Text Society.

The Turks, with the zeal of recent converts, were intolerant of Christianity. Christian residents and the numerous pilgrims began to suffer indignities and injuries at their hands. Many holy places and things, objects of enthusiastic reverence and devotion to Christians, were wantonly defiled by the Turks. The pilgrims on their return filled Europe with the story of the profanation of holy places, and of the insults and dangers the faithful had to endure when visiting the birthplace and sepulchre of the Lord. The Byzantine emperors being unwilling or unable to help, Symeon, Patriarch of Jerusalem, in A.D. 1093, commissioned Peter the Hermit, on his return home from pilgrimage, to ask help from the Western Church.

The idea of a crusade was not altogether a new one. Nearly a hundred years before, Pope Sylvester had issued a letter in the name of Jerusalem to the universal Church, beseeching all Christians to sympathise with the afflictions of the Holy City, and to aid her by gifts if they could not do so by arms ; and an expedition recovered Sardinia from Saracen rule, but effected nothing further. Gregory VII. also, in 1074, in a letter to the emperor, Henry IV., stated that 50,000 men from both sides of the Alps were ready to march against the infidels of the East if the pope would lead them, and said that he earnestly wished to undertake the expedition, especially as it might lead to reconciliation with the Greek Church.

Peter the Hermit duly presented the request of the patriarch to the pope, Urban II., and claimed to have had a vision in the Church of the Holy Sepulchre, in which our Lord bade him rouse the Western nations to deliver the Holy Land from the infidel. The pope authorised Peter to preach a crusade. Peter went through Italy and France, preaching in churches and highways, drawing an affecting picture of the desecration of the holy places by the infidels, and of the indignities and injuries they inflicted on Christian pilgrims, and so moving people by his impassioned eloquence that a religious enthusiasm spread like a contagion among all classes throughout Europe, and produced one of the most remarkable movements which Christendom had witnessed. In the spring of 1095 the pope held a council at Piacenza, attended by 200 bishops, 4,000 clergy, and 30,000 laity.

No building could contain the multitude, and the sessions were held in the plain outside the city. A holy war was proposed ; ambassadors from the Greek emperor, Alexius Comnenus, stated the distress of the Christians and the danger of an invasion of Europe by the formidable and fanatical Turks. People were moved to tears, and many on the spot bound themselves by oath to engage in the crusade. Another council, at Clermont, in France, in the autumn of the same year, was still more numerous and enthusiastic. Fourteen archbishops, 225 bishops, 100 abbots, and vast numbers of clergy and people filled the town, and encamped in the surrounding country. The pope addressed the people from a pulpit in the market-place ; his exhortation to a crusade was interrupted by a cry from the whole assemblage : " God wills it ! " and when he ceased thousands took the vow and attached the cross upon their shoulders. The contagion seized all classes—knights and nobles, bishops and abbots, monks and clergy, artizans and peasants, old men and children, and women of all ranks. Landowners sold or pledged their lands and artizans their tools, and those who had nothing to sell begged, to raise funds for their equipment and expenses. Every one who assumed the cross was taken under the protection of the Church ; the monk left his cloister, the servant his master, and the debtor his creditors ; women put on men's dress, and clerics appeared with armour and weapons. The impatience of the people could not be restrained. Before the nobles could complete their military arrangements a vast crowd set out, with Peter the Hermit for their leader and a knight named Walter the Penniless for military commander ; another followed under a priest named Gottschalk ; a third under a priest named Folkmar. Without order or discipline, unprovided with armour or money, encumbered by numbers of infirm old people, women, and children, these companies of pilgrims straggled across Europe ; no depots of provisions or arrangements for their reception had been made ; they were reduced to theft and plunder ; their progress was consequently opposed by the inhabitants, and they perished in multitudes by the way. The strongest and best-provided found themselves at last at Constantinople. They were ferried across the Bosphorus, and marched on Nicæa, the capital of the newly-established Turkish sovereignty of Roum. A great battle was fought under its walls, and the Christians were defeated. A pitiless massacre ensued of the helpless multitude, and their bones were gathered into a great heap, which remained for many years a monument of the luckless enterprise.

Meantime the responsible chiefs of the crusade were maturing their preparations. Among them were Godfrey of Bouillon (son of that Count Eustace of Boulogne who was one of the chief followers of William the Conqueror in his invasion of England), with his brothers Eustace and Baldwin ; Robert Duke of Normandy, the Conqueror's eldest son ; Hugh of Vermandois, brother of the King of France ; Count Raymond of Toulouse ; Count Robert of Flanders ; Stephen of Blois (whose son succeeded to the throne of England). They were subsequently joined by the Norman Bohemund of Tarentum, and his nephew Tancred the hero of the crusade. Each leader was in absolute and independent command of his own followers. They took different routes through Europe, some by land, some by sea, and rendezvoused at Constantinople. Nicæa fell before their arms, and a second victory at Dorylæum made them masters of the kingdom of Roum. Here Baldwin was induced to separate from the rest, and march with his followers upon Edessa, where he at once won himself a principality. The rest marched, with frequent skirmishes and much suffering from want of necessaries, as far as Antioch. For eight months they lay round Antioch, suffering the utmost extremity of famine, before the crafty Bohemund negotiated with a traitor an entrance for his troops into the town. They were in turn besieged by a Turkish army ; but sallied out, defeated the Turks, and captured provisions and spoil.

While before Antioch, they received news that the Fatimite caliph had attacked the Turks, and recovered Jerusalem ; and that he offered peace to the Christians and the old freedom of access to the sacred places. They, however, disdained to turn back without accomplishing the task for which Europe had already made such heavy sacrifices. After a siege of forty days, Jerusalem was taken and given up to slaughter and sack.

Godfrey was chosen king of the new kingdom. At its greatest extent, in the time of Baldwin II., the Latin kingdom of Jerusalem comprehended all the sea-coast from Tarsus, in Cilicia, to El Arish, with the exception of Ascalon and Gaza ; in the north it extended inland to Edessa, beyond the Euphrates ; and in the south the ranges of Lebanon and the Jordan formed its boundary. This territory was divided into states, which all owned fealty to the kingdom of Jerusalem. A code of law was drawn up, called the Assizes of Jerusalem, which is the completest monument we possess of the feudal constitution of the Middle Ages. The princes of the states subdivided the land among their followers, castles were built in commanding situations, and the European adventurers entered into the enjoyment of the Syrian fields and vineyards. The Latin conquest of this portion of the territory of the ancient Greek Church, instead of helping to heal the schism, only widened and embittered it ; for the crusaders got rid by one means or another of the Greek patriarchs of Antioch and Jerusalem, and everywhere substituted clergy of the Roman obedience.

The succession of Kings of Jerusalem was, Godfrey (A.D. 1099), Baldwin I. (A.D. 1101), Baldwin II. (A.D. 1118), Fulk (A.D. 1131), Baldwin III. (A.D. 1144), Amaury I. (A.D. 1162), Baldwin IV. (A.D. 1174), Baldwin V. (A.D. 1185), Guy of Lusignan (A.D. 1186), Conrad (A.D. 1192), Henry (A.D. 1192), Amaury II. (A.D. 1197–1205).

In 1118 Hugh de Payens founded the order of the Knights of the Temple, and shortly afterwards the Hospitallers were reorganised on the same military basis. The two orders had head-quarters in Jerusalem, and dependent houses, which were in fact castles, in various parts of the Holy Land. They were gradually endowed with estates in all countries of Europe, and drew recruits from the noblest families. They formed two divisions of a standing army, with whom war was not so much a profession as a religion.

The Latin dominions in the East owed their stability for many years as much to dissensions amongst the Mohammedans as to the valour of the Frankish defenders. But in the time of Baldwin III. the Turkish power was reunited, and the Latins weakened by mutual jealousies and distrust.

The consequences were soon felt in the fall of Edessa (A.D. 1147), and the loss of all territory east of the Euphrates. The peril of the Latin kingdom again aroused the West. Pope Eugenius proclaimed a second crusade ; at his request the illustrious St. Bernard preached it throughout Italy, France, and Germany, and it excited almost as wild an enthusiasm as the first holy war.

The second crusade consisted chiefly of French and Germans, who set out in the spring of A.D. 1157. The Germans numbered 71,000 knights and men-at-arms, with a great multitude of light horse and foot, commanded by Emperor Conrad in person. The French army numbered about 60,000 harnessed knights and foot in proportion, and was led by its monarch, Louis VII. The treachery of the Greeks left them without supplies, and the Turks harassed every foot of their march across Asia Minor. The great majority perished miserably by famine and sword. The scanty remnant assisted the Latins in a siege of Damascus, but when the attempt failed, through treachery as was believed, the Germans returned home in disgust. The French king wintered in Jerusalem, and returned home by sea at Easter without further achievement. Europe had been drained of men and treasure with no results but defeat and disgrace.

The contest continued in the Holy Land in a series of battles and sieges, with occasional truces, between the Latins and their Turkish and Saracen neighbours. The kingdom was often aided by noble pilgrims with large armed trains, who visited the holy places, fought a campaign against the infidel, and returned home again. But even these successes would hardly have sustained the kingdom, but for the contest between the Turkish sultans of Baghdad and the Fatimite viziers of Cairo, which prevented both from efficiently prosecuting the Christian war. This old strife was now about to end. In A.D. 1173, Shawer was the Vizier of the Fatimite caliph, Nureddin was Sultan of Baghdad. The Arabs, hard pressed by the attempt of King Amaury, in conjunction with a Greek force, to seize Egypt, asked the Turks for help. Nuraddin sent a large force into Egypt under Shirkuh, his commander-in-chief, with whom was his nephew, the well-known Saladin. Meantime Shawer had got rid of the Christians by a treaty.

But the Turks seized Shawer while on a visit to their camp.
The Fatimite caliph in terror for himself sent to demand
Shawer's execution, and named Shirkuh vizier in his stead.
Soon afterwards Shirkuh died, and Saladin succeeded him
both as commander-in-chief of the Sultan of Baghdad and
Vizier of the Caliph of Egypt, and soon made himself
undisputed master of Egypt. In the same year Nureddin
died, and Saladin succeeded as sultan, and thus united two
of the long-severed sections of the Mohammedan power
—the Saracenic and the Turkish—a union which threatened
speedy destruction to the kingdom of Jerusalem. The new
king, Guy of Lusignan, had not the qualities needed at such
a crisis, the princes were divided by rivalries, the nobles had
fallen into the luxurious habits of the East, the two military
orders were insubordinate ; the Templars suspected of
treachery ; the general state of morals was excessively
depraved.

Saladin, in A.D. 1187, provoked by assaults upon his
territory, and especially by the plunder of a caravan of
travellers, of whom his mother was one, invaded the country,
defeated the Christian forces with terrible slaughter in
the battle of Hattin, or Tiberias, marched to Jerusalem,
which fell after a fortnight's siege, overran the country,
admitting the Syrian Christians to submission and tribute,
until the sea-port of Tyre alone remained in the hands of
the Christians.

Moved by this great misfortune the pope, Clement III.,
proclaimed a third crusade, and the great sovereigns of
Europe responded to the call—Richard of England, Philip
of France, Frederick of Germany, the Dukes of Austria and
Burgundy, the Count of Flanders, and many lesser princes
and nobles, and the great trading republics of Genoa and
Pisa. But again these vast forces were wasted. The Germans marching by the old overland route were harassed by
the old treachery of the Greeks, and by assaults of the Turks.
The generalship of their great emperor, however, carried
them successfully through both. They conquered the
Turks with great slaughter in a battle before Iconium, took
the city, and marched boldly through the rocky defiles of
Cilicia. But in the passage of a river near Tarsus the
emperor was drowned ; the discipline of the army was no

longer maintained. On reaching Antioch many died of the heat and intemperance ; many returned home. Of all the German hosts the younger Frederick brought only 5,000 to assist in the siege of Acre ; and there he too fell a victim to the climate. Richard of England, who displayed a genius for military affairs, had built a great fleet, with which he sailed from Marseilles straight to Acre. Philip had been conveyed by the fleet of the Genoese. But when the various princes assembled at Acre, their operations were hindered by a thousand jealousies, and after two years Acre surrendered to Saladin and the French king returned home in disgust. Richard continued another year and more, and recovered a large part of the coast from the enemy. But the Christian forces were thinned by war and disease ; Richard's strength began to give way under the climate, and after having advanced within a day's march of Jerusalem, he was at last obliged to conclude a three years' truce with his great foe and leave his enterprise unachieved.

Other crusades were from time to time undertaken.

On the death of the great Saladin (A.D. 1173), the inferior ability of his successor seemed to promise success to a renewal of the crusade, and the new pope, Celestine III., urged it. Richard of England declined to take part ; the King of France levied taxes from his people for it but diverted them to other uses. The emperor, however, sent a considerable force to the Holy Land, which recovered the sea coast ; but there was no concerted action between them and the Latins of the East, and the conquests were ephemeral. On the death of Henry (A.D. 1197) the Germans concluded a six years' truce with the enemy and returned home.

Innocent III. (A.D. 1178–1216) earnestly promoted the holy war. But Richard was now dead, Philip of France occupied with difficulties at home, and in Germany Otho and Henry were contending for the empire. A great excitement, however, was kindled in France by the preaching of a priest named Fulk, of Neuilly-on-the-Marne, and a number of French princes took the cross, the chief being the young Count Theobald of Champagne, brother of Henry, the late King of Jerusalem. They made an alliance with Venice—which at this period had surpassed her rivals,

Genoa and Pisa, and was the greatest oi the trading republics—for the transport and provisioning of their armies, on condition that conquests made should be equally divided between the allies. The great object of this crusade was an invasion of Egypt, which the statesmen of the West held to be the most vulnerable point of the Saracen monarchy. When the main body of the crusaders mustered in Venice, they agreed as part of the price to be paid to the Venetians, to aid them in the recovery of Zara, in Dalmatia, lately taken from the republic by the King of Hungary. Old Dandolo, the doge, though ninety-four years of age, took the cross and accompanied the expedition. At Zara they were invited by Alexius, the son of Isaac Angelus, the Emperor of Constantinople, who had been dethroned by his brother Alexius, to aid him in recovering the throne. He promised them in return the co-operation of the empire in the crusade, and the re-union of the churches. The crusaders accepted the offer, and sailed for Constantinople. The magnitude, strength, beauty and riches of the city astonished the Western visitors. After the first assault the usurping Alexius fled, his blinded brother Isaac was brought out of his prison, replaced upon the throne, and unwillingly ratified the terms his son had made. But dissensions soon arose, and the terms on which the Latins had come to Constantinople were unfulfilled ; so they resolved to take possession of the city. They took it in a second assault, and gave it up to slaughter and pillage. The plunder in gold and silver and objects of ancient art was immense, and Western Europe was enriched with the spoils. The Sainte Chapelle in Paris was built by St. Louis to enshrine the " crown of thorns," which was among the Constantinopolitan treasures, and the bronze horses which adorn the front of St. Mark's at Venice were part of the Venetians' share of the spoil. The conquerors elected Count Baldwin of Flanders to the vacant throne ; a Venetian, Morosini, was elected patriarch, and the Greek empire and Church received a Latin sovereign and hierarchy.

The Latin empire, however, never established itself, and after fifty-seven years (1204–1261) the Greeks, in alliance with the Genoese, deposed Baldwin II., and restored the Greek sovereignty in the person of Michael (VIII.) Palæologus.

The celebrated Simon de Montfort, one of the princes of this crusade, had refused to turn aside to the attack on Zara, and proceeded straight to the Holy Land, but with his scanty forces nothing could be effected.

The successor of Innocent III. was equally bent on the prosecution of the holy war. Some reinforcements were sent to Acre. A larger body sailed for Egypt in November, A.D. 1219, and after a siege of sixteen months took Damietta, but marching thence to Cairo found the way barred by the enemy; a pestilence broke out in their camp, the country round them was inundated by opening the sluices of the Nile, and the Christian army was compelled to make peace and return. In 1228 the Emperor Frederick sailed in person with a considerable force to Acre, and by a treaty with the Sultan Kameel, obtained possession of Jerusalem (with the exception of the Temple, which was to remain in the custody of the Saracens, but to be open to Christians), Nazareth, Bethlehem, Sidon, and other places, and entered Jerusalem in triumph.

Fifteen years afterwards, viz., in A.D. 1244, both Moslem and Christian succumbed before a new power. The Chorasinians, who had gained possession of Persia, were now pressed by the advance of the Tartars. That numerous race, inhabiting the plains of Asia, had been formed into a great empire by Genghis Khan early in the thirteenth century; had appeared in a vast swarm and overwhelmed Russia in 1226; had been turned aside from Germany by a brave resistance; had overrun Poland, and poured down towards the south. The Chorasinians, pressed on by this irresistible force, fell upon Syria and Palestine, captured Jerusalem, slaughtered the people, robbed the churches, and violated the tombs and sacred places. The pope vainly tried to rouse Europe to its rescue. At this time Louis IX. of France—St. Louis—being hopelessly ill, desired to receive the cross, and from that time began to recover. He displayed the Oriflamme, raised the forces of France, and sailed for Cyprus, and thence to Damietta. Damietta was taken with ease, but on the march to Cairo famine, pestilence, and the cutting of the Nile, again reduced the

Christian army to surrender to the enemy. St. Louis undertook a second crusade in 1270, landed in Tunis, but died there, and the expedition came to nothing. Edward, the heir of England, who had taken the cross, did not arrive till after the death of the French king, and sailed to Acre, where he fulfilled his vow in the defence of the city. The Christians finally lost their last footing in the Holy Land A.D. 1291.

The two hundred years of the crusades dissipated the power and distributed the possessions of the great nobles, and this helped to build up a middle class with civil rights, to emancipate the peasants, and establish the authority of the popes. It also introduced into the West the learning and arts of the East.

CHAPTER XXXV

WALDENSES AND ALBIGENSES

THE medieval Church was not free from the erroneous doctrines and schismatical movements which have distracted the Church in all ages. In the eleventh and twelfth centuries there was a movement of religious earnestness among the people, and the abuses of the Church set earnest minds in antagonism to the established order, while their lack of sound religious knowledge left them a prey to error and fanaticism. The Paterines of the eleventh century were chiefly disaffected opponents of the clergy; the Cathari (or Puritans) of the twelfth century had derived from the East doctrines of a pronounced Manichean complexion, such as that matter is the source of evil; that the world was made by a secondary deity; that men's bodies are the production of a creator of evil, and their souls imprisoned in them; that our Lord had not a real body, was not really born, or really died. Among opponents of the existing order was Peter de Bruys, who in the early half of the twelfth century, in Languedoc and Provence, established a sect called Petro-Brussians. He preached against infant baptism and the grace of the Eucharist; and, since God will accept sincere worship wherever offered, advocated the pulling down of churches. He was at last seized and burnt by the populace. Henry, a monk and hermit, a little later held clandestine assemblies in Poitiers, Bordeaux, and Toulouse, in which he preached somewhat similar doctrines. He was at last brought before Eugenius III., at the Council of Rheims (A.D. 1148), and committed to prison. At the same period a sect of violent fanatics sprang up in Antwerp, who rejected all external ordinances of religion and the ordinary ties of morality. They were suppressed by St. Norbert, the founder of the Premonstratensians.

The most remarkable sect of this century was that of the Waldenses. These sectaries have excited much interest at various times among ourselves, from the fact that in the thirteenth century they claimed to have existed continuously as a distinct body, in the valleys of Piedmont, from the pure early ages of the Church, and to have maintained unbroken primitive doctrine and discipline ; and some continental reformers, who held the whole medieval Church to have apostatised, regarded these Waldenses and their successors, the Wyclifites and Hussites, as a continuous chain of witnesses for the pure Gospel. The question has been very carefully examined, and it seems certain that the sect of the Waldenses was founded about A.D. 1170, by Peter Waldo, a rich merchant of Lyons, who employed two ecclesiastics to translate for him the Gospels used in Divine service, and other portions of Scriptures, and passages of the Fathers. With the desire to live more closely after the example of our Lord and His apostles, he gave all his wealth to the poor, associated others with him, and began to preach in the streets of the city and in neighbouring villages. The Archbishop of Lyons forbad this unauthorised teaching, and, when Peter declined to desist, excommunicated and expelled him from the diocese. Peter sent two of his party to Rome to request the pope, Innocent III., to sanction their labours. Had the pope done so, the foundation of an order of preaching friars would have been anticipated by half a century. He refused, and they became a sect, under the name of the Poor Men of Lyons, and gradually developed doctrines in opposition to those of the Church. They spread into the south of France, Lombardy, Aragon, and Germany. In the year 1198, the Bishop of Turin obtained from the Emperor Otho authority to use forcible measures against them. Their adherents became very numerous ; they taught publicly, established schools, proselytised energetically. Their claim for laymen to preach rapidly developed, as in similar cases, into a claim for their preachers to administer all Christian rites, and they finally limited salvation to their own sect, as the only one like Christ and His apostles. They were sound in faith as to the doctrines which relate to God, and received all the articles of the creed ; so that in many respects they bore a striking resemblance to modern Protestant sects, who look back to them with natural interest.

About the beginning of the thirteenth century sects multiplied so greatly as to call for the serious notice of the authorities. In the south of France especially the doctrines of the Cathari had spread even among higher classes ; the gentry ceased to put their sons into holy orders, the clergy were held in general contempt. Bishops issued sentences of excommunication and banishment, but heretics were protected by the princes ; the pope sent special legates, but their mission was not very successful.

It was the age of the crusades, and the pope proclaimed a crusade against the heretics of southern France, commonly known by the name of Albigenses who were akin to the Catharists and Paulicians of earlier days.

A large army was assembled of Frenchmen, Normans, and Flemings. Simon de Montfort, Earl of Leicester, was appointed chief in this holy war. Beziers was the first town they attacked. Catholics joined with Catharists in patriotic resistance to the invaders. The besiegers repulsed a sally, and pressing close on the retreating townsmen, entered the place with them, and a general massacre ensued. Arnold, Abbot of Citeaux, the pope's legate with the crusading army, when asked how Catholics were to be distinguished from heretics, answered, " Kill them all ; the Lord knoweth them that are His." After the massacre the city was plundered and set on fire. At Carcassonne, which made a prolonged resistance, its viscount was decoyed into a conference by an assurance of safe conduct, and then treacherously seized, Abbot Arnold declaring that no faith was to be kept with one who was faithless to his God. He was cast into prison, where he died. Raymond, Count of Toulouse, who had at first given a forced adherence to the crusade, at length took up arms in defence of his territory with the help of the King of Aragon. The war continued for six years, with alternating fortunes and great cruelties on both sides. Raymond submitted in 1214. Simon de Montfort was confirmed by the Council of the Lateran in possession of the greater part of his conquests, a small part being reserved for Raymond's son. The council also enacted (for the first time) that heretics should be made over to the secular arm, which should exterminate heresy under pain of ecclesiastical censures.

[A useful summary of the two faiths and of their ultimate fate has been recently given in *The Albigensian Heresy*, by the Rev. H. J. Warner (S.P.C.K. 1922), from which we quote part of his concluding words (p. 91); after pointing out the Catharist dualism as one of the main causes of the failure of Albigensianism he continues : " The Albigensian Christ offered no atonement, all-sufficient and complete, for the sins of men, and so brought to men no peace which passeth all understanding. Their ' perfect ' life was impracticable and would have brought society to an end. All agree that the Waldenses, who started *de novo* from the Scriptures and endeavoured to live and teach according to their precepts, began solely as reformers and not schismatics. Yet even they could not keep themselves untainted by the stronger and more numerous Catharists, and it was easy for their enemies to convince an uncritical age that there was no difference between them. The Albigenses have perished ; the Waldenses remain " ; while on the historic side a reviewer of the book added two valuable comments : " The strength of the Cathari lay in the weakness and scandals of the Church," and Catharism " perished not under the sword of the Crusaders, but before the higher morality displayed by the Franciscans and Dominicans in the early days of those orders."—ED.]

CHAPTER XXXVI

THE POPES AT AVIGNON AND THE GREAT SCHISM

THE death of Boniface VIII., the result of the bold violence of William of Nogaret, the minister of Philip the Fair (p. 245), closed the great period of the papacy which began with the rise of the Hildebrandine influence in the pontificate of Leo IX.

Boniface's successor, Benedict XI., rescinded many of his predecessor's obnoxious acts, and conciliated the French king. His pontificate lasted only a few months, and Philip, after long intrigue, secured the election of a Frenchman, who was entirely in his interests. The new pope, Clement V., summoned the cardinals to attend his consecration, not at Rome, but at Lyons. He lived in various parts of France for five years and then fixed his permanent residence at Avignon, where, nominally beyond the French territory but entirely under the influence of the kings of France, the papal see continued for the next seventy years, the pope being always a Frenchman, as were also the majority of the cardinals. A papal delegate, usually the Bishop of Orvieto, represented the pope in Rome. A new race of noble families —the Colonnas and Orsini, Gaetani and Savelli, tyrannised over the imperial city. The short-lived tribunate of Rienzi was an attempt to realise the dream of an independent Italy by the revival of the ancient republic, an attempt which had the enthusiastic adhesion of Petrarch ; Dante's mind turned rather to a restoration of an universal empire, with Rome for its capital ; while both plans contemplated the reformation and maintenance of the spiritual authority of the pope. Rome was still the religious capital of Christendom, pilgrims still flocked to its shrines ; but the papal court was at Avignon. The pope built a vast palace fortress there, which still remains ; around it the cardinals built noble houses. Ecclesiastical causes from all countries were brought there for decision ; canonists attended upon the courts ; crowds of suitors filled its streets, and the city grew to accommodate them ; streams of gold flowed to this centre. Clerks seeking ordination, clergy and prelates seeking promotion, usurers and merchants, scholars and artists, swelled the crowd. The luxury of the papal court was great, the licence of the papal city shameless.

The rapacity of the popes * increased. John XXII., the most insatiate of pontiffs, reserved to himself all the bishoprics in Christendom. Benedict XII. assumed the privilege of nomination to all benefices vacant by cession, deprivation, or translation, and this soon became a permanent rule of the Roman chancery. Benefices were sold without disguise, and so managed as to bring in the greatest revenue possible. A rich vacancy was made the first link in a chain of translations, each bringing its own profit. John XXII. first imposed upon all benefices the tax called annates, or first-fruits, being the first year's income paid into the coffers of the pope.

The countries of Europe were thus drained of vast sums. England, the last to submit to the papal pretensions and now the first to oppose these extortions, set the example of refusal to submit any longer to this rapacity. The Parliament of Carlisle, *temp.* Edward I., addressed a strong remonstrance to the pope. A Parliament of Edward III. passed the Statute of Provisors, refusing the pope the patronage of English benefices.

The death of Gregory XI. was the commencement of the Great Schism between two lines of popes, who for above forty years divided Western Christendom into two almost equal camps.

The origin of the schism was as follows. Gregory XI. dying in Rome, the cardinals proceeded to elect his successor. The Roman populace surrounded the place of meeting with clamours for a Roman, or at least an Italian, pope, who should reside in Rome and not at Avignon. The cardinals elected a Neapolitan archbishop, under the

* The succession is : (1305) Clement V. ; (1316) John XXII. ; [Nicholas V., anti-pope, 1328-9 ;] (1334) Benedict XII. ; (1342) Clement VI. ; (1352) Innocent VI. ; (1362) Urban V. ; (1370) Gregory XI.

name of Urban VI. (A.D. 1378). This satisfied the people.
The pope began his reign by a sentence of excommunication
against cardinals who had been guilty of simony. The
cardinals, in return, withdrew to a neighbouring town,
declared their own previous selection null, because made
under compulsion, and chose a French cardinal, under the
name of Clement VII., who took up residence at Avignon
with the cardinals of his party, Urban remaining at Rome.
In similar cases of rival popes in former times there had been
little doubt who was the legitimate pope ; the anti-pope
was usually the creature of some prince or faction, with only
a scanty local recognition. But now the question of right
was doubtful, and each received wide and conscientious
support. To Urban adhered Italy, the German Empire,
England, and the nations of N. Europe ; to Clement France,
Spain, Scotland, and Sicily. The general wish was for a fresh
undisputed election. But personal ambitions and interests
prevented this. The Roman succession was continued by
the successive elections of Urban VI. (1378), Boniface IX.
(1389), Innocent VII. (1404), and Gregory XII. (1406).
The Avignon line was continued in Clement VII. (1378) and
Benedict XIII. (Peter di Luna) (1394). Christendom had
to support two papal courts instead of one, both unwilling
to submit to any diminution of the customary wealth and
splendour. The exactions and venality of the earlier
Avignon popes appeared light in comparison with the
practices of both rivals during the schism. The popes of
both lines were continually pressed to abdicate ; some
solemnly swore to do so, and evaded their oaths. It was
even said that there was a tacit collusion between them.
The spectacle of two papacies, each anathematising the
other as antichrist, and both behaving like antichrists,
shook the authority of the papacy ; there was universal
uncertainty and distress of conscience throughout the
Western Church. If schismatical ordinations and sacraments were invalid, who could feel sure that it was not his
own party which was in schism ? Persons since accounted
as saints by the Church anathematised one another, while
the whole Church cried aloud for a settlement and for a
general reformation " in its head and in its members."
At length the cardinals of both parties deserted their popes

and summoned a general council. The Council of Pisa (1409), deposed both popes, and elected a new pope in Alexander V. But the deposed popes continued their pretensions and found supporters, and the action of the council had only created a third line of rival popes. From 1378 to 1409 the Western Church was divided into two, and from 1409 to 1415 into three, obediences. Alexander V. was succeeded by John XXIII. (1410), who very reluctantly summoned another council to meet at Constance, in A.D. 1414. This council at once deposed John himself, and then proceeded to consider fully the state of the Church.

CHAPTER XXXVII

REFORMING COUNCILS OF THE FIFTEENTH CENTURY

A GENERAL reform of the Church " in her head and her members " was now the watchword throughout Europe, and was understood to mean that the necessary reform must begin with the papal see. The Church must maintain the superiority of a general council to that of the pope. Nicholas I. had enunciated the theory of the supreme sovereignty of the pope over the whole Church, and the Hildebrandine popes had forced this principle upon the Church. The Council of Pisa enunciated the theory that the Church represented in a general council was superior to the pope, and might depose him ; and the Council of Constance forced the acceptance of this principle upon the popes.

At the Council of Constance the first step of importance was a return to primitive precedent by the appointment of the Emperor Sigismund to protect and preside over the council. The next important step was holding the council out of Italy. A third was the admitting to the council, besides prelates and bishops of whom the majority owed their positions to the abuses it was desired to reform, representatives of universities, canonists, and theologians. There were actually assembled 300 bishops, deputies of fourteen universities, and 300 doctors. A fourth step was the method of voting by nations. The Italian bishops were then (as ever since) so much more numerous than those of other churches, that individual voting would have given them a very unfair advantage. It was therefore resolved that the council should divide itself into four nations—the Italian, German, French, and English—each with equal rights, and that the majority of the four should prevail. The deposing of the rival popes left a clear course for the contemplated reforms.

The famous decrees of the fourth and fifth sessions of this council declared that " every lawfully convoked œcumenical council representing the Church derives its authority immediately from Christ ; and every one, the pope included, is subject to it in matters of faith, in the healing of schism, and the reformation of the Church." This decree was passed without a dissentient voice. That the council was œcumenical cannot be disputed. The two small fractions of the Church which still obeyed Gregory XII. and Benedict XIII. ultimately gave their adherence to the council, as is shown in the concordat of Narbonne, and John XXIII. had been deposed with universal consent. A committee of reformation made recommendations to the council, which, if carried into effect, would have destroyed the machinery by which Rome had absorbed so much of the revenues and patronage of the Church, and corrected many of the evils which had so long oppressed the Christian commonweal. But the council disagreed on the next great step. The Germans and English joined the Italians in favour of an Italian candidate, the Cardinal Colonna, and he was elected as Martin V. The new pope used all his power and influence to evade any real reformation ; continued the policy of playing off the nations one against another ; concluded separate concordats with them ; and terminated the council as soon as possible. Only a few reforming ordinances came into force ; most of the articles of these few were so drawn as to leave open a door for the renewal of abuses, and in a short time things reverted to their former course.

One important feature in the history of the Council of Constance must not be omitted here, viz., its action against Wyclif, Huss, and Jerome of Prague. The council extracted forty-five propositions from the writings of Wyclif, which it condemned as unsound, and decreed that since he had died an impenitent heretic his bones should be exhumed and cast out of ecclesiastical sepulture. The sentence was duly executed by the English ecclesiastical authorities.

It next dealt with the religious controversy which was disturbing Bohemia. Huss, a man of learning and distinction, Rector of the University of Prague, confessor to the queen, preacher at a chapel in the capital founded for the purpose of encouraging preaching in the vernacular tongue, had taught the doctrine of Wyclif.* His teaching found many adherents in Bohemia, but also excited great opposition. Cited to appear before the pope, he had appealed to a general council. The Emperor Sigismund wished the council to settle these Bohemian troubles, and requested his brother Wenceslaus, the King of Bohemia, to send Huss to Constance, promising him a safe-conduct. Jerome of Prague, one of his chief followers, voluntarily joined Huss at Constance. The council induced Sigismund to allow his safe-conduct to be set aside, on the plea that the council was greater than the emperor, and that no safe-conduct extended to the protection of a heretic from the punishment of his heresy. The two men were imprisoned and treated with rigour, and ultimately condemned and burnt at the stake—Jerome on May 30th, Huss on July 6th, 1416. This provoked an outbreak of resistance to Rome throughout Bohemia, which brought the most terrible misfortunes upon the kingdom. The opposing parties engaged in a ferocious civil war, extended their hostilities into neighbouring countries, and thus brought upon themselves repeated invasions in return.

Huss and Jerome were regarded by their party as martyrs, their pictures were placed in the churches, and leading Hussites bound themselves to maintain their doctrines. Nicholas of Hussinecz and John Ziska came to the front— the one as the political, the other the military, chief of the movement. The right of the laity to the sacramental cup was their watchword. Ziska gathered a powerful force, displayed the chalice embroidered on his banners, and wherever he went enforced the administration of the Eucharist in both kinds. On the 22nd July, 1419, a great number of Hussites encamped on a hill near Aust, and inaugurated their enterprise by a general celebration of the Holy Communion in the open air. The previous confession was omitted, the clergy celebrated without any distinctive vestments, the altars, 300 in number, were uncovered tables, the chalices of wood. Forty-two thousand persons—men, women, and children—communicated, and the celebration

* Except on the subject of the Eucharist, on which he held the current Roman doctrine.

was followed by a great love feast. This camp became permanent, and grew into a town called Tabor—tabor being the Bohemian for tent. Ziska and his armed followers marched upon Prague, where they killed some magistrates, and plundered the convents. The excitement threw King Wenceslaus into an apoplexy, of which he died. Bohemia fell to his brother, the Emperor Sigismund whom the Hussites especially hated, as the traitor who had given Huss his safe-conduct and then abandoned him to his fate. They broke out at once into open rebellion, renewed their attack on the convents of Prague, and slaughtered the monks. The movement spread to other places. Churches and monasteries were plundered, their ornaments destroyed, and in many places the buildings reduced to ruin. A small proportion of the Bohemians, especially among the higher classes, adhered to the Roman Church ; the University, the inhabitants of the capital, and many among the middle classes were in favour of a moderate reform ; a numerous party, chiefly of the populations of the towns and the peasantry, went to fanatical lengths, and mixed up with their religious extravagances political opinions of a republican and socialistic complexion. The more moderate reformers were called Calixtines (from calix, chalice) ; the more extreme Taborites, and camp meetings formed an important feature of their system, where the people assembled in tens of thousands to receive the Eucharist in both kinds, and where their fanaticism was kept alive by fervid oratory. Ziska, the Taborite leader, possessed extraordinary military genius, and made his followers into a formidable army, which was everywhere victorious. The war was carried on with horrible ferocity. On the taking of a town all the inhabitants were slain, except, perhaps, a few women and children ; churches were burnt, with those who had taken refuge in them ; priests and monks were burnt in pitch. The Catholics made equally cruel reprisals. Palaces, castles, even whole towns, were destroyed ; manufactures and foreign commerce ruined, tillage neglected, adventurers flocked to both sides for the sake of plunder. The emperor collected a great army to subdue the country, but the Bohemians suspended their mutual hostilities and under Ziska defeated the invaders. A second and third time Sigismund invaded the country, but each time recoiled with disgrace before the heroic defence.

When the Council of Bâle met (p. 271), the Bohemians were invited to send a deputation for the discussion of their differences, and four articles, known as the *Compactata*, were agreed upon as terms of peace. The clergy were to be permitted to administer the Eucharist in both kinds to such adults as should desire it ; in all other points the Bohemians were to conform. The more moderate were willing to accept these terms, the more violent refused, and in a battle at Lipau between the two parties the moderates were victorious, and the power of the fanatics was effectually broken. In 1436, at a great assembly at Iglau, the *Compactata* were received as a settlement of the religious state of Bohemia, and a few days later Sigismund was formally accepted as their king. But the death of Sigismund in the following year was followed by a disputed succession and a long minority. The Taborites were not silenced, and not until after a diet held at Prague in 1444 was the Calixtine doctrine generally accepted. The Taborite practices gradually died out, except in the town of Tabor itself. But next the pope repudiated the *Compactata*, as having only been agreed upon by the Council of Bâle after its rupture with the pope ; and on the refusal of George Podiebrad, the king, to reduce Bohemia to entire conformity, he declared him a heretic, pronounced sentence of deposition, and proclaimed a crusade against him. Matthias Corvinus, King of Hungary, responded to the invitation, to wrest the sceptre out of the hands of George, but was unsuccessful. On the death of George the Bohemians elected Ladislaus, a Polish prince, who made good his claims by force of arms, and eventually succeeded Matthias in his Hungarian kingdom. A fresh settlement of religion was concluded. Each of the great parties was to enjoy perfect religious freedom, and on a vacancy in any parish the new incumbent was to be chosen from the party to which the old one had belonged.

By one of the decrees of Constance another general council was to be held in five years, a second after another seven years, and thenceforward every ten years. Accordingly at the end of five years Martin V. summoned a council at Pavia, which, on account of plague, was removed to Siena, and then dismissed by the pope on account of the fewness of those present.   Shortly before his death, however, he summoned a new council at Bâle. Eugenius IV., the new pope, immediately after its opening proceedings pronounced the council dissolved, with a view to its reassembling a year and a half later at Bologna. Relying, however, on the decrees of Constance, it refused to suspend its session. It received the adhesion of kings, princes, universities, and bishops ; even many cardinals and papal officials, in spite of sentences of excommunication, deserted the pope and went to Bâle ; the public opinion of Europe was against the pope, who prudently gave way, retracted his hostile bulls, and professed his devotion to the Universal Church and the holy Œcumenical Council of Bâle. He sent four cardinals to preside over the council as his legates, who were admitted to the presidency on swearing, in their own names, to the decree already passed in the second session, that a general council has its authority immediately from Christ, and that all men, including the pope, are bound to obey it in matters relating to faith, to the extinction of schism, and the reform of the Church in head and members.

The subjection of the papacy to the authority of a general council seemed irrefragably established. For three years and a half the council continued its sessions ; decrees of reform were drawn up, and the pope signified his agreement with them ; but at the end of that time a plausible pretext arose for the removal of the council to Italy, of which the pope took advantage.

The Emperor John Paleologus, threatened by the power of Amurath II., sought aid from the West for the preservation of the Greek empire and Church. The pope invited him to a conference with a view to the reunion of the churches, and desired that the meeting should take place in some Italian city. A majority of the council passed a decree that the meeting should be north of the Alps ; but the minority of the council passed an irregular decree in accordance with the pope's wishes, got it by a stratagem signed with the seal of the council, had it read in one corner of the cathedral, while the decree of the majority was read from the pulpit, and sent it to the pope. The pope accepted it as the legitimate act of the council, and issued a bull transferring the council to Ferrara.

The pope's council opened at Ferrara, January 8, 1438. Of the fathers assembled at Bâle only two transferred themselves to Ferrara. Of the great nations only England obeyed the summons of Eugenius. The Bâle council declared Eugenius deposed, and elected Amadeus, ex-Duke of Savoy, under the title of Felix V. The feeling of the Church was, however, opposed to the creation of another schism; the sovereigns, many bishops, and other important members of the council, absented themselves; and though the council continued to sit, it grew continually feebler. Nicholas V., the successor of Eugenius, induced Felix to resign, and the schism soon came to an end.

The rival council of Ferrara meanwhile was busy with its negotiation with the Greeks. The differences between the Eastern and Western divisions of the Church had grown up gradually. A rivalry of honour began when Constantine removed the seat of empire to the shore of the Bosphorus, and this lay at the bottom of all subsequent dissensions, and was the real cause of the final schism. The question of the worship of images was the first doctrinal question on which the two churches took opposite sides; but the addition in the Western Church of the " filioque " to the creed without the authority of a general council was, and has continued to be, the chief doctrinal cause of division. There were other minor questions, as the use of leavened or unleavened bread in the Eucharist, the marriage or celibacy of the clergy; but the great obstacle was the pretensions of the Roman see to supremacy over the whole Church, and the refusal of Constantinople to surrender the liberties of the independent patriarchates to Rome, and to sacrifice the ancient constitution of the Church to the papal system of a monarchy.

Since the final breach in 1054,* when the two churches formally excommunicated one another, several efforts for reconciliation had been made. The present crisis offered

* Page 278.

hope. All Europe desired reconciliation, on the broad general ground of the wickedness of the schism.

Both the pope and the Council of Bâle, each professing to be the true representative of the Western Church, sent a pressing invitation to the emperor and the patriarch, each sent a fleet to convey them, and the rival fleets were with difficulty prevented from engaging in combat within sight of Constantinople. The emperor and the dignified ecclesiastics and their numerous suites accepted the pope's invitation, and came to Ferrara. The discussion of the disputed points occupied fifteen months, in the course of which the plague broke out at Ferrara, and the council was removed to Florence. The Greek theologians showed skill and courage, but were not fairly treated. The pope had engaged to defray their expenses, but doled out rations to them, withheld supplies in order to coerce the unwilling, and gave liberal bribes to those open to such inducements; while their own emperor also put pressure upon them. In the end they arrived at a compromise on the four principal points : (1) as to the procession of the Holy Spirit, the Greeks explained that in limiting themselves to the ancient words of the Niceno-Constantinopolitan Creed, " proceeding from the Father," they did not intend to exclude procession from the Son, but only procession from the Father and the Son as from two principles, while the Latins declared that they did not hold the double procession in this latter sense. Each party was to retain its own form of the creed. (2) As to the Eucharist, either leavened or unleavened bread might be used and each church should retain its own custom. (3) It was agreed that souls are purified by suffering after death and may be benefited by the prayers and alms of the living ; but on the difference as to the nature of purgatory nothing was decided contrary to the opinion of either Church. (4) The Roman pontiff was declared to have the primacy of the whole world, as the successor of St. Peter who was chief of the apostles and vicar of Christ ; and that to him, in St. Peter, was given by the Saviour full power of teaching, directing, and governing the Church, according as contained in the acts of the œcumenical councils and in the sacred canons. The other patriarchal sees—Constantinople, Alexandria, Antioch, and

Jerusalem—were to hold the same order as of old, to wit, with all their privileges and rights preserved.

The fourth decision was the critical one, and was arrived at with great difficulty.

The pope claimed a recognition of his supremacy over the whole Church, " according to Scripture and the sayings of the saints." The emperor pointed out that the sayings of the saints—*i.e.*, the courtly rhetoric to be found in the letters of ancient bishops and emperors to the bishops of Rome—could not be accepted as definitions of the legal relations subsisting between the two parties, and that the canons of councils ought to be taken as the rule. When the papal theologians sought to overwhelm the Greeks with the mass of forged and corrupted passages in the pseudo-Isidore and Gratian, they answered shortly and drily, " All these canons are apocryphal." The compromise at length effected was ambiguous. It ran that the pope had authority from Christ to rule and feed the Church " according as contained in the acts of the œcumenical councils and in the sacred canons." But the text of this famous passage has been corrupted ; and whatever text be taken, its meaning is disputed. The Greeks say that they intended to acknowledge the pope's authority only so far as it was in accordance with the ancient councils and canons. The Latins say that the reference to ancient councils and canons was not a limiting clause, but only a confirmatory reference, and was not only an acknowledgment of the plenary authority claimed, but also that this authority was according to ancient rule and precedent.

This attempt at a reconciliation of the schism between East and West thus utterly failed. Everywhere on their return journey the Greeks were met with marks of disapprobation. The patriarch of Constantinople had died a month before the conclusion of the treaty, and leading ecclesiastics refused to accept the vacant dignity ; and when one was found to accept it the people turned their backs upon his benediction. The patriarchs of Alexandria, Antioch, and Jerusalem held a council, at which they denounced the Council of Florence, and declared the new patriarch of Constantinople, and all bishops appointed by him, to be deposed, and threatened the emperor with the censures of the Church.   The Primate of Russia, who had attended the council and accepted its decrees, on his return was upbraided by Prince Basil, at the public service of the Church, as a traitor ; the clergy deserted him, he was imprisoned in a monastery, and at length escaped to Rome.

The King of France, on the occasion of the quarrel between the pope and the Council of Bâle, summoned an assembly, which was attended by the dauphin and princes of the blood, many nobles, bishops, and other ecclesiastics and laymen, at Bourges.   It was resolved to continue to recognise the pope, but also to accept the reforming decrees of the council, with certain modifications required by the circumstances of France.   Thus originated the " Pragmatic Sanction of Bourges," the first comprehensive codification of what have since been called the Gallican liberties.   They recognised the supreme authority of general councils, secured the freedom of Church elections, and rejected the papal encroachments on rights of patronage and the revenues of benefices.   Twenty years later Pius II. (Æneas Silvius Piccolomini, who, as secretary to the Council of Bâle, had written in its defence), at a council held at the Lateran, condemned the Council of Bâle, and declared the Pragmatic Sanction to be heresy.   Nevertheless it continued to be the law of France till Pius II. induced Louis XI. to abrogate it, bribing the king by conceding to the Crown the patronage of the Church.   The Parliament of Paris remonstrated with the king, refused to register his edict, and continued to act on the Sanction as legal, and it continued to be law till the time of Francis I.   Leo X. induced that king to agree to a Concordat, and he, with great difficulty, coerced the Parliament and Church into its acceptance.

The German electors also, at the Imperial Diet of Mayence (1439), recognised Eugenius as pope, but accepted the reformation decrees of Bâle.   But the pope, by intrigues and bribes, and by giving the princes large rights over the German churches, triumphed over the opposition, and in 1448, by the Concordat of Vienna regained many of the advantages he had surrendered.

On the whole, the Church relapsed into its old state of

corruption. The popes steadily resisted any attempt to summon a new council. They proceeded by honours and preferments to win over men of literary talent ; a new race of writers set themselves to rehabilitate the old theories of papal power. The popes never, indeed, assumed anything like the Hildebrandine attitude towards the Christian sovereigns, and the sovereigns were careful to maintain their power over their national churches, and their rights as against the pope ; but the abuses of the court of Rome even increased, and, from Rome, corruption and vice spread over Europe. From 1464 to 1503 the Christian world endured the rule of such popes as Paul II., Sixtus IV., Innocent VIII., and Alexander VI., each of whom seems to have striven to exceed the vices of his predecessors. The Church cried out against the universal wickedness and corruption, but no one could see from what source a reformation could arise. A Dominican preacher, about 1484, said, " The world cries for a council, but how can one be obtained in the present state of the heads of the Church ? No human power avails any longer to reform the Church through a council, and God Himself must come to our aid in some way unknown to us."

CHAPTER XXXVIII

THE GREEK EMPIRE AND CHURCH FROM THE EMPRESS IRENE, 780, TO THE FALL OF THE EMPIRE, 1453

WE continue our sketch of the Eastern empire in chapter XXVI from the reign of the Empress Irene. She was dethroned by her treasurer Nicephorus (802), and in exile on the Isle of Lesbos earned a scanty subsistence by the labours of her distaff.

A series of usurpations followed: Stauracius; Michael I.; Leo (V.), the Armenian; Michael (II.), the Stammerer; Theophilus; Michael (III.), the Drunkard, the Elagabalus of the Eastern empire. In his reign (842) occurs one of the chief points of contact between the Eastern and Western Churches. Ignatius, Patriarch of Constantinople, was deposed by Michael (or rather by his uncle, the Cæsar Bardas, who administered state affairs while his nephew wallowed in vice), and the able and learned Photius was consecrated in his place. Ignatius appealed to his brother-Patriarch of Rome, Nicholas I., not to recognise the intruder. Nicholas excommunicated Photius, who retorted the excommunication. The quarrel between the churches was embittered by their rival claims to the ecclesiastical obedience of Bulgaria.* Next came Basil, the Macedonian (867), who founded a dynasty which lasted through the reigns of five emperors, for one hundred and sixty years.

On the death of Constantine IX., the last male heir of the Macedonian family, its blood still occupied the throne in the person of his daughter Zoe, who brought the imperial title and power to her successive husbands, Romanus III., Michael IV., and Constantine Monomachus; and next in the person of Theodora, married to Michael IV., Stratisticus. While Theodora, now a widow, was sole empress, the final

* See page 230.

rupture of the Eastern and Western branches of the Church
was consummated. The swords of the Normans had terminated the Greek power in Apulia, which had formed part
of the Greek empire since Justinian's reign, and brought
its churches under the Roman obedience. The patriarch,
Michael Celularius, issued a pastoral to the flock thus torn
from his care, warning them against the errors of the Latins.
The pope, Leo IX., sent ambassadors to complain of this
insult, and obtaining no redress, the papal envoys laid on
the altar of Sta. Sophia a formal sentence of excommunication, which the patriarch retorted (1054). The pretensions
of the popes to sovereignty over the whole Church had by
this time been matured ; all future attempts at reconciliation failed in that point, and the breach continues to the
present hour.

By a bloodless revolution the noble family of the Comneni succeeded to the throne ; first Isaac Comnenus (1057),
then, after an interval Alexius (1081), the emperor in whose
reign the first crusaders passed through Constantinople on
their way to the Holy Land. He was succeeded by his son
John, the Handsome, an able and warlike sovereign, who
ruled well, and kept the Saracens in effectual check.
Manuel, his son, was the greatest hero of the imperial line
of the East ; he extended his conquests in the West,
strengthened himself by marriages and alliances with
Western princes ; made overtures to the pope, Alexander III., for a reconciliation of the churches, and aimed
at the reconstitution of the ancient grandeur of the Roman
empire by recovering the obedience of the West. Andro-
nicus, the last of the Comneni, the hero of a most romantic
career, usurped the imperial throne in 1183. A revolt of
the people dethroned him and raised Isaac Angelus to the
purple. He was dethroned and imprisoned by his brother,
Alexius Angelus ; but his son escaping fled to the West,
repaired to Venice, where the warriors of Europe were
assembling for the second crusade, and induced them by
great promises to undertake his father's cause (p. 255).
But the people of Constantinople rose against the Angeli
and their Latin allies. A second siege put the city into the
hands of the crusaders with the rights of conquerors (1204).
They plundered the city of its wealth and art treasures, the

accumulation of a thousand years, and divided the empire among themselves; the French took the city and title of emperor, and seven Latin emperors succeeded one another during a period of fifty-five years. A Latin patriarch was appointed, and the Latin Church established as that of the new empire. The Greek nobles fled to the other great cities of the empire, and set up independent sovereignties. " Whatever was learned or holy, whatever was noble or valiant, rolled away into the independent states of Trebizond, Epirus, and Nice."

Theodore Lascaris (1206–1222) set up his standard at Nicæa, and he and his son-in-law and successor, Ducas Vataces, whose reigns extended over fifty years, gradually won back the whole of the European provinces, hemmed in the imperial city, and reduced its Latin emperors to seek in vain for Western succours to avert their impending fate. In 1261, under Michael Paleologus, the city itself was surprised, and the Greek empire restored at Constantinople in the family of the Paleologi. Several islands (Lesbos, Chios, Rhodes) were soon afterwards wrested out of the hands of the Franks; but the Asiatic side of the empire was left exposed to the Turks.

Michael sought to avert a Western assault upon the restored empire by an ecclesiastical reconciliation with the pope. This was effected (for the time) at the Council of Lyons (1274). But the subject despots of Ætolia, Epirus, and Thessaly refused the union; the immediate subjects of Michael resisted it, and endured severe persecution; on the emperor's death the whole Eastern Church and people abjured the enforced and unreal union.

In the reign of John Paleologus (1341—1391) the Ottoman Turks conquered nearly all the empire, excepting only the city. The emperor again sought in person the succour of the West, offering as its price a reconciliation with Rome. The history of the Council of Ferrara, in which this was effected with imperfect and transitory success, has been told in the preceding chapter.

The emperor submitted to the pope, but on his return with empty coffers his person was detained at Venice for sums borrowed there, till his son Manuel raised money in Constantinople and sailing with it to Venice relieved his father, and pledged his own person as a security for the rest of the debt. Thirty years later, when the empire was on the verge of ruin, Manuel again visited the chief states of Europe to beg for aid. He was received everywhere with imperial honours and respectful pity; but the King of France was a lunatic (Charles X.); the King of England (Henry IV.), a usurper, whose throne was threatened by internal discord; while the power of the papacy was paralysed by the great schism.

But the impending fate of the empire was postponed for another fifty years. The invasion of the Mongul leader Timour (or Tamerlane) called the Sultan Bajazet away to the defence of his own dominions, and his defeat and capture in the battle of Angora (1402) shattered the Turkoman power.

The severed portions of the Turkoman dominions were reunited in Mahomet I., who was succeeded by two warlike sovereigns. But the armies of Amurath II. were occupied with John Hunniades, who at Belgrade arrested the westward progress of the Ottoman arms, and with Scanderbeg, Prince of Albania, who for twenty-three years kept up a war of independence among his mountains.

The end of the empire of Constantine was, however, approaching. On the death of the Emperor Manuel Paleologus, his son Constantine was chosen as his successor (1448). Three years afterwards the young and enterprising Mahomet II. succeeded Amurath, and at once resolved on the conquest of the imperial city. The fall of the city is, perhaps, the noblest chapter of its history, and the last of the emperors died the death of a hero after a protracted and desperate defence in the breach, resisting the last overwhelming assault, and his body was found buried under a heap of slain, May 29, 1453.

The Turks tolerated the Church in their dominions, the sultans retaining the power which the emperors exercised of instituting and deposing the Patriarch of Constantinople. The organisation of the ancient churches has been maintained. There are still the four Patriarchs of Constantinople, Alexandria, Antioch, and Jerusalem, but they rule over a scanty, scattered, and oppressed people [and the Great War of 1914–18 made their position sadder and more difficult rather than better].

CHAPTER XXXIX

MEDIEVAL DEVELOPMENTS

SOME of the most striking features in the general aspect of the Church and the popular religion of the Middle Ages are as follows :—

In the general external aspect of the Church : (1) the papal supremacy, and all which flowed from it ; (2) the disciplinary organisation of the Church ; (3) the constitution of the various bodies of the clergy.

In the popular doctrinal system : (4) the popular idea of the Eucharist ; (5) the cultus of the Blessed Virgin Mary ; (6) the cultus of local saints, with the pilgrimages and indulgences which sprang out of it ; (7) the belief in purgatory and masses for the dead.

1. The papal supremacy. We must not suppose that people generally submitted willingly to the papal rule. On the contrary, we know that princes questioned and resisted his authority, that national churches complained bitterly of infringements of their rights and the people generally of the venality and rapacity of the papal officials, and that some theologians questioned the Divine right of their rule. But the fact remains that the papacy had gradually grown up to a spiritual empire over the whole West, practically recognised by all men, and making itself everywhere felt. People might murmur, but they submitted as to a power they could not resist ; they might complain of venality and rapacity, but they went on bribing the officials of the Curia when they had any business at Rome.

2. The disciplinary action of the Church then presents a striking contrast to the utter and lamentable absence of discipline among ourselves. People were condemned to open penance for notorious sins, while to-day most lay offenders are unconscious that the Church even claims to exercise any control over their conduct. In those days the

Church took cognisance of every man's life. The canonical obligation of confession at least once a year subjected every man to paternal rebuke for sin and to private penance. But besides this private exercise of discipline, open vice subjected the offender to open rebuke and Church censures exposed him to the action and penalties of the civil law ; in short, the Church had laws, and those laws were regularly enforced. The archdeacon's apparitor, bearing a summons to some neighbour to appear before the ecclesiastical court for the scandal with which the neighbourhood was ringing, or for the Easter dues which he was backward in paying, was a familiar personage in town and village.

3. The outward status of the clergy more than anything else, perhaps, made the Church of those times differ in external aspect from the Church of this day. For two whole organisations of clergy, three if we include the military orders, have almost or entirely disappeared from several countries of Europe, and the status of the remaining order has been much modified in all. The great and wealthy monasteries, which were scattered over the face of Europe, are for the most part in ruins, and the learned and dignified members of the orders of Benedict and Cluny and Citeaux have disappeared from many parts of Christendom. The friars, whose houses existed in the suburbs of every town, and whose frocks, black, brown, or grey, were familiar in town street and on village green, in the castles of the nobles and the cottages of the poor, are no longer seen. Hermits and recluses have entirely vanished from their cells by road-side and churchyard. Prince-bishops have been reduced to the status of modestly-portioned officials of a struggling Church. The number of the secular clergy (except perhaps in Italy) is greatly reduced. The whole status and prestige of the Church is altered by the growth of other constituents of our modern society.

4. In the popular religion one great difference between pre-Reformation and post-Reformation days was in public worship.

At the former period the Church put the Holy Communion in its right place, as the chief act of Divine worship, and all attended it. But the sacrificial aspect of the Eucharist had been allowed to attain exaggerated proportions,

and the sacramental aspect of it to fall into neglect.
Though the great body of the people attended the eucharistic service every Sunday and holy day, they only communicated once a year. In modern days Morning Prayer and
sermon came to be popularly regarded as the chief service,
and Holy Communion as a supplementary and entirely
voluntary act of special devotion ; and in the reformed
churches this is only gradually being altered.

5. The cultus of the Blessed Virgin Mary entered very
largely into the popular religion. Elevated in popular
theology into some such mid-way place between God
and the mass of mankind as that into which Socinianism
would depress our Lord, she was accepted as the favourite
mediatrix between God and man. Her maternal relation
and authority were supposed to give her special power
with her Divine Son, while her sex and character were
supposed to make her specially accessible to feelings of
compassion. There probably was a distinction in the
worshipper's mind between the worship offered to God and
that which he paid to Mary, but it is not too much to say
that the Virgin shared with God the worship of the people.
The devout went to mass in the morning, and paid their
homage to the Virgin in the evening. Sunday was the
Lord's day, and Saturdays and all eves were devoted to the
Virgin. The Psalter and the Book of Hours were adapted
to the worship of the Virgin, and the Athanasian Creed
parodied into an assertion of all the medieval inventions
about her, ending with the clause, " This is the faith concerning the Virgin Mary, which except every one believe
faithfully he cannot be saved." The rosary consisted of
ten aves * to every paternoster.

6. The special devotion to local saints was also a very
prominent feature in medieval religion. Special saints
were adopted by nations, towns, families, and individuals
as their special guardians—St. George of England, St.
Denis of France, St. James of Spain, St. Bride of Douglas.
The holy places of Palestine were, as early as the fourth
century, objects of pilgrimage from all parts of the world ;
the shrines of the apostles and other numerous holy places

* The " ave " is an address to the Blessed Virgin Mary, the
Paternoster is our Lord's Prayer.

of Rome were next, in the popular estimation of Western
Christendom, to the holy places of Palestine. Each country
had its great shrines or relics which were famous throughout the West. Pilgrims came from all countries to visit
St. James of Compostella, the three kings of Cologne, the
crown of thorns at Paris, the Holy house of Loretto, the
holy coat of Trèves, and the shrine of St. Thomas of Canterbury. Every country had, besides, a number of saints
of merely national repute ; every diocese, every neighbourhood, its tomb, relic, or holy well. Pilgrimages to these
places formed a considerable feature in the religious and
social habits of the people, and connected with them were a
multitude of superstitions.

7. Lastly, the notions about purgatory and the efficacy
of masses for the dead exercised a considerable influence on
the popular mind. These notions influenced, though not
nearly so largely as is commonly supposed, the number of
donations given to the Church. When a new monastery or
a new church was built, the natural condition that prayers
should be said there for the donor and his relations was not
the sole object of his donation. Still a considerable number
of chantries were specially built and priests endowed for
perpetual mortuary masses, and nearly everybody
bequeathed some small sum to those who should attend
and pray for him at his funeral. The whole subject of
purgatory loomed large in the popular imagination. It
probably did both good and harm. Some it would deter
from sin by the belief that they would certainly have to pay
for every sin by terrible suffering. It would undermine in
others the resistance to a pressing temptation by the
thought they could pay for the indulgences of this life by
posthumous penalties, and so win heaven at last.

There was much which was false and corrupt in the
Church of the Middle Ages ; but we must not fall into the
notion that everybody held all these erroneous opinions,
or that they believed all these superstitions and carried
them all to their logical conclusions. In this medieval
Church there was a widespread tone of earnest religious
feeling, and it perhaps cultivated a high degree of saintli-
ness of character more successfully than modern times
have done ; it especially kept alive two great ideas which in

later times fell into neglect—the idea of worship and the idea of self-sacrifice.

Some of the further developments of the medieval Church are so important in relation to our present religious controversies that their history must be considered more fully.

The Holy Communion.—The Acts of the Apostles shows us that our Lord's institution of the memorial of His sacrifice at once took its place as the great act of worship in Christ's Church. St. Paul briefly enunciated the doctrine : " The cup of blessing which we bless, is it not the communion (the partaking) of the blood of Christ ? The bread which we break, is it not the communion of the body of Christ ? " (1 Cor. x. 16). The apostolic fathers speak of this sacrament in language which is vague as to doctrine, but shows that they held it in high estimation. Thus Ignatius says : " I desire the bread of God, which is the flesh of Christ ; and His blood I desire to drink, which is love incorruptible."

Justin Martyr describes the Eucharist in his Apology to Antoninus. He speaks first of the bread and wine as blessed by the presiding presbyter, and then says : " This food is called by us Eucharist, of which no one is allowed to take but he who believes our doctrines to be true, and has been baptized in the laver of regeneration for the remission of sins, and lives as Christ enjoined. For we take not these as common bread and common drink ; for like as our Saviour Jesus Christ, having been made flesh by the Word of God, had flesh and blood for our salvation, so we are taught that the food which is blessed by the prayer of the Word that proceedeth from Him by assimilation of which our flesh and blood are nourished, is the flesh and blood of Him, the Incarnate Jesus." We have not space to quote the long catena of passages from Irenæus, Tertullian, Origen, Cyprian, Athanasius, Cyril of Jerusalem, Jerome, Augustine, Theodoret, and later writers. They all speak n high terms of the sacredness and mystery and grace of the Sacrament and often in warm rhetorical language. They clearly believed in a real spiritual presence of Christ in the Sacrament ; they believed that the faithful communicant did receive the body and blood of Christ in the Sacrament ; and they sometimes use language of startling strength, which at first looks like a plain assertion of modern Roman doctrine. But the truth is, this doctrine had not arisen in their days ; they did not therefore speak with the caution which afterwards became necessary. Side by side with the most startling of these passages are others which serve to limit and define the meaning of the writer.

The modern Roman doctrine was not put forward till towards the middle of the ninth century. Paschasius Radbert, a monk of the Abbey of Corbie, was master of the monastic school, and a commentator on the Scriptures, and had attained some celebrity among the theological scholars of the age. He afterwards became abbot of his monastery. At the request of the abbot of the daughter house of New Corbie, Paschasius drew up a treatise on the Eucharist for the instruction of the younger monks of that house. The treatise obtained a reputation, and the Emperor, Charles the Bald, requested a copy of it. In this treatise the rhetorical phrases of the Fathers were literally understood and the doctrine of transubstantiation broadly expressed.* That this was the received doctrine of the Church was immediately contested. Rabanus Maurus, Archbishop of Mayence, Walafrid Strabo, Florus, and Christian Druthmar, all of them among the most learned men of the age, declared that there was no other than a spiritual change in the Eucharist, and that Paschasius' teaching was a novelty. On the other hand, Hincmar, the great Archbishop of Rheims, seems to show more or less sympathy with Paschasius' view, and Haymo, Bishop of Halberstadt, a commentator of great reputation, strongly supports the novel doctrine. At the request of the emperor

---

* He gives, however, no clear definition of the doctrine, and it was still later that it crystallized into the form best quoted in words used by the Council at Rome in 1059 under Pope Nicholas II., which required of Berengarius to pronounce an anathema rejecting in anticipation the consubstantiation theory of Luther, and defining the official Roman doctrine :—" If any one shall say that in the Holy Sacrament of the Eucharist there remains the substance of Bread and Wine, together with the Body and Blood of our Lord Jesus Christ, and shall deny that singular or wonderful conversion of the whole substance of Bread into His Body and of the whole substance of Wine into His Blood, there remaining only the species, *i.e.* accidents of Bread and Wine, which conversion the Catholic Church very aptly calls Transubstantiation, let him be accursed."—Ed.

the book was answered by Ratramnus, another monk of Corbie, in a work which had a great influence on the minds of the English reformers. He holds that " the change in the elements is not wrought corporally, but spiritually and figuratively ; under the veil of the material bread and wine, the spiritual Body and Blood of Christ exist. . . . One and the same thing in one respect hath the nature of Bread and Wine ; and in another respect is the Body and Blood of Christ. Both (the bread and wine), as they are corporally handled, are in their nature corporal creatures, but according to their virtue and what they become spiritually, they are the mysteries of Christ's Body and Blood." " By all that hath been hitherto said, it appears that the Body and Blood of Christ, which are received by the mouths of the faithful in the Church, are figures in respect of their visible nature ; but in respect of the invisible substance, that is, the power of the Word of God, they are truly Christ's Body and Blood."

The doctrine of Paschasius rapidly gained ground ; less rapidly in the Gallican Church ; and in the Saxon Church the primitive doctrine still held its ground to the time of the Norman Conquest.

A new controversy on the subject broke out a hundred years later. Berengarius had been the master of the cathedral school of Tours, and was now Archdeacon of Angers. He had a clearness and vivacity of method in his teaching, an originality and independence of mind, and had a high reputation throughout France for learning and piety. He was an opponent of the doctrine which Paschasius had introduced, and which had now become generally accepted. In 1049 he wrote to Lanfranc, then Abbot of Bec, in Normandy, expressing his surprise that he should maintain the doctrine of Paschasius. Lanfranc was absent, and the letter fell into other hands, and its contents became known at Rome. At a council held at Rome by Leo IX., in 1050, Berengarius was condemned unheard as a heretic. From this time to the end of his life in 1088, Berengarius lived a life of controversy and persecution. Twice he made his submission to a council of the Church,* overborne, not by arguments, but by clamour and threats, but did not cease

* See note, p. 286.

to retain and teach his own opinions. He entered into a controversy with Lanfranc on the subject. Lanfranc's book has been always preserved, and that of Berengarius was recovered in the last century. Berengarius's doctrine is not that mere figurativism which is sometimes attributed to him. " He distinguishes between the visible sacrament and the inward part or thing signified ; it is to the outward part only that he would apply the terms for which he had been so much censured—sign, figure, pledge, or likeness. He repeatedly declares that the elements are ' converted ' by consecration into the very body and blood of our Saviour ; that the bread, from having been something common, becomes the beatific body of Christ, not, however, by the corruption of the bread, or as if the body, which has so long existed in a blessed immortality, could now again begin to be ; that consecration operates not by destroying the previous substance, but by exalting it. It is not a portion of Christ's body which is present in each fragment, but He is fully present throughout." *

Successive councils condemned the views of Berengarius, and the doctrine of transubstantiation became the accepted doctrine of the Western Church. After the Norman Conquest, Lanfranc, one of the foremost champions of the new doctrine, became Archbishop of Canterbury, and the doctrine spread into England also.

In the early part of the thirteenth century the doctrine was formally defined and put forth as part of the authoritative teaching of the Roman Church. This was done under Pope Innocent III., by the famous Lateran Council, A.D. 1216. Its first chapter declares that " Christ's body and blood in the sacrament of the altar are really contained under the species of bread and wine, the bread being by the Divine Omnipotence, *transubstantiated* into His body and the wine into His blood." Lastly, the Council of Trent, A.D. 1551, carried this further by decreeing that by conse cration " there is made a conversion and change of the whole substance of the bread and wine into the substance of Christ's body and blood, which change has been fitly and properly termed transubstantiation " ; and the creed of Pope Pius IV. (A.D. 1563) declared that " the body and

* Robertson, iv. 363.

blood of Christ, together with His soul and divinity, are truly and really and substantially in the Eucharist, and that there is a conversion of the whole substance of the bread into His body, and of the whole substance of the wine into His blood, which conversion the Catholic Church calls transubstantiation."

In scholastic language the substance of a thing is that by which it is what it is ; the accidents comprise its form, texture, colour, taste, etc., *i.e.* all by which it is cognisable by the senses. Now the definition of transubstantiation is, that it is only the substance of the elements which is changed, the accidents remaining. But the distinction between substance and accidents cannot be scientifically held to-day, and this particular explanation of the Presence of Christ in the Eucharist is thus ruled out by a truer philosophy. As a matter of fact, while the unlearned multitude of the Middle Ages, and of modern times, have held the doctrine in the grosser form, the more learned and liberal-minded have from time to time put forth statements which show that there have always been those who interpreted the definition of the Presence in a sense which differed little if at all from that of the primitive Church. St. Bernard of Clairvaux (A.D. 1115) acknowledged no feeding but a spiritual feeding. Peter Lombard, the famous master of the Sentences (A.D. 1141), though speaking of the conversion of the bread and wine, declines to define whether that conversion be formal or substantial, or of some other kind. Thomas Aquinas (A.D. 1255) spoke of Christ's body as present, not bodily, but substantially—a distinction not easy to explain. Durandus (A.D. 1320) said that though we believe the presence, we know not the manner of the presence. Cuthbert Tunstall, Bishop of Durham (1474—1559), said that " before the Lateran Council it was free to every one to hold as they would concerning the manner, and it would have been better to leave curious persons to their own conjectures." Cardinal Cajetan, " the classical theologian of the Roman court," writes that " the real body of Christ is eaten in the Sacrament, yet not corporally but spiritually. Spiritual manducation, which is made by the soul, reaches to the flesh of Christ, which is in the Sacrament." Finally, Gardiner, in his controversy with Cranmer, says : " The Catholic teaching is, that the manner of Christ's presence in the Sacrament is spiritual and super-natural, not corporal nor carnal, not natural, not sensible, not perceptible, but only spiritual, the how and manner whereof God knoweth." *

Martin Luther † substituted a theory of consubstantia-tion (see note, p. 286), for the Roman doctrine of transub-stantiation, and other continental reformers imperilled the truth of the Real Presence itself, Zwingli representing the sacraments as " mere badges and tokens of a Christian man's profession." The reformed English Church rejected (art. xxv.) this low view, and also the false philosophy of the theory of transubstantiation, while accepting the Pauline definition of the Presence, in its art. xxviii. :—
" The Bread which we break is a partaking of the Body of Christ. . . . Transubstantiation (or the change of the substance of Bread and Wine) in the Supper of the Lord, cannot be proved by Holy Writ ; but is repugnant to the plain words of Scripture, overthroweth the nature of a Sacrament, and hath given occasion to many superstitions. The Body of Christ is given, taken and eaten only after a heavenly and spiritual manner. And the means whereby the Body of Christ is received and eaten in the Supper is Faith." But both here and constantly in the Prayer Book of 1662 is emphasised the Reality of the Presence after consecration. In the third exhortation in the Holy Com-munion service it is stated that " we spiritually eat the flesh of Christ and drink His blood " ; in the Catechism the " inward part is " the Body and Blood of Christ which are verily and indeed taken and received by the faithful in the Lord's Supper " to " the strengthening and refreshing of our souls by the Body and Blood of Christ as our bodies are by the Bread and Wine," and most clearly the faith of our Church in the Real Presence is shown by the use of our Lord's own words : " This is my Body, this is my Blood," at the most solemn moment of the Consecration

* Bishop Harold Browne's " Exposition of the Thirty-nine Articles," ii. 468.
† This passage beginning "Martin Luther" and ending "unhappily arisen," is an editorial addition to the original text. On the general subject of the asserting of a Real Presence in our Communion Office, see the still valuable section vi. in Sadler's *Church Doctrine, Bible Truth.*

and the repetition of this assertion in the administration ; statements which are driven home in the Prayer of Thanks-giving : " Thou hast vouchsafed to feed us . . . with the spiritual food of the most precious Body and Blood of Thy Son " ; while a warning against a crude material view of this Presence is added in the so-called Black Rubric which rejects " any corporal presence of Christ's natural Flesh and Blood." As Dr. Strong rightly says, " The fact that the Presence of Christ is *spiritual* is a reason for, not against, calling it *real*."

The English Prayer-book as proposed in 1928 emphasized the same doctrine as the following excerpts will show : (1) The Third Exhortation (already quoted), instead of being so seldom heard, was placed in the "Deposited Book " as a Preparation. The omissions made, though they leave one difficult phrase (" we are guilty of ") in the air more than before, do not include anything which would lessen the emphasis of its teaching on the point with which we are concerned. (2) Prayer of Consecration. Here is added : " with Thy Holy and Life-giving Spirit vouchsafe to bless and sanctify both us and these Thy gifts of Bread and Wine that they may be unto us the Body and Blood of Thy Son." (3) Alternative words of Summons to Com-municants. " Draw near and receive the Body of our Lord Jesus Christ . . and His Blood . . . take *this*, etc." (4) Thanksgiving. " Having now by faith received the precious Body and Blood of Christ " precedes the Prayer of Thanksgiving of the 1662 book. (5) Thanksgiving for the institution of Holy Communion. Here is provided as an alternative collect, the well-known form: "O Lord, Who in a wonderful sacrament . . . has given to us," etc., and as the Epistle and Gospel, 1 Cor. xi. 23–28, and St. John vi. 53–63.

The Church thus continues in its wisdom to emphasize the fact of the Real Presence without a dangerous attempt to define the " how." Out of such attempts most of the divisions in the Church have unhappily arisen.

The dogma of transubstantiation has never been adopted by the Greek Church.*

The Temporal Power.—" The ecclesiastical hierarchy

* It is difficult to see in what sense the writer meant this. The facts may be best given in a condensed extract from *A Dict. of the Eastern*

never received any territorial endowment by law, either under the Roman empire or the kingdoms erected upon its ruins." * "The early endowments of the Roman see consisted of estates, not only in Italy and the adjacent isles, but also in distant countries, as Gaul, Africa, Asia, the gifts of many different benefactors." †

The first accession to the Roman see of temporal authority over cities and provinces came through the connection of the popes with the Carlovingian family (p. 201).

If it was the intention of Pepin to give to the Pope the territory taken from the Lombards in supreme and absolute dominion, the subsequent history shows us that his son, at least, exercised sovereign rights over it, and treated the popes as feudatories, and the popes accepted the position, conferring on Charlemagne the title of emperor, and acknowledging themselves his subjects.

In the dissolution of the Lombard kingdom the inhabitants of the duchy of Spoleto sought a refuge from the storm by declaring themselves the subjects and servants of St. Peter, and completed by this voluntary surrender the circle of the ecclesiastical state.

At the same time that the forged Isidorean decretals (p. 205) were issued there appeared also another remarkable literary forgery, perhaps by the same hand, of a document

---

Orthodox Church in the art. "Transubstantiation:"—The Synod of Beth-lehem (1672), commonly called the Council of Jerusalem, accepted the term transubstantiation, approved a real change "into the real Body of the Lord itself," asserted that the substance of the bread and wine no longer remains, but there is the Body itself and the Blood of the Lord in the species and form of the bread and wine, that is to say under the accidents of the bread ; though the Russian Catechism of Philaret (1839) adds the qualification, if such it be, that "the word Transub-stantiation is not to be taken to define the manner in which the bread and wine are changed into the Body and Blood of the Lord, for this none can understand but God ; but this much only is signified that the bread truly, really, and substantially becomes the very true Body of the Lord and the wine the very Blood of the Lord," while the Catechism of Mogilas emphasizes that "under the appearance of bread and wine, really and properly, that is in actual fact, Jesus Christ is present." Dr. Darwell Stone (*Hist. of the Doctrine of the Holy Eucharist*) says that "these declarations of the Council of 1672 reassert the main lines of traditional earlier doctrine."—ED.

* Hallam, "Europe during the Middle Ages."
† Robertson, ii. 376.

known as the " Donation of Constantine." This was introduced to general notice in an Epistle of Pope Hadrian I., in which he exhorts Charlemagne to imitate the liberalty and revive the name of the great Constantine. According to the legend, the first of the Christian emperors was healed of leprosy, and baptized by Pope Sylvester, and in gratitude Constantine withdrew from the seat and patrimony of St. Peter, declared his resolution to found a new capital in the East, and resigned to the popes the free and perpetual sovereignty of Rome, Italy, and the provinces of the West. This gross fiction was in those uncritical days generally accepted without opposition and enabled the popes to represent their claims to territory and sovereignty in the West as being only a resumption of rights which the first Christian emperor had conferred, and which had been lost by the invasion of the barbarians. Possibly influenced by this claim, Countess Matilda, daughter and heiress of Boniface, Duke of Tuscany, the powerful supporter of Gregory VII. against the Emperor Henry IV., settled all her vast estates upon the see of Rome. The possession of this splendid inheritance was disputed by the Emperor Henry V. and by other princes, and some portions of it were lost ; but the Roman see remained in possession of a considerable part, which it continued to hold down to the nineteenth century, when at last this temporal sovereignty of the popes was reduced to the dimensions of a palace, a church, and a garden, to be slightly enlarged in 1929.

The Papal Infallibility.—There is no trace of this doctrine in the early centuries. The early Church believed that the promise of Christ that the indwelling Spirit should guide His disciples into all truth, and that Christ would be with them always to the end of the world, involved the belief that the Church would be supernaturally preserved from error and kept in the truth. In primitive times it was held that this authoritative and infallible voice of the Church was to be looked for in a general council, and this derived support from the words of the decree of the Council of Jerusalem : " It seemed good to the Holy Ghost and to us." Accordingly, when questions of doctrine troubled the Church, councils were summoned to determine them. The history of general councils is an evidence of this belief that a general council was the Church of Christ by representation and possessed these promises of Christ.

The opposite theory that this infallibility of the Church resided in the pope could not originate till the pope had begun to be regarded as in some sense the organic head of the Church, accordingly we hear nothing of it for the first eight centuries of the Church's history. Not till the forged Isidorean decretals had laid a foundation for the papal assumptions did Nicholas I. venture to claim that the decrees of a pope were a rule for the whole Church, and to pronounce an anathema on all who should refuse to receive them. The circumstances of the papacy for the next 200 years prevented any further growth of the seed thus planted. It burst into leaf in the Hildebrandine period (Ch. XXXIII.). Gregory VII. assumed that the pope in uttering his decrees had the Divine guidance, and that his utterances were therefore infallible. Writers of the period, Anselm of Lucca, Cardinal Damiani, Cardinal Gregory of Pavia, supported the papal pretensions and began to claim a sort of vague infallibility for the popes. Pope Agatho had said at a Roman synod in 680 that all the English bishops were to observe the ordinances made in former Roman synods for the Anglo-Saxon Church. Cardinal Damiani represented this as a decree issued by Agatho to all bishops in the world, saying they must receive all papal orders as though attested by the very voice of Peter, and therefore of course infallible. A passage of St. Augustine said that all those canonical writings (of the Bible) were pre-eminently attested which apostolical churches had first received and possessed. He meant the Churches of Corinth, Ephesus, Rome, etc., which had received St. Paul's Epistles. Anselm of Lucca took the passage and corrupted it into " the epistles issued by the apostolical see are part of the canonical Scriptures." This corruption was adopted by Gratian and Peter Lombard, whose works were the text-books of the medieval Church; and so the Church was taught that St. Augustine had declared every papal decree to stand on a level of inerrancy side by side with the apostolical epistles.

The two great authors of the doctrine of papal infallibility are Gratian and Aquinas—the one the great authority for medieval canon law, the other for medieval scholastic

theology. Gratian in his "Decretum" adopted in good
faith all the forgeries and falsifications of previous ages.
His work became the great repertory from which succeeding
canonists and theologians derived their knowledge of
fathers and councils. Gratian plainly lays down that the
pope is the source of all law, and himself above all law,
and compares him in this respect to Christ.

When Aquinas wrote his "Summa Theologiæ" (about
1250), which became the theological text-book of the succeeding ages of the Church, he assumed the truth of all that
Gratian had written, and adopted all the mass of matter
which had accrued or been invented in the intervening period
in support of the papal pretensions. Especially he adopted
the forgeries published in his own time of a collection of
passages from Greek councils and fathers, which were
calculated to establish that the Roman Bishop was from
primitive times recognised as sole authority on doctrinal
questions. Aquinas probably believed these extracts to be
genuine ; influenced by them, he, for the first time, lays
down that the pope is not only the absolute ruler but also
the infallible teacher of the Church. "Christ," he says,
" is fully and completely with every pope in sacrament and
authority. The apostolic see rules, ever remaining un-
shaken in the faith of Peter, while other churches are
deformed by error ; and thus the Roman Church is the sun
from which they all receive their light. A council derives
its whole authority from the pope ; he has the right of
establishing a new confession of faith, and whoever rejects
his authority is a heretic, for it belongs to him alone to
decide on every doctrinal question." * The popes were
delighted. John XXII. declared that Thomas (Aquinas)
had worked as many miracles as he had written articles, and
could be canonised without any other miracles, and in his
bull affirmed that Thomas had not written without a special
inspiration of the Holy Ghost. Innocent IV. said that
whoever assailed his teaching incurred suspicion of heresy.

Still the doctrine met with much opposition. The
Dominican order were the special champions of all that
Aquinas (one of their order) had taught, and among these
of the papal infallibility. But great theologians, notably

* Summa, ii. 2, Q. I., Art. 10 ; Q. XI., Art. 2, 3.

those of the University of Paris, the great theological university of the Middle Ages, opposed the doctrine. Besides, it was a received maxim of the Church that popes could err, and the error of Liberius was constantly quoted as an illustration of it. The papal champions invented a theory that as soon as a pope erred he, *ipso facto*, ceased to be pope.

The great schism, however, brought the doctrine of the Pope's infallibility into disrepute, and the councils of Constance and Bâle (Ch. XXXVII.) formally enunciated the doctrine that a general council is superior to a pope, and obtained the assent and submission of the contemporary popes. For 130 years (1320–1450) not a single book was written in support of the papal claims until Cardinal Torquemada revived the ultramontane theory. Cardinal Cajetan and others followed, and the new Order of Jesus became its influential champions. The two theories continued to be held by two parties within the Roman Church down to the Vatican Council of 1870, when the pope's infallibility was proclaimed as a dogma of the Christian faith.

The Cultus of the Blessed Virgin Mary.—From the time of the Council of Ephesus, which assembled to determine the controversy which Nestorius had raised about the title Theotokos (God-bearer) commonly attributed to the Blessed Virgin, we find titles of reverence and affection, gradually growing in extravagance, attributed to her, and a legend growing up about her.

Sophronius (Bishop of Jerusalem when it fell into the hands of the Mohammedan conquerors) in the seventh century mentions that the notion of her Assumption had already been suggested: "Many of our people doubt whether Mary was taken up with her body, or went away leaving the body. But how, or at what time, or by what persons her body was taken hence, or whether removed, or whether it rose again, is not known, although some will maintain that she is already revived, and is clothed with a blessed immortality with Christ in heavenly places, which very many affirm also of blessed John the Evangelist." The belief in the Assumption gradually became popular. In Italy a festival in honour of it was introduced as early as the seventh century, and adopted in France and Germany in the ninth. In the time of Gregory VII. offices in her honour were said in some monasteries. It became a pious custom to repeat frequently the angelical salutation, " Hail, Mary, full of grace ! blessed art thou among women." The title " Queen of Heaven " was attributed to her. St. Bernard encourages the idea of her being invoked as a mediatrix by those who feared to approach the Saviour directly.

The first idea of any mystery in the birth of the Virgin occurs in the twelfth century ; and St. Bernard, highly as he was accustomed to exalt the Virgin, vigorously opposed this new step. Some monks of Lyons desired to establish a festival in honour of the immaculate conception of the blessed Virgin. Bernard wrote them a letter, still extant, which furnishes us with sound and sufficient arguments against the doctrine. He is willing to grant that the Virgin, like John Baptist and Jeremiah, may have been sanctified from the womb, but he denies that she was conceived without sin. He shows that if freedom from sin in conception were required for the Virgin, it must equally be required for the parents of the Virgin ; and so it must be carried back to all her ancestors, which would be absurd. He calls the doctrine a " novelty," an " error," and a " superstition." He sums up thus : " The prerogative of a holy conception should be reserved for One Who Himself should sanctify all, and bring remission of sins. It is only the Lord Jesus Christ Who was conceived of the Holy Ghost, Who alone was holy in conception."

For a long time the doctrine did not make way in the Church. Peter Lombard, Hugo de St. Victor, St. Thomas Aquinas, even Buonaventura, the author of the " Psalter of the Virgin " and of the " Creed of the Virgin," are all opposed to it. We may include three popes—Innocent II., III., and V.—among its opponents. Innocent II. says in a sermon on the Assumption, " The glorious Virgin was conceived in original sin." Innocent III., comparing Eve and Mary, says, " Eve was formed without sin, but she conceived in sin ; while, on the contrary, Mary was conceived in sin, but she conceived without sin." Innocent V. (towards the close of the thirteenth century), attempting to explain the mystery, says she was sanctified before her birth, but not in her conception, for " if that had been so, she would have been exempt from original sin." Aquinas enters at great length into the argument, and concludes that " Christ in no way contracted original sin, but His very conception was holy, according to St. Luke i., ' That which is born of thee shall be called the Son of God ' ; but the blessed Virgin did contract original sin, although cleansed from it before she was born from the womb." Buonaventura proves that St. Thomas Aquinas' opinion was most agreeable to the faith and authority of the Fathers, and that Mary was not sanctified until after she had contracted original sin.

In the fourteenth century the doctrine of the Immaculate Conception of Mary began to spread. Duns Scotus admitted that it was not an accepted doctrine of the Church, but argued that God might have done it, and that it may possibly be true. Duns was a Franciscan, and his order, devoted to the honour of Mary, took up the doctrine as a new jewel in her crown. The two great orders of friars were divided upon the question, the Dominicans maintaining the conclusions of their champion Aquinas. Sixtus IV. issued a bull in 1476, censuring the disputants for their violence against each other, and condemning them equally for charging each other with heresy, since the point was not yet decided by the Roman Church and the apostolic see. Pius V., in 1570, issued a similar bull. Still later Paul V. (1617) and Gregory XV. issued bulls forbidding any to assert in private conversation or in sermons that the blessed Virgin was conceived in sin ; but forbidding the use of the word " immaculate " as applied to her conception in any public office of the Church. In the Council of Trent it was attempted to get the dogma defined, but the opposition was successful, and nothing was determined either way.*

So the two opinions existed side by side in the Church till 1854, when pope Pius IX. astonished the world by issuing a bull, in which he decreed that the doctrine of the immaculate conception was an article of the faith, and that any one who from that time should deny it would be guilty of heresy, and imperil his salvation.

* This section is chiefly extracted from the Rev. J. E. Bennett's " Broken Unity of the Church."

CHAPTER XL

THE REFORMATION

IN the year 1517 Leo X., of the great Florentine family of the De Medici, was pope, a young prince of ability and education, with a taste, like all his family, for literature and the arts, and for splendour and luxury, but a very unsuitable person for head of the Church of Christ. The three chief sovereigns of Europe were, Maximilian I., Emperor of Germany; Francis, King of France; and Henry VIII. of England, powerful princes, rivals in European politics, in the splendour of their courts, and in personal fame.

The Church was peaceful. Francis had successfully imposed the concordat in France; the English king maintained the laws his predecessors had enacted, restraining all encroachments of the pope on the rights of the crown. Germany had its concordat, but allowed greater privileges to the pope than any other country. In Spain the king had from an early date possessed the rights which other sovereigns had only recently and hardly won. The pope and Curia, on the other hand, derived a very large revenue from all countries of Europe, through bulls of confirmation to bishoprics, annates, appeals, &c.; a jubilee every twenty-five years brought in vast sums as offerings; and if between times a Julius wanted money to maintain his wars, or a Leo to support his magnificence, he issued an indulgence, farmed it out to the different countries, and so replenished his exchequer.

But the venality and exactions of Rome, the wealth and idleness of monasteries, the non-residence of the secular clergy, the rapacity of the friars and their defence of superstitions and abuses, the general decay of discipline and corruption of morals, filled all lands with complaint. The revival of learning and the study of antiquity and the

Scriptures had made the learned acquainted with the false-
ness of the foundation on which the system of the papacy
was reared, and had led men to question some of the received
religious doctrines ; while the discovery of the art of print
ing was spreading this disquieting knowledge among the
people. The Church was on the eve of the greatest con-
vulsion which had happened to it for a thousand years ;
and what princes, councils, universities, doctors, prelates,
and saints had attempted in vain during two hundred years
was effected at last through an obscure German friar.

The magnificent young pope wanted money, and issued
an indulgence, nominally for the rebuilding of St. Peter's.
The indulgence was farmed as usual. A Dominican friar
called Tetzel was engaged to conduct the sale in Germany.
By indulgences the pope professed his power to give pardons
for all sins which a man had committed, or even might
hereafter commit. But Tetzel made them still more
offensive, as he travelled from town to town, by the grossness
and profanity of his addresses, outraging common sense and
Christian feeling by his assertions of the efficacy of the papal
pardons, and deluding ignorant and superstitious people
into the purchase of his wares.

Wittenberg, the chief town of Saxony, was the seat of a
university, in which Doctor Martin Luther, an Augustine
friar, was Professor of Philosophy. He had read the great
work of the mystic Tauler, knew his Thomas à Kempis, and
was translating some of St. Paul's Epistles into German.
He was shocked at the corruptions of religion and the
wickedness of the people ; and this sale of indulgences was
one of the most shameful of the corruptions and calculated
to encourage men in their wickedness. He acted boldly
where he felt strongly. On the eve of All Saints, the day on
which Tetzel was to exhibit his relics and sell his pardons in
the Church of Wittenberg, in the presence of pilgrims
from the neighbouring villages and of the townspeople and
students of the university, Luther posted upon the door of
the church a paper containing ninety-five theses against
indulgences, which he undertook to defend in disputation.

Thus commenced that movement for the Reformation
of the Church which shook all Europe and produced
immediate consequences of the greatest magnitude.

The challenge was taken up by several papal champions, and a sharp controversy followed ; it attracted wide attention and keen interest. Leo summoned Luther to appear before him at Rome. Frederick (surnamed the Wise), Elector of Saxony, sympathised with the Reformer and steadily protected him, and claimed that the cause ought to be decided by the ecclesiastical laws of the empire. Luther was accordingly ordered to appear before the Diet of the Empire at Augsburg, where Cardinal Cajetan appeared as Papal Legate. The pope thought to settle the controversy by the issue of a bull, commanding all men to acknowledge his power to deliver from all punishments (eternal as well as temporal) due to sin and transgression (not against ecclesiastical ordinances only, but) of every kind. Luther appealed to a general council, but was induced to write a submissive letter to the pope, promising silence on the controversy, provided the other side were also silenced. But Eckius, one of the papal champions, challenged Luther to a disputation at Leipzig on the authority and supremacy of the Roman pontiff. Luther accepted the challenge, and also published a vast number of popular tracts, preached constantly, and renewed the demand for a Reformation of the Church in head and members, in a book entitled *The Reformation of Christendom*.

The reply from Rome was a bull of excommunication, unless he retracted within sixty days. On the 10th of December, 1520, outside the city of Wittenberg, in the presence of a great concourse of people, Luther formally burnt the bull of excommunication and also the Book of Decretals and Canons, the basis of the whole papal system.

The bold act of Luther fanned into flame the doubts smouldering in men's minds. Wittenberg became famous ; students from all parts flocked to its university to read Greek with Melancthon and theology with Luther ; and their principles passed with great rapidity throughout Europe, and excited a great and general ferment.

Leo demanded of the emperor, Charles V., the punishment of the audacious friar, who had set all ecclesiastical authority at defiance and was disturbing the whole Church. Luther was accordingly summoned before the Diet assembled at Worms (A.D. 1521). He was condemned and declared an enemy of the empire, and it was forbidden to give him aid or shelter. But the Elector Frederick had provided for his safety. As he returned homeward he was seized by agents of the Elector in disguise, who carried him to the Castle of Wartzburg, where he lay concealed for ten months, occupying himself especially in his German translation of the Scriptures.

Tired, however, of absence from the active conduct of the movement, which was rapidly spreading, he returned to Wittenberg. In 1524 he abandoned his monastic vows and costume and married an ex-nun. The progress of the reform was disturbed and imperilled by the excesses of the Anabaptists and the revolt of the peasants. Munzer, a leader of the new sect of Anabaptists, threw himself into the revolt and frightened men as to the possible consequences of the movement for reformation. The revolt, however, was suppressed, and the Reformation went on.

In 1525 the Elector Frederick died. He was succeeded by his brother John, who at once assumed the supremacy over the ecclesiastical affairs of his own dominions ; engaged Luther and Melancthon to draw up a body of laws relating to the form of ecclesiastical government, the method of public worship, the rank, offices, and revenues of the clergy, and other matters of that kind ; established it as law, and proclaimed it by heralds throughout his dominions (1527). Other princes and states of Germany followed his example ; renounced the papal supremacy, and established a like form of worship, discipline, and government. Some princes who had joined in the cry for reformation drew back from this abrogation of the papal supremacy, and an open rupture ensued. The papal party soon gave indications of an intention to proceed to hostilities against the Reformed states. The Reformed princes began to consider measures of mutual defence. In the midst of these preparations the Imperial Diet met at Spires (A.D. 1526), presided over by Ferdinand, the brother of the emperor who was himself fully occupied in regulating the troubled state of his dominions in France, Spain, and Italy. These political troubles favoured the cause of the Reformers. The imperial ambassadors had orders to keep Germany quiet, only requiring the execution of the decree of the Diet of Worms

against Luther and his adherents. But the majority of
the princes declined to assent to that until the whole
question had been determined by a general council, which
the diet unanimously requested the emperor to summon ;
and it was agreed that the princes and states of Germany
should meantime manage the ecclesiastical affairs of their
several dominions as they should think expedient.

Political events still further aided the Reformation, for
the pope, after the defeat of Francis I. at Pavia, entered into
a treaty with the French and Venetians against him ; and
the emperor in return repudiated the papal authority in
his Spanish dominions, made war upon the pope, laid siege
to Rome, and blockaded the pope in the Castle of St.
Angelo. These events encouraged more German princes
to join the reforming party.

But the emperor came to an agreement with the pope.
Another Diet was held at Spires (A.D. 1529). The liberty
of the princes to manage ecclesiastical matters was revoked
by a majority, and it was declared unlawful to introduce any
changes in doctrine, discipline, or worship until a general
council had been held. The Elector of Saxony, the Landgrave of Hesse, and others entered a solemn protest against
this decree, appealing to the emperor and a future council.
Those who adhered to this protest were the first called by
the name of Protestants.

The next important step was the Diet of Augsburg, at
which the emperor was present. The Protestants, at the
emperor's desire, had prepared a formal statement, in
twenty-eight chapters, of which twenty-one clearly enunciated their chief doctrines and seven pointed out the errors
and abuses which had occasioned their separation from
Rome. This Confession of Augsburg was signed by John,
the Elector of Saxony, and four other princes of the empire,
and by the imperial cities of Nuremberg and Reutlingen.
It was afterwards adopted by other bodies of seceders from
Rome as the expression of their faith, and was largely used
in the articles of religion drawn up by the English Reformers
under the guidance of Cranmer and Ridley.

The case of the Reformers was argued by Melancthon
and others, while Luther, in safe keeping in the Castle of
Coburg, kept up a constant communication with his friends

and influenced their proceedings. Conferences failing to reconcile differences, the diet made a decree, in the absence of some of the chief Protestant princes, censuring the changes which had been made in religion; ordering all princes, states, and cities of the empire to return to allegiance to Rome; and the emperor and the popish princes undertook to enforce the observance of the decree (Nov. 19, 1531).

The Protestant princes entered into a defensive league, and sought the aid of other sovereigns and states, especially the King of England, then engaged in that controversy with the pope on the question of his marriage, which shortly ended in his rejection of the papal supremacy; the King of Denmark, who had already broken with the pope; and the King of France, who sometimes favoured and sometimes burnt the Reformers, but who was in political antagonism to the emperor. The emperor, threatened by this confederacy and by the advancing power of the Turks, arranged a peace, in which, in return for help in his Turkish war, he conceded freedom of religion till a rule of faith should be fixed either at a general council or, failing that, in a diet of the empire.

Clement VII. died in 1534. Paul III., his successor, convoked a general council at Mantua, but the Protestants protested against an Italian council, claiming that a controversy which had arisen in Germany should be decided within the empire. The pope proposed Trent as the place for the council, and the emperor assented; but the Protestants still refused to attend it. The emperor and pope thereupon resolved to reduce the recusants by force of arms. The Elector of Saxony and the Landgrave of Hesse raised forces in self-defence; but at the battle of Muhlberg, on the Elbe (April 24, 1547), the Protestant armies were defeated. At the ensuing diet, the emperor required the Protestants to leave the decision of religious matters to the council then sitting at Trent. But the council was soon after adjourned from Trent to Bologna, and thereby in effect dissolved, and the pope could not be induced to reassemble it.

The emperor then engaged a number of divines to draw up a formulary to serve as a rule of faith and worship for both parties within the empire till the decision of a council could be obtained; and this *formula ad interim*, which satisfied neither party and was not very strictly observed by either, served to tide over the difficulty for a few years.

It was believed that Charles was making use of the religious divisions among the princes and states to strengthen himself at their expense, while, on the other hand, using the religious dissensions to coerce the pope into a general council, by which also his imperial authority would be aggrandised. His plans, if he entertained such, were frustrated by a bold move on the part of Maurice, Duke of Saxony. Suddenly with a powerful army he surprised the emperor at Innsbruck, and obtained terms which were ever after considered by German Protestants as the basis of their religious liberty. The rule of faith called the *Interim* was to be void; all should enjoy the free exercise of their religion till a diet should determine amicably the dispute; and if it were impossible to arrive at uniformity in doctrine and worship, then this religious liberty should continue always. The diet met at Augsburg in 1555, when it was finally decreed that the Protestants who followed the Confession of Augsburg should be exempt from the jurisdiction of the Roman pontiff and of the bishops and should be at liberty to enact laws for themselves relative to religious faith, discipline, and worship; that all inhabitants of the empire should be free to join which Church they preferred; and that any one injuring another on account of his religious opinions should be proceeded against as an enemy of the empire, an invader of its liberties, and a disturber of its peace.

The Lutheran body thus became a rival community, side by side with the unreformed German Church. But Luther always regretted this, acknowledged the authority of the episcopate, and still sought a reformed national Church.

The Reformation in Switzerland.—The followers of Zwingli, a canon of Zurich, claim that he anticipated Luther, and had already begun to preach a reformation before the German reformer posted his famous theses on the doors of the church of Wittenberg. He opposed

x

the sale of indulgences in Switzerland, and thus began the movement for reform in the Helvetic cantons. His revolt from the ancient system of doctrine and discipline was more violent than that of Luther. In doctrine he denied the grace of sacraments ; in discipline he attributed to the civil magistrate such authority in ecclesiastical affairs as is inconsistent with the Divine constitution of the Church. The disputes between the followers of Luther and Zwingli, chiefly on the doctrine of the Eucharist, weakened the reform movement. A conference at Marburg (1527) failed to produce an agreement. Many German cities embraced the Zwinglian system, and not until 1577 was a *Form of Concord* between the two parties arrived at which allowed both to hold and preach their views within the same Church. What Zwingli effected at Zurich, Œcolampadius carried through at Bâle, the system of the latter being, however, in doctrine more nearly in agreement with Luther than with Zwingli.*

The reputation of the school of Zurich was, however, soon eclipsed by that of Geneva, organised by the genius of Calvin. The son of a notary of Picardy, he was educated at the University of Paris. His father destined him for the priesthood, and had procured a benefice for him, when the talent he developed led his father to think that such extraordinary abilities might find a more profitable career in the law. He had already come under the influence of Olivetan, the first translator of the Scriptures into French, and willingly abandoned the ecclesiastical career and continued his law studies in Orleans and Bourges, where he became still more decidedly attached to the reformed doctrines then widely spreading, though secretly, in France.

When Calvin returned to Paris he gave himself once more to theology, became a teacher of the reformed doctrine, and was soon regarded as the head of that party in France. In 1532 his friend Nicholas Cop was elected rector of the Sorbonne, and engaged Calvin to write for him the customary oration, in which he gave an exposition of the new doctrines. Both were summoned before Parliament, but took refuge at the court of the Queen of Navarre, the sister

* The mass was abolished in Zurich in 1525. By 1529 the reformed doctrines were established in Berne and other Swiss cantons.

of Francis I., who had embraced the Reformation, and gave shelter to the Reformers.

In 1536, being only twenty-five years of age, Calvin published his " Institutes of the Christian Religion," which contains a full development of the theological system known by his name. Geneva, which had thrown off the yoke of Rome, requested that he would devote himself there to the organisation of religion. Here he spent the remainder of his life, establishing and administering the system of doctrine and Church government already laid down in his Institutes.

In doctrine he adopted, on the whole, the position of Luther. He believed in the grace of sacraments, though he is not always consistent in his utterances on the subject, and many of his followers adopted the Zwinglian theory. The great feature of his system is his teaching on election. This he founded on the teaching of St. Augustine, which had been generally received, though not authoritatively sanctioned, in the Western Church ; but he made an advance upon St. Augustine's doctrine. Calvin's teaching on predestination may be summed up in what are called the Five Points—viz., (1) election (and non-election or reprobation) ; (2) redemption ; (3) the bondage of the will ; (4) grace ; (5) final perseverance. " He maintained that God not only foresaw, but from all eternity decreed the fall of Adam and the total corruption of his posterity by sin ; all from birth inherit his fallen nature, with its hereditary bond of sin and guilt, and are in a state of utter alienation from God ; free-will can do nothing but sin, and that continually. God is pleased, for reasons known to Himself and independently of the foreseen merits of the objects of His mercy, to elect some from the fallen race to salvation. They are made willing by His grace, which is irresistible, or necessarily effectual, to obey the Gospel call ; are regenerated by His Spirit, and live in holiness and obedience to His will, and cannot finally fall from a state of grace. The rest of mankind God predestines to eternal destruction, not on account of foreseen sin, though it may aggravate their doom, but in fulfilment of His sovereign purpose or decree." Augustine did not teach that God had predestined the fall of Adam and the ruin of his race. Unlike

Calvin, he believed that Christ died for all men, and that all who are baptized are regenerated and receive grace. But there is another grace—the grace of perseverance—which he believed that only the elect receive. The great difference is that Calvin makes God chargeable with the fall of man, Augustine does not. Augustine believed in the universal bestowal of baptismal grace, and that a man may fall away from it and be lost; Calvin believed that it was only bestowed on the elect, and that they would necessarily be saved.*

Calvin also introduced a novel system of Church government, which, under his own superintendence, became a stern spiritual tyranny. The government was vested in a Consistory of six clerical and twelve lay elders, Calvin retaining the presidency to the end of his life. This body met weekly. It only professed to enforce discipline by spiritual censures; but when these were insufficient it handed over the offenders to the secular arm, to be dealt with in no gentle way; and it was a principle of the system that the State was bound to give its support to the Church and to enforce her censures by temporal penalties. Not only crimes but sins were severely punished; not only libertinism but innocent merriment were sternly checked. Persons were imprisoned for playing a Twelfth Night game, and for reading old romances. Unchastity was sternly punished. One case is recorded of a person sentenced to death for adultery. One child was beheaded for striking his parents; another, condemned to death for an attempt only to strike its mother, with difficulty escaped the sentence. All kinds of blasphemy were visited with heavy penalties, and it was held to be blasphemy to speak against the Reformers. Witchcraft was severely dealt with. Watchmen—*i.e.* spies—were established, whose duty it was to report all breaches of discipline. There was an annual visitation of every house in the city, which was a formal inquisition by a minister and a lay elder into the habits of the household. To this in 1550 was added a system of catechising from house to house, and attendance on sermons was enforced. The idea

* The English Reformers put predestination and election into an important place in their theological system, but their theory was that of Augustine, or nearly so, not that of Calvin.

of religious toleration no more entered the mind of Calvin
than of any of his contemporaries, and the burning of
Servetus for Socinianism is an illustration of this. Calvin's
system had a great attraction for the sterner minds among
the Reformers, and at Geneva for many years they sought
refuge from persecution in their own countries, and from
it emissaries propagated this system throughout Europe.
In the end the Palatinate, several German cities, the Seven
United Provinces, seven Swiss Cantons, Scotland, and the
numerous body of Huguenots in France adopted the
Calvinistic doctrine and discipline.

The massacres of Vaudois at Calvrières and Merindol
stained France deeply with " the blood of the saints."
Henry II. ascended the throne determined to prevent the
Reformation from spreading in France, and among the
festivities on the coronation of the queen were interposed
four burnings, at which the king and court attended ; and
in 1552 he issued the edict of Chateaubriand, which dis-
qualified all persons holding reformed opinions from civil
office, and established a censorship of books. It was not
till 1555 that a reformed church with a settled pastor was
opened in Paris. On one occasion the worshippers were
surprised, and five of them condemned and burnt ; nevertheless congregations were organised in the provinces. In
1556 the reformed made a public demonstration by walking
in procession through the streets to the number of 4,000,
singing psalms of the version of Clement Marot, which did
so much to popularise the cause. Two Bourbon princes
joined openly in this demonstration. The Reformers held
a synod in 1559, and issued a Confession of Faith. After
the accidental death of Henry II., the antagonism of the
two parties became still more embittered. The reformed,
under the Prince of Condé, tried to possess themselves of
the person of the young king at Blois. The king issued the
Edict of Romorantin, which declared all who attended the
reformed worship traitors and transferred the jurisdiction
in their causes from the civil to the ecclesiastical courts.
At the assembly of notables which met at Fontainebleau
soon afterwards, the Admiral Coligny, with a retinue of
800 horsemen, presented a petition from Normandy,
demanding freedom of religious opinions. On the death of

Francis II., the queen-mother Catherine of Medicis, became regent and a theological discussion on the reformed doctrine took place at the meeting of the States General in which Beza was the champion of reform, and a more tolerant edict was issued.

An accidental collision between the two parties at Vassy, in which sixty reformed were killed and two hundred wounded, was the prelude to the civil wars of religion, which, with occasional truces, lasted for nearly 40 years. The first war ended with the Peace of Amboise, which gave the reformed party several towns in which they might freely exercise their religion, of which Rochelle was the most important, and gave the nobles a right to have reformed worship in their own houses for their families and tenants. Space does not permit us to recount the subsequent wars. We must mention the famous Massacre of St. Bartholomew, A.D. 1572, in which, with the king's assent, the troops were let loose on the Huguenots in Paris, and they were hunted out and killed on the spot. Similar massacres occurred in other towns, and the number killed is variously estimated at from 30,000 to 100,000. When news of the massacre reached Rome, by the pope's order it was received with a salute of artillery, a general illumination, and a thanksgiving service, and a medal was struck to commemorate the event.

The murder of Henry III. by Jacques Clement placed Henry IV. of Navarre upon the throne. Jeanne d'Albret, the sister of Francis I., the widowed Queen of Navarre, had established the reformed religion in her little independent sovereignty of Bearn about 1570, which became a refuge for the persecuted Reformers, and had brought up her son Henry in the reformed religion, and though he was induced for the peace of France to conform to the established religion, yet by the Edict of Nantes (May, 1598) he gave large freedom of opinion and worship to the reformed, and removed all disqualification for civil office.

Richelieu, by the capture of Rochelle, the chief stronghold of the Huguenots, broke their strength as a political party, but left them toleration of religion and worship.

Louis XIV., under the influence of Madame de Maintenon resolved to reduce them to conformity. He forbad their ministers to preach and destroyed their places of worship ; and when they began to emigrate, in order to enjoy religious freedom in other countries, he forbad them to quit the kingdom on pain of the galleys. In 1684 and 1685 Roman ecclesiastics were sent among the reformed to convert them, attended by troops of dragoons. In 1648, the Edict of Nantes was revoked, the Huguenot preachers were banished, and the exercise of their religion was entirely forbidden. Many were driven to conform ; many in secret maintained the religion made dearer to them by persecution, and some half million or more emigrated from France within three years, and enriched England, Holland, and North Germany, with that number of intelligent, industrious citizens, who brought some wealth and still more valuable trades with them.

Louis XIV., however, strenuously upheld against the pope his own royal authority and the rights of the Gallican Church. In 1681–82 he summoned an assembly of French clergy, which was attended by thirty-five bishops and as many representatives of the other orders, at which the following propositions were accepted by the whole assembly : 1. The pope's power only extends to spiritual things ; kings are not subordinate to popes ; and the doctrine that kings may be deposed by them is contrary to God's Word. 2. The pope's authority in spiritual things is subject to the limitations defined by the Council of Constance. 3. The authority of the holy see can only be exercised in France according to the laws, usages, and ordinances of the Gallican Church. 4. The pope's decisions on matters of faith are only valid when received by the Church.

In Sweden the doctrines of the Lutheran Reformation were early introduced, and the reorganisation of its Church was effected by the king, Gustavus Vasa. The Church had been very wealthy ; the king divided between the crown and the landowners two-thirds of its revenues. The legal succession of its bishops has been disputed,* the first bishop

* The Lambeth Conference, 1920, was satisfied as to " the unbroken succession of the episcopate in Sweden, and on the conception of the office of a priest held by that Church " and recommended, in the case of Sweden, but not of " the other Scandinavian Churches," that their communicants might communicate at our altars, and the priests, properly ordained, might preach in our churches. (Resolution 24, cf. p. 153.)—ED.

of reformed opinions, Laurentius Petri, received his consecration as Archbishop of Upsala, after a long vacancy of that see, in 1531 from Petrus Magni, Bishop of Vesteras (the actual record of Magni's consecration is not forthcoming, but there is no ground to doubt the fact), and Magnus Sommar, Bishop of Strengnäs, both anti-Lutherans, and by 1536 both their sees were filled by men in sympathy with the new teaching (see Wordsworth: *The National Church of Sweden*, 1911). There was usually only one consecrating bishop, with two assistant canons, who might be presbyters; but the validity of consecration by one bishop is universally allowed. King Sigismund, favouring the party of reaction towards Rome, was dethroned; a council was held at Upsala in 1593, whose acts, establishing the Lutheran doctrine as the religion of Sweden, are regarded as the great charter of the Swedish Church. The king is the head of all Church courts, assisted by an ecclesiastical council of laymen.

In Denmark the doctrines of the Lutheran Reformation, introduced about 1526, received legal sanction at the Assembly of the Estates, held at Odensee, 1527. The Reformation was not, however, established till 1544, and the constitution of the Church was the work of King Christian V. in the year 1683. Only Lutheranism was tolerated; no man could fill any office, civil or military, unless of the national religion. The Danes retain many customs of the ancient Church; confession before Communion; at the celebration a cross and lighted candles on the altar; surplice and chasuble of red velvet, with a cross embroidered in gold on the back; wafer bread; the ancient sentences of administration: " *Hoc est verum Jesu corpus ; Hoc est verus Jesu sanguis.*"

The Church of Norway was anciently part of the Church of Denmark. At the cession of Norway to Sweden early in the nineteenth century the Danish Church became independent. By the cession of Finland to Russia in 1809 another independent Lutheran Church was created, and an Archbishop of Abo created as its ecclesiastical head.

The history of the so-called Jansenist Church of Holland is an interesting and important episode. When the pope required all bishops to subscribe to the condemnation of

Jansenius, the Archbishop of Utrecht and his suffragans demurred. They were willing to condemn the incriminated propositions, but not to aver that they were held by Jansenius. The popes endeavoured to prevent the continuance of the line of bishops thus refusing submission to the demand of Rome. The bishops, however, took care to continue their succession ; each successive bishop dutifully reports his election and consecration to Rome, and Rome returns an excommunication as its reply. Still the ancient Church of Holland maintains itself, and presents the spectacle of a Church Catholic but not Roman. The " Old Catholics " of Germany in the last century obtained episcopal consecration from the Archbishop of Utrecht.

In all provinces of Italy the reformed doctrines found many adherents, especially in Venice, Tuscany, and Naples, Ochino and Peter Martyr being the most conspicuous preachers of the reform. But the Inquisition drove many to seek safety in exile. In Naples the people resisted the introduction of that tribunal with such success that the emperor was glad to accommodate matters and issue a general pardon.

In Spain the new doctrines were introduced by stealth ; but the Inquisition, already long established here, acted with such promptitude and vigour that the movement made less way than in any of the other countries of Europe.

England was the last country in the West which fell under the Roman supremacy in the eleventh century ; it was the first country which in the fourteenth protested against the papal abuses and restrained them by legislative enactments. Its insular position and strong nationality helped its independent action. The reforming doctrines spread from Germany into England. Wolsey, the great minister of Henry VIII., was in favour of a general reformation, and had taken steps in that direction in the visitation of the monasteries, the encouragement of the new learning at the universities, and by his lenient treatment of those charged with heretical opinions. Warham, the Archbishop of Canterbury, and a great number of the prelates and clergy inclined in the same direction. The king at first defended the ancient order, and, proud of his ecclesiastical knowledge, wrote an answer to one of Luther's early books but the affair of the divorce enlisted his passions against the papal supremacy and engaged him in the Reformation. The special feature of the English Reformation was that it was not, as in Germany, the setting up of a rival system in opposition to the ancient ecclesiastical organisation, nor, as in Geneva or the United Provinces, the total subversion of the old organisation and the planting of a new one in its place, but it was a real reformation of the Church undertaken by sovereign and clergy; and thus in England alone the historical organisation and status of the Church were preserved, while its doctrine and discipline were reformed.

We must refer to other works for a fuller account of the English Reformation *; we can only here point out its salient features. In 1534 Cranmer, the new archbishop, declared the king's first marriage null and void, and thus virtually set aside the pope's supremacy by deciding a cause which had long been before the papal court. Already, in 1531, the Convocation, with Archbishop Warham at its head, had petitioned the king to relieve the clergy of the payment of annates, and of the fees for bulls for consecrations of bishops, and requested that, if the pope refused, the obedience of England might be withdrawn from the see of Rome. An Act of Parliament had accordingly abolished annates, offered five per cent. on the value of the see as fees for bulls of consecration, and enacted that if the pope should refuse the bulls, bishops should be consecrated by the archbishop of the province and other bishops; and that if the pope proceeded to excommunication and interdict, his sentence should be disregarded. Two years afterwards, by Acts of Parliament, all reference to the pope, and all interference on his part, in the appointment of bishops was done away, all appeals to the papal courts and all applications to Rome of any kind forbidden. In the same year (1534) the two Convocations endorsed what Parliament had done, declaring that the Bishop of Rome has no greater jurisdiction conferred on him by God in this kingdom of England than any other foreign bishop. There seems to have been no difficulty in obtaining the assent of

* For the chief causes, see Arrowsmith: *The Prelude to the Reformation*, and works on the Renaissance movement.—ED.

the clergy generally, even in the monasteries, to this final repudiation of the papal supremacy, and the bishops were zealous in preaching it to the people. The mendicant orders were suppressed in 1535, and five years later monasticism was altogether abolished, and the king seized the monasteries for his own use, or distributed them in grants to his nobles and courtiers. Chantries were suppressed and their property confiscated in 1547. Convocation drew up ten articles of religion in 1536, briefly setting forth the doctrines of the English Reformation. Several translations of the Bible were published—Coverdale's in 1535, and the Great Bible in 1539, besides others—and the Service Book slightly altered. On the accession of Edward VI. a new Book of Common Prayer, prepared during the last reign, was published, thus completing the first stage of the English Reformation. The young king fell, however, into the hands of the Duke of Somerset, the Lord Protector, who was influenced by the Calvinistic Reformers. Calvin entered into correspondence with the king and Cranmer ; Bucer and Peter Martyr were invited to England, and made divinity professors at Cambridge and Oxford ; John a Lasco, a Zwinglian, was allowed to establish a congregation in London, and Calvinistic views of doctrine and discipline were encouraged. The doctrines and liturgy of the Church of England were revised. A new Prayer-book was drawn up, which made alterations in the Genevan direction, and many changes in the Holy Communion service in the the direction of Zwinglian doctrine. This second Prayerbook, however, did not get into general use, for before the day fixed an order in council suspended its further issue, and before anything further was done the young king died.

Mary on her accession obtained from Parliament the repeal of all the Reformation laws, and steps were taken to root out the Reformation by the fires of persecution. Many fled abroad—some to Frankfort, some to Geneva. During the three years that the persecution continued it is computed that 277 persons were brought to the stake, besides those punished by imprisonment, fine, and confiscation. The majority, terrified by the persecution, conformed ; but the fires of Smithfield burnt into the heart of the nation an undying hatred of Romanism. Mary died Nov. 17th, 1558, and Cardinal Pole on the following day.

Elizabeth and her advisers desired to take up the Reformation as it stood at the end of its first stage, accepting the first Prayer-book of Edward as the standard of doctrine and ritual. But to conciliate the Puritan party, which, encouraged in the reign of Edward VI., had become much more influential through the return of the Marian exiles, who had brought Genevan ideas and fashions back with them, the second book was taken as the standard, and some few alterations made as to vestments and eucharistic observances, which raised the tone of its orthodoxy. The Marian bishops, except Kitchen, of Llandaff, declined to accede to the changes; the parochial clergy (one hundred only excepted) accepted them; and the mass of the people received them with joy. The Thirty-nine Articles of Religion received the assent of Convocation in June, 1563. Pope Pius V. in 1560 made overtures for a reconciliation, offering to accept the English Reformation and approve of the Prayer-book on condition of the recognition of his supremacy, acknowledging that the book contained nothing contrary to the truth and comprehended all necessary to salvation. Finding a return of England to the obedience of the Roman see hopeless, he published in 1570 a bull of excommunication and deposition against the queen, fomented conspiracies against her, and called upon Spain to execute his sentence. The queen was strong in the affection of her subjects, the conspiracies proved abortive, and God delivered England from the Spaniard by the wreck of the Armada.

The antagonism between England and Scotland prevented the English Reformation from spreading into the northern country. John Knox, a disciple of Calvin, is the hero of the Scottish Reformation, and chiefly by his influence the Genevan system was established there. The first overt act of the Scottish Reformation was the presentation of a petition in 1559 to the queen-mother, Mary of Guise, regent on behalf of her daughter, Mary Queen of Scots, praying for prayer, sacraments, and preaching in the vulgar tongue, and for reformation of the lives of the clergy. The petition not meeting with a favourable answer, some

laymen entered into a Covenant to stand by one another
with life and fortune in the attempt to obtain reform.
The clergy held a provincial council at Edinburgh, and
passed some constitutions for the improvement of discipline ;
the synod also condemned several persons for heresy, and
required them to make recantation at the market-cross ;
but the mob riotously rescued their friends.

The reforming party, who styled themselves " the Congregation," in allusion to the Old Testament name for the
ancient Church of God, made Perth their head-quarters,
and there introduced the novelties in religion for which they
had in vain asked authority. After a sermon by Knox,
the mob defaced the images of the Church and plundered
the monasteries, an example followed at Cupar, in Fife.
The regent ordered troops to move upon Perth, whereupon
the Lords of the Congregation summoned their friends
there to the number of 7,000, besides the burgesses of Perth.
An accommodation was arrived at, and the forces on both
sides disbanded. But the regent violating the conditions,
the Congregation met at Crail, when, after one of Knox's
inflammatory addresses, they proceeded to destroy altars
and images, and proceeding to St. Andrews did likewise.
The regent ordered troops to march towards St. Andrews ;
the Congregation mustered forces to oppose them, and open
war began. The insurgents marched upon Perth, and
obliged the garrison to surrender ; thence to Edinburgh,
defacing churches and destroying monasteries on their
route. The mob of Edinburgh rose, despoiled the churches,
and plundered and destroyed the religious houses of the
capital. The regent not being strong enough to put down
the outbreak by force concluded a truce with the Congregation, on condition that Edinburgh should be restored
into the hands of the government, no further violence done,
and that the preachers and the reformed should not be
disturbed, pending a meeting of Parliament. He, however, fortified Leith, the port of Edinburgh, and garrisoned
it with French soldiers ; whereupon the Congregation concluded a treaty with Queen Elizabeth and with the help
of English troops laid siege to Leith. The queen regent
died and a peace was concluded with an act of oblivion for
the past and a promise of a settlement of religion at the

next Parliament. The King of the French and the Queen of Scots refused to ratify the treaty, but the Parliament was held without their authority, and proceeded to abrogate the ancient ecclesiastical order and doctrine and to establish a system of doctrine and government framed after the model of Geneva, but adopting the second Book of Common Prayer of Edward VI. An order for destroying monastic churches and houses having been issued, the mob included in it many other churches, on the ground that places where idols had been worshipped ought to be destroyed. "Thus every building with a steeple was a mark of the beast, a seat of idolatry, and a house of devotion of the Amorites. The churches were all rased or battered, the beauty of the great towns scandalously blemished, and the public ornaments of the kingdom laid in rubbish. The communion plate was made prize, and the bells, timber, and lead sent to sale in the market. Registers and libraries were destroyed, and the remains of learning and antiquity thrown into the fire " (Collier, Book vi.).

In 1581 James, his nobles, and all ranks of people subscribed the Covenant. In 1610 he, having succeeded to the throne of England and adopted its religion, endeavoured to restore the episcopal form of government in his native country. Three bishops were consecrated in London to three of the ancient sees ; they consecrated an archbishop of St. Andrews, who proceeded to fill the other sees. The step was unpopular and occasioned riots, but was maintained by the civil authority. Charles I. on his accession to the throne endeavoured to introduce a Book of Common Prayer, taken, with some modifications, from the English Book. When the Dean of Edinburgh (1633) appeared in the cathedral church in a surplice and began to read prayers from the book a riot broke out * ; the resistance thus initiated spread throughout the country. The Covenant was again brought forward and signed by the Assembly of the Kirk, and the Scots Parliament (1640) ratified the act of the Assembly ; Charles, now embroiled with English rebels, was obliged to connive. The Covenant slightly

* When the dean began to read, one Jenny Geddes threw her three-legged stool at his head, exclaiming, "Thou false loon, wilt thou read the mass at my lug ? "

altered was adopted by the Westminster Assembly of Divines and the Parliamentary party in England and the king died a martyr for his absolute refusal to accept the Presbyterian system in England. When Charles II. was restored, the Scots Parliament (1661) rescinded the Covenant, and left the settlement of religion in the king's hands. It was resolved to re-establish the Church of Scotland, and Sharp was consecrated Archbishop, but was murdered by the " covenanters." A resolute resistance was maintained by a section who, under that name, refused to conform and continued to meet for public worship. They suffered fine, torture, and death, with the result of keeping up their enthusiasm and prejudicing mankind in favour of a cause which produced so many " martyrs." Not until the Revolution did the persecutions cease, and William III. establish in Scotland the Presbyterian form of Church government and doctrine, of which he was himself an adherent.

INDEX

PRINTED IN GREAT BRITAIN BY WILLIAM CLOWES AND SONS LIMITED
LONDON AND BECCLES.

The Historic Monuments of England

Edited by A. HAMILTON THOMPSON, M.A. Cantab., Hon. D.Litt. (Durham), F.S.A., Professor of Mediæval History in the University of Leeds.

∽ ∽ ∽

THE CATHEDRAL CHURCHES OF ENGLAND.

By A. HAMILTON THOMPSON, M.A., Hon. D.Litt. (Durham), F.S.A. With copious Illustrations. 8s. 6d.

The Builder says: "This vast amount of really useful information, orderly arranged and lucidly expressed . . . the result of much painstaking research."

PARISH CHURCH ARCHITECTURE.

By E. TYRRELL-GREEN. With 64 Illustrations, chiefly from drawings by the Author and a Map. 8s. 6d.

The Architect says: "This is a very good book indeed."

ENGLISH MONUMENTAL SCULPTURE SINCE THE RENAISSANCE.

By KATHARINE A. ESDAILE. With many Illustrations. 10s. 6d.

Mr. Edmund Gosse in "The Sunday Times": "She has made the subject of English eighteenth-century sculpture her own, and it is a field in which she has no rival."

BAPTISMAL FONTS, classified and Illustrated.

By E. TYRRELL GREEN, author of "Parish Church Architecture. 10s. 6d.

Architects' Journal: "The book is unusually well arranged . . . and exceptionally well written."
The Church Times: "This handy and exhaustive work."

ENGLISH MEDIÆVAL PAINTED GLASS.

By J. D. LE COUTEUR. With about 50 Illustrations. 8s. 6d.

Country Life says: "We have not met with a book on the subject which within a small space gives so much well-digested information."

THE PAINTED GLASS OF YORK. An Account of the Mediæval Glass of the Minster and the Parish Churches.

By the Rev. F. HARRISON, M.A., F.S.A., Librarian of the Dean and Chapter Library, York. With a Preface by W. FOXLEY NORRIS, D.D., Dean of Westminster. With four coloured Plates and numerous Illustrations. 12s. 6d.

Journal of the Society of Glass Technology says: "A vast store of information about the stained and painted windows in the greatest treasure-house of that art in England."

The Historic Monuments of England—*continued*.

SUNDIALS. Incised Dials or Mass-Clocks.

A Study of the Time-Markers of Mediæval Churches, containing Descriptions, Photographs, Diagrams, and Analysis of Dials, chiefly in Hampshire, but also in various other counties. By ARTHUR ROBERT GREEN, M.R.C.S. (England), L.R.C.P. (London). 10s. 6d.

The Times Literary Supplement says: "Covers ground which has been very little worked, and should lead readers . . . to explore a subject which is curious and has its own engaging problems."

FRENCH CHURCH ARCHITECTURE.

By E. TYRRELL GREEN. With about 70 Illustrations. 10s. 6d.
Few people have any adequate idea of the wealth and splendour of France's splendid architectural possessions. The writer tells the traveller what to see in the places he may visit. At the same time the student of architecture may find in the book a useful introduction to its subject and a handy work of reference.

The Scotsman: "It goes through practically the whole country, and will be cordially welcomed by tourists and travellers of the more studious sort."

THE BEDE HISTORIES.

Edited by Miss H. L. POWELL.

HISTORY OF THE PEOPLE OF ENGLAND.

By ALICE DRAYTON GREENWOOD, F.R.Hist.Soc. Series III.

Vol. I., 55 B.C. to A.D. 1485. With 27 Illustrations and 15 Maps. 7s. 6d. net.

The Church Times says: "It is astonishingly accurate: it is on occasion humorous, it is alive with human interest, and, above all, it is honest."
The Manchester Guardian says: "It is clearly written and well furnished with maps, genealogies, and illustrations."
History says: "The book is characterised by a general accuracy of detail."

Vol. II., A.D. 1485–1688. With 16 Illustrations and 7 Maps. 7s. 6d. net.
History says: "Should be invaluable to the highest forms of schools and to undergraduates. . . . One has a sense that everything is here which is wanted."

Vol. III., A.D. 1689–1834. With about 20 Illustrations and Maps. 7s. 6d. net.
The Times Literary Supplement says: "Fully maintains the high standard of the earlier volumes . . . should be of great value to the young University student. The facts are accurate, well co-ordinated and clearly set forth. . . . The maps, illustrations and reproductions are numerous and excellent."

HISTORY OF THE PEOPLE OF ENGLAND FROM THE EARLIEST TIMES TO 1066. (Series II. Vol. I.)

By ADELINE I. RUSSELL, M.A. With 122 Illustrations and 8 Maps. 2s. 6d. net [*The first volume of a junior series.*]

The Teacher's Times says: ". . . Presented in a most attractive form. . . . Incidents and quotations are taken, where possible, from contemporary authorities."
The Journal of Education says: "Scholarly, well-balanced, and thoroughly interesting."

THE CONVERSION OF THE ENGLISH.

By the Rev. H. CURTOIS. With many Illustrations. 6s. net.

The Guardian says: "It is delightful reading. Bede's fascination is perennial . . . a jolly book to give to boys and girls, or as a school prize."

ENGLISH ECCLESIASTICAL STUDIES. Being some Essays in Research in Medieval History.

By ROSE GRAHAM, M.A., F.S.A. With Illustrations. 15s. net.

SKETCHES OF CHURCH HISTORY. (New Edition.)

By J. C. ROBERTSON, M.A., revised by C. B. Moss, M.A. Vol. I. From A.D. 29 to A.D. 604 Vol. II. From A.D. 604 to the Reformation. Limp cloth, 2s. 6d. each. The two in one volume, cloth boards, 5s. net.

By the Rev. E. L. CUTTS, D.D.

PARISH PRIESTS AND THEIR PEOPLE IN THE MIDDLE AGES IN ENGLAND.

With numerous Illustrations. 7s. 6d. net.

TURNING POINTS OF ENGLISH CHURCH HISTORY.

5s. net.

TURNING POINTS OF GENERAL CHURCH HISTORY.

Condensed and revised by WILLIAM C. PIERCY, M.A. 6s. net.

STUDIES IN CHURCH HISTORY.

A selection from the Series.
Complete List post free.

THE PRELUDE TO THE REFORMATION.

By the Rev. R. S. ARROWSMITH. 8s. net.

The Month says: "Learned, up-to-date and sympathetic volume."

THE ALBIGENSIAN HERESY.

By the Rev. H. J. WARNER, B.D. 3s. 6d. net. Vol. II., 6s. net.

The Times says: "A safe and scholarly guide."

THE MONASTIC CHRONICLER AND THE EARLY SCHOOL OF ST. ALBANS.

By CLAUDE JENKINS, D.D., Canon of Canterbury. 3s. 6d. net.

G. C. Coulton in *The Hibbert Journal* says: "An interesting and instructive little book. . . ."

THE EARLY FRANCISCANS AND JESUITS. A Study in Contrasts.

By ARTHUR S. B. FREER, M.A. 6s. net.

The Times Literary Supplement says: "An admirable introduction to the study of the Friars."

THE VENERABLE BEDE. His Life and Writings.

By the Right Rev. G. F. BROWNE, D.D. With Illustrations. 10s. net.

The Morning Post says: "The final and complete history of the scholar-saint."

ESSAYS CATHOLIC AND CRITICAL.

By members of the Anglican Communion. Edited by EDWARD
GORDON SELWYN, D.D. Second Edition. 10s. 6d. net.

Contributors :

The Rev. Dr. E. J. BICKNELL.
The Rev. Sir EDWYN C. HOSKYNS.
The Rev. Dr. E. O. JAMES.
The Rev. K. E. KIRK.
The Rev. W. L. KNOX.
The Rev. E. MILNER-WHITE, D.S.O.
The Rev. Dr. J. K. MOZLEY.

The Rev. Dr. A. E. J. RAWLINSON.
The Rev. Dr. E. G. SELWYN.
W. SPENS.
Prof. A. E. TAYLOR.
Prof. A. HAMILTON THOMPSON.
The Rev. L. S. THORNTON.
The Rev. Dr. N. P. WILLIAMS.

Dean Inge in the *Sunday Times* says : "A very able and well-written book of
essays, quite equal to the famous 'Lux Mundi.'"
The Church Times says : "A very notable contribution to thought and theology."

ESSAYS CATHOLIC AND MISSIONARY.

Edited by E. R. MORGAN, M.A., Warden, College of the Ascension,
Selly Oak.

The authors are :

ROBERT H. BAKER.
C. H. BOUTFLOWER, Bishop of
  Southhampton.
LAURENCE E. BROWNE.
GODFREY CALLAWAY.
W. J. CLISSOLD.
MOTHER EDITH.
H. H. KELLY.
H. A. JONES.

P. H. LOYD, Assistant Bishop of
  Bombay.
W. V. LUCAS, Bishop of Masasi.
E. R. MORGAN.
E. L. STRONG.
REGINALD TRIBE.
M. N. TROLLOPE, Bishop in Corea.
EVELYN UNDERHILL.
STACY WADDY.

The Church Times says : "A piece of work of quite first-rate importance. . . .
The book is opportune. It will count for something. We believe it will help in
its degree to make history. . . . A great deal of thought is packed into this
volume. . . . The volume contains notable contributions. . . . It is representative of the best of English Catholicism."

CONFIRMATION, OR THE LAYING ON OF HANDS.

Vol. I. Historical and Doctrinal.   Vol. II. Practical.

12s. 6d. net.   8s. 6d. net.

By various writers, including Bishop A. J. MACLEAN (Moray), Bishop
TAYLOR, Archdeacon JOYNT, Revs. W. P. T. ATKINSON, A. CHILTON,
H. LOVELL CLARKE, W. K. LOWTHER CLARKE, D.D., HAROLD ELLIS,
C. L. FELTOE, D.D., T. J. HARDY, E. GROSE HODGE, K. D. MACKENZIE,
S. L. OLLARD, H. M RELTON, D.D., J. F. LOVELL SOUTHAM, REGINALD
TRIBE, Miss F. R. GRAY, R. M. FRENCH, and W. W. VAUGHAN, Head-
master of Rugby School.

These two volumes are a great contribution to practical-theology.

HOMES OF THE PSALMS. Their Original Meaning and Structure illustrated by the Surroundings in which they were First Used.

By STACY WADDY, M.A., Secretary of S.P.G. With four Plans. 6s. net.

THE SPIRIT OF WISDOM, LOVE AND POWER. Instructions and Material for Meditation.

By PAUL B. BULL, C.R. Paper cover, 1s. 6d. Duxeen boards, 2s. 6d. net.

THE GOSPEL FOR ASIA. A Study of Three Religious Masterpieces : Gita, Lotus, and Fourth Gospel.

By KENNETH SAUNDERS, Litt.D. 10s. 6d. net.

The Church Times says: "This is a book of the greatest value ; and we owe a debt, not only to Dr. Saunders, but to the S.P.C.K. for introducing it to England. . . . The book is full of information. . . . we hope that it will be widely read.''

S. FRANÇOIS DE SALES, 1567–1622.

By E. K. SANDERS. 12s. net.

THE TEACHING CHURCH. A Handbook of Adult Religious Education.

Edited by A. L. WOODARD. Paper cover, 2s. 6d. Cloth boards, 3s. 6d. net.

THE DOCTRINE OF GOD. Three Lectures.

By J. K. MOZLEY, D.D. 4s. net.

CHRISTIAN THOUGHT. A Grammar of Reinterpretation or Christianity and Nature.

By F. W. BUTLER. 6s. net.

WHAT DO WE MEAN BY GOD? Some Studies in the Objectivity of Christian Experience.

By CYRIL H. VALENTINE, M.A., Ph.D. (Lond.). 7s. 6d. net.

THE HOLY SPIRIT.

By the Rev. A. J. MACDONALD, M.A., B.D., F.R.Hist.S. With a Foreword by the Right Rev. A. A. DAVID, D.D., Bishop of Liverpool. 3s. 6d. net

THE HALLOWING OF HOME. Studies of Our Lord's Words spoken to Women.

By H. MAYNARD SMITH, D.D. Paper cover, 1s. 6d. Duxeen boards, 2s. 6d. net.

THE CHURCH'S YEAR. Prayers for Holy Seasons and other Anniversaries.

Compiled by ARTHUR MCCHEANE, M.A. Paper Cover, 1s. Cloth boards, 2s. Ornamental cloth, gilt top, 3s. net.

MY FAITH.

By VERNON F STORR, Canon of Westminster. Paper cover, 1s. Cloth, 2s. net.

[*A popular manual of faith and practice on evangelical lines*.]